PHONETIC
FIRST NAME
TRANSLATIONS
INTO HAWAIIAN

PHONETIC FIRST NAME TRANSLATIONS INTO HAWAIIAN

OVER 15,500 FIRST NAMES PHONETICALLY TRANSLATED INTO HAWAIIAN

KIM CRINELLA

CONTENTS

Phonetic Name Translations

Phonetic translations are based on sounds and have no literal meaning or intentional translation. This resource of over 15,500 first names translated phonetically into Hawaiian is a useful resource if you are having a Luau, Hawaiian theme wedding, or Hawaii theme celebration to translate the names of your guests for invitations, name badges, and table place cards. If you are a teacher teaching your students about Hawaii you can translate the names of your class. This is also a great resource if you are looking for a name for your baby or pet!

What is a Phonetic Name Translation?

When outsiders began visiting the Hawaiian Islands, adaptations were made to "translate" non-Hawaiian names into "Hawaiian names" phonetically based on the Hawaiian alphabet and word structure. In the Hawaiian language there are

Five vowels: A-E-I-O-U

Eight Consonants: H-K-L-M-N-P-W

and ' (which is called a glottal stop)

In the Hawaiian language a consonant is always followed by a vowel which also means all Hawaiian words end in a vowel. Please note that the glottal stop, ', is not used in phonetic name translations, only in literal Hawaiian words and translations.

How to Pronounce Hawaiian Words

Hawaiian words and names are more easily pronounced when they are broken down into single syllable chunks. Take the name of Hawaii's state fish, Humuhumunukunukuapua'a. It looks overwhelming to try and say! But when broken down into single syllable chunks it is easier to say...

Hu-mu-hu-mu-nu-ku-nu-ku-a-pu-a-a

Phonetically it is pronounced:

who-moo-who-moo-new-coo-new-coo-ah-poo-ah-ah

Sometimes the letter W is pronounced the same as V as in the traditional pronunciation of Hawai'i which is phonetically pronounced huh-vi-ee rather than huh-why-ee.

Stressed Vowels

A – phonetical sound: ah, as in spa. Hawaiian word: Ānuenue
E – phonetic sound ay, as in sway. Hawaiian word: Nēnē
I – phonetic sound ee, as in tree. Hawaiian word: Honi
O – phonetic sound oh, as in mango. Hawaiian word Mahalo
U – phonetic sound oo, as in blew. Hawaiian word Honu

Unstressed Vowels

A- phonetic sound uh, as in about. Hawaiian word Pua.
E – phonetic sound eh, as in met. Hawaiian word Wahine.

Literal Translations of Hawaiian Words Above

Ānuenue = Rainbow
Nēnē = Hawaiian Goose, State Bird
Honi = Gentle Kiss, a Traditional Hawaiian Greeting
Mahalo = Thank you
Honu = Sea Turtle
Pua = Flower
Wahine = Woman

Meanings of Traditional Hawaiian Names

A Traditional Hawaiian Name has a specific meaning behind it and is given to a child when they are born by their parents or a Kapuna, a family elder. The child is typically named after something that came to the family member in a dream, by distinguishing characteristics the child displays when born, or characteristics the family would like the child to display. For example, the male Hawaiian name Koa means brave, bold, fearless, warrior.

Meanings of Phonetic Hawaiian Names

The phonetic first name translations provided have no intentional literal meaning. The phonetic translations are created based on the sounds the name makes when said and the Hawaiian alphabet and word structure. Because there are only 13 letters in the Hawaiian language there are many names which sound similar and have the same phonetic translation.

How to Get A Literal Translation of
a First Name In Hawaiian

To get a literal Hawaiian translation of a name the literal meaning of the name would be needed in the originating language then the literal translation would be the Hawaiian word for that literal meaning.

For example, the Irish name Brian. The literal translation is strong, noble. In Hawaiian the word and name Ikaika (phonetically pronounced ee kai kuh) means strong, powerful. Ikaika would be a good literal name translation for Brian.

Where Did These Phonetic
First Name Translations Originate?

In 1999 the Author, Kim Crinella, began compiling a list of first names of her friends, family, and office co-workers then phonetically translated them and published the list on her website AlohaFriends.com along with tips for creating a Luau or Hawaii theme wedding anywhere. As people from all over the World began using her resources for their celebrations they would email asking to have names translated that were not listed. The names were phonetically translated and added to the list which over 25 years has grown to a list of over 15,500 phonetic first name translations.

How to Request A Phonetic First Name Translation

If you have a first name that is not translated in this book you may submit your name translation request to **afriendintheislands@gmail.com**. The name will be added to the website resource of translations at WeddingsOnoahu.com and will also be added in future editions of this book. Names submitted for phonetic translation must not already appear in this book. Requests of more than one first name must be submitted in alphabetical order.

A

FIRST NAMES

AACHARIAH - AKALIAHA
AADEN - AKENI
AADILA - AKILA
AAKASH - AKAKA
AALIYA - ALIIA
AALIYAH - ALIIAHA
AAMAN - AMANA
AAMIR - AMILE
AAMURIE - AMULIE
AANDRANEE - ANAKALANE
AANUND - ANUNOKO
AARIC - ALIKE
AARON - ALONA
AARTI - ARILI
AARYA - ALIA
AARYN - ALINE
AAYESHA - AIEKA
ABA - APA
ABAZ - APAKA
ABBEY - APEI
ABBHA - APAHA
ABBIE - API
ABBIGALE - APIKALE
ABBOT - APOKU
ABBY - API
ABCDE - APAKAKE
ABDALLAH - APAKALAHA
ABDERRAHIM - APAKELAHIME
ABDOULAYE - APAKOULAIE
ABDUL - APAKULO

ABE - APE
ABED - APEKI
ABELARD - APELALAKA
ABELINO - APELINO
ABENA - APENA
ABHINAV - APAHINAWA
ABHIJEET - APAHIIEKI
ABIGAIL – APIKALIA
ABIGALE - APIKALE
ABIGAYLE - APIKAILE
ABIONA - APIONA
ABITHA - APIKA
ABEER - APELI
ABEL – APELA
ABERIANE - APELIANE
ABET - APEKI
ABHA - APAHA
ABHIGNA - APAHIKENA
ABHINOV - APAHINOWU
ABHISHEK - APAHIKEKI
ABIEL - APIELI
ABIGAIL – APIKAILA
ABIGALE - APIKALE
ABIGAYLE - APIKAILE
ABILENE - APILENE
ABILIO - APILIO
ABISHAI - APIKAI
ABNER - APENELA
ABO - APO
ABONATAR - APONAKALA

ABRA - APALA
ABRAHA - APALAHA
ABRAHAM – APELEHAMA
ABRAM - APALAMA
ABRAXAS - APALAKAKA
ABRE - APALE
ABREANNA - APALEANA
A'BRESHA - A'APALEKA
ABREY - APALI
A'BRIAHN - A'APALIAHANA
ABRIAL - APALIALA
ABRIELLE - APALIELE
ABRYN - APALINE
ACACIA - AKAKIA
ACADIA - AKAKIA
ACE - AKE
ACEL - AKELI
ACHICOSE - AKIKOKE
ACHILLE - AKILE
ACHIM - AKIME
ACIE - AKIE
ACIEL - AKIELI
ACK - AKAKA
ACYAN - AKIANA
ADA – AKA
ADAEZE - AKAEKE
ADAIR - AKAILE
ADALBERT - AKALAPEKI
ADALGIZA - AKALAKIKA
ADALIA - AKALIA

ADALINDA - AKALINEKA
ADALINE - ALAKINE
ADALITZA - AKALIKEKA
ADAM – AKAMU
ADAMO - AKAMO
ADARA - AKALA
ADARAIN - AKALAINE
ADARSH - AKALAKA
ADDARIUS - AKALIUKO
ADDESSA - AKEKA
ADDIE - AKIE
ADDILYNN - AKILINE
ADDISON - AKIKONU
ADEA - AKEA
ADEAH - AKEAHA
ADEANA - AKEANA
ADEEN - AKENI
ADEJUWAN - AKEIUWANA
ADELA - AKELA
ADELAIDA - AKELAIKA
ADELAIDE - AKELAIKA
ADELALDA - AKELALA
ADELE – AKELE
ADELFA - AKELIPA
ADELINE - AKELINA
ADELMA - AKELIMA
ADELORE - AKELOLE
ADELYNNE - AKELINE
ADEN - AKENI
ADENA - AKENA

ADI - AKI

ADIAM - AHAKEUMO

ADIDA - AKIKA

ADIE - AKIE

ADIEL - AKIELI

ADIL - AKILE

ADILENE - AKILENE

ADILINA - AKILINA

ADINA - AKINA

ADINO - AKINO

ADIT - AKIKE

ADITA - AKIKA

ADITYA - AKIKIA

ADLI - AKALI

ADMILSA - AKAMILEKA

ADNAN - AKANANA

ADOLF - AKOLUPU

ADOLPH - AKOLUPU

ADONIS - AKONIKE

ADONNA - AKONA

ADONTI - AKONUKI

ADORA - AKOLA

ADORACION – AKOLAKIONU

ADORAN - AKOLANA

ADRA - AKALA

ADREA - AKALEA

ADREINA - AKALEINA

ADRI - AKALI

ADRIAN – AKILIANO

ADRIANA - AKALIANA

ADRIANDRO - AKALIANAKALO

ADRIANN – AKILIANA

ADRIANNA - AKALIANA

ADRIANNE - AKALIANE

ADRIANO - ALAKIANO

ADRIEL - AKALIELI

ADRIELLE - AKALIELE

ADRIENNE – AKALIENE

ADRIESE - AKALIEKE

ADRIONNA - AKALIONA

ADRIONNE - AKALIONE

ADVAITH - AKAWAIKE

ADWYN - AKAWINE

ADYS - AKIKE

ADYSON - AKIKONU

AEDAN - AEKANA

AEISHA - AEIKA

AELAINIA - AELAINIA

AELENE - AELENE

AELIENAH - ALELIENAHA

AENA - AENA

AENIJAH - AENIIAHA

AERIAL - AELIALA

AERIK - AELIKE

AERYN - AELINE

AETNA - AEKINA

AETO - AEKO

AFEWORK - APEWOKU

AFIYA - APIIA

AFON - APONU

AFREEN - APALENI
AFRICA - APALIKA
AFSHAN - APAKANA
AFSOON - APAKONU
AFTAB - APAKAPA
AFTON - APAKONU
AGATHA - AKAHA
AGEE - AKE
AGENA - AKENA
AGENOR - AKENOLU
AGGIE - AKIE
AGNE - AKANE
AGNES - AKENEKI
AGNESE - AKANEKE
AGNESSA - AKANEKA
AGNETA - AKANEKA
AGNIESZKA - AKANIEKIKIKA
AGRANDECE - AKALANAKEKE
AGRIPINA - AKALIPINA
AGUEDA - AKUEKA
AGUINALDO - AKUINALO
AGUSTA - AKUKA
AGUSTIN - AKUKINE
AGUSTINA - AKUKINA
AGUSTUS - AKUKUKO
AHAB - AHAPA
AHAD - AHAKA
AHJA - AHIA
AHKIKIYAE - AHAKIKIIAE
AHKIMIYAE - AHAKIMIIAE

AHLEIA - AHALEIA
AHMAD - AHAMAKA
AHMAEL - AHAMAELI
AHMAYA - AHAMAIA
AHMED - AHAMEKI
AHMET - AHAMEKI
AHNA - AHANA
AHNI - AHANI
AHOLIBAMA - AHOLIPAMA
AHSAN - AHAKANA
AHULANI - AHULANI
AIBHLIN - AIPEHELINE
AICA - AIKA
AICHA - AIKA
AIDA - AIKA
AIDALYN - AIKALINE
AIDAN - AIKENI
AIDEN - AIKENI
AIDIE - AIKIE
AIDIN - AIKINE
AIDYN - AIKINE
AIESHA - AIEKA
AIGNER - AIKINELA
AIJA - AIIA
AIK - AIKE
AIKO - AIKO
AILA - AILA
AILEEN - AILINA
AILIONORA - AILIONOLA
AILSA - AILEKA

AILISH - AILIKE

AIM - AIME

AIMAL - AIMALA

AIMAN - AIMANA

AIMEE - EME

AINA - AINA

AINAT - AINAKA

AINE - AINE

AINO - AINO

AINSLEE - AINEKELE

AINSLEIGH - AINEKELEIKEHE

AINSLEY - AILINA

AIRA - AILA

AIREL - AILELI

AIRAN - LAWIKE

AIREA - AILEA

AIRIAN - AILIANA

AIRIE - AILIE

AIRIKA - AILIKA

AIRSTINE - AILEKINE

AIRYN - AILINE

AISEL - AIKELI

AISHA - AIKA

A'ISHAH - A'IKAHA

AISHWARYA - AIKEWALIA

AISLEY - AIKELEI

AISLING - AIKELINE

AISLINN - AIKELINE

AISLYN - AIKELINE

AISLYNN - AIKELINE

AISSA - AIKA

AISTE - AIKE

AIVERY - AIWELI

AIXA - AIKA

AIYANA - AIIANA

AIYANNA - AIIANA

AIZAZ - AIKAKA

AJA - AIA

AJAMU - AIAMU

AJANI - AIANI

AJAY - AIAI

AJHALAH - AIHALAHA

AJI - AII

AJINI - AIINI

AJITINDER - AIIKINEKELI

AJITPAL - AIIKEPALA

AJOHNA - AIOHUNA

AKAIDA - AKAIKA

AKANKSHA - AKANAKAKA

AKARI - AKALI

AKASH - AKAKA

AKBAR - AKAPALA

AKEED - AKEKI

AKEEM - AKEMI

AKEENA - AKENA

AKELA - AKELA

AKEYLAH - AKEILAHA

AKHILESH - AKAHILEKI

AKI - AKI

AKIA -AKIA

AKIBA - AKIPA

ALASIA - ALAKIA

AKIJAH - AKIIAHA

ALASKA - ALAKAKA

AKIRAH - AKILAHA

ALASTAIR - ALAKAILE

AKKU - AKU

ALAUNA - ALAUNA

AKSHA - AKAKA

ALAURA - ALAULA

AKSHAY - AKAKAI

A'LAYCIA - A'ALAIKIA

AKSHITA - AKAKIKA

ALAYLA - ALAILA

AKSHUN - AKAKUNO

ALAYNA - ALAINA

AKTA - AKAKA

ALAYSIA - ALAIKIA

AKUA - AKUA

ALAZAE - ALAKAE

AL - ALE

ALBA - ALAPA

ALA - ALA

ALBAN - ALAPANA

ALADDIN - ALAKINE

ALBANY - ALAPANI

ALADRIANN - ALAKALIANA

ALBERIC - ALAPELIKE

ALAETRA - ALAELA

ALBERT - ALAPAKI

ALAIN - ALAINE

ALBERTA – ALEPEKA

ALAINA - ALAINA

ALBERTIA - ALAPEKIA

ALAINE - ALAINE

ALBERTINA - ALAPEKINA

ALAIS - ALAIKE

ALBERTINO - ALAPEKINO

ALAJUJUAN - ALAIUIUANA

ALBERTO – ALEPEKO

ALAN - ALENA

ALBIE - ALAPIE

ALANA - ALANA

ALBIN - ALAPINE

ALANAH - ALANAHA

ALBREA - ALAPALEA

ALANDIS - ALANAKIKE

ALBRIE - ALAPALIE

ALANEYER - ALANEIELI

ALBUS - ALAPUKO

ALANIE - ALANIE

ALCHAMY - ALAKAMI

ALANIS - ALANIKE

ALCINE - ALAKINE

ALANNA - ALANA

ALCIRA - ALAKILA

ALARIC - ALALIKE

ALDA - ALA

ALASAUNDREA - ALAKAUNOKOLEA

ALDEAN - ALEANA

ALDEN - ALEKENA
ALDO - ALO
ALDONA - ALONA
ALDRENA - ALALENA
ALE - ALE
ALEA - ALEA
ALEAH - ALEAHA
A'LEAHA - A'ALEAHA
ALEASE - ALEAKE
ALEATHEA - ALEAKEA
ALEC - ALIKA
ALECIA - ALEKIA
ALECTA - ALEKA
ALEDA - ALEKA
AL'DESHA - ALA'AKEKA
ALEESE - ALEKE
ALEESHA - ALEKA
ALEEYA - ALEIA
ALEGNA - ALEKINA
ALEGRA - ALEKILA
ALEGRIA - ALEKILIA
ALEIDRA - ALEIKELA
ALEIGH - ALEIKEHE
ALEISHA - ALEIKA
ALEIYA - ALEIIA
ALEJAGA - ALEIAKA
ALEJANDRA - ALEIANAKALA
ALEJANDRIA - ALEIANAKALIA
ALEJANDRINA - ALEIANAKALINA
ALEJANDRO - ALEIANAKALO

ALEK - ALEKI
ALELI - ALELI
ALENA - ALENA
ALENE - AILINA
ALERO- ALELO
ALESA - ALEKA
ALESHA - ALEKA
ALESSANDRA - ALEKANAKALA
ALESSANDRO - ALEKANAKALO
ALESSI - ALEKI
ALESSIA - ALEKANIA
ALESSIO - ALEKIO
ALETA - ALEKA
ALETH - ALEKI
ALETHA - ALEKA
ALETHEA - ALEKEA
ALETHIA - ALEKIA
ALEX - ALIKA
ALEXA - ALEKA
ALEXANDA - ALEKANAKA
ALEXANDER - ALEKANEKELO
ALEXANDRA - ALEKANEKA
ALEXANDRE - ALAEKANAKALE
ALEXANDREA - ALEKANAKALEA
ALEXANDRIA - ALEKANEKALIA
ALEXANDRINA - ALEKANAKALINA
ALEXEI - ALEKEI
ALEXENIA - ALEKENIA
ALEXEY - ALEKEI
ALEXI - ALEKI

ALEXIA - ALEKIA

ALEXINA - ALEKINA

ALEXINE - ALEKINE

ALEXIS - ALEKI

ALEXSANDRA - ALEKIKANAKALA

ALEXUS - ALEKUKO

ALEXX - ALEKI

ALEXYS - ALEKIKE

ALEXZANDRIA - ALEKIKANAKALIA

ALFER - ALAPELI

ALFIE - ALAPIE

ALFILITA - ALAPILIKA

ALFINA - ALAPINA

ALFLITA - ALAPALIKA

ALFOND - ALAPONUKU

ALFONSO - ALAPONUKO

ALFORD - ALAPOLUKU

ALFRED - ALEPELEKE

ALFREDA - ALEPELEKO

ALFREDO - ALEPELEKO

ALGALANA - ALAKALANA

ALGERNON - ALAKELINONU

ALGIS - ALAKIKE

ALGONDA - ALAKONUKA

ALI - ALI

ALIA - ALIA

ALIAH - ALIAHA

ALIANA - ALIANA

ALICE - ALEKA

ALICEN - ALIKENI

ALICIA - ALIKIA

ALICIONA - ALIKIONA

ALICK - ALIKEKE

ALIDA - ALIKA

ALIE - ALIE

ALIEA - ALIEA

ALIFIA - ALIPIA

ALIJA - ALIIA

ALIJANDRA - ALIANAKALA

ALIN - ALINE

ALINA - ALINA

ALINE - ALINE

ALIRIS - ALILIKE

ALISA - ALIKA

ALISE - ALIKE

ALISHA - ALIKA

ALISHIA - ALIKIA

ALISIA - ALIKIA

ALISON - ALEKONA

ALISSA - ALIKA

ALISTAIR - ALIKAILE

ALITHEA - ALIKEA

ALIVEA - ALIWEA

ALIVIA - ALIWIA

ALIVYA - ALIWIA

ALIX - ALIKE

ALIYA - ALIIA

ALIYAH - ALIIAHA

ALIZA - ALIKA

ALIZE - ALIKE

ALIZEA - ALIKEA
ALJANAE - ALIANAE
ALJEAN - ALIEANA
ALJENDRA - ALIENIKILA
ALJON - ALIONU
ALJOSHA - ALIOKA
ALJUAN - ALIUANA
ALJUANA - ALIUANA
ALKA - ALAKA
ALKEISHA - ALAKEIKA
ALKEST - ALAKEKI
ALLA - ALA
ALLAKREA - ALAKALEA
ALLAN - ALENA
ALLANA - ALANA
ALLBRIE - ALAPALIE
ALLEE - ALE
ALLEGRA - ALEKILA
ALLEN - ALENA
ALLENBACH - ALENIPAKA
ALLENNA - ALENA
ALLEON - ALEONU
ALLERY - ALELI
ALLESSANDRA - ALEKANAKALA
ALLEY - ALEI
ALLI - ALI
ALLIE - ALIE
ALLIEE - ALIE
ALLISON - ALEKONA
ALLISSA - ALIKA

ALLIVIA - ALIWIA
ALLIX - ALIKE
ALLOCH - ALOKU
ALLORA - ALOLA
ALLURE - ALULE
ALLY - ALI
ALLYAH - ALIAHA
ALLYN - ALINE
ALLYNE - ALINE
ALLYSA - ALIKA
ALLYSON - ALIKONU
ALLYSSA - ALIKA
ALMA - ALEMA
AL-MALIK - ALA, AMALIKE
ALMAS - ALAMAKA
ALMAZ - ALAMAKA
ALMEA - ALAMEA
ALMEEN - ALAMENI
ALMERINDA - ALAMELINEKA
ALMIRA - ALAMILA
ALMOND - ALAMONUKU
ALMUT - ALAMUKO
ALNOOR - ALANOLU
ARLO - ALO
ALONA - ALONA
ALONDRA - ALONUKULA
ALONSO - ALONUKO
ALONZO - ALONUKO
ALOSINA - ALOKINA
ALPESH - ALAPEKI

17.

ALPHONSE - ALAPONUKE
ALPHONSO - ALAPONUKO
ALPHONSUS - ALAPONUKUKO
ALTA - ALAKA
ALTAGRACIA - ALAKAKALAKIA
ALTAIR - ALAKAILE
ALTAMESE - ALAKAMEKE
ALTHEA - ALEKEA
ALTHIS - ALAKIKE
ALTHONIO - ALAKONIO
ALTON - ALEKONA
ALTOVISE - ALAKOWIKE
ALTRAVIOUS - ALALAWIOUKO
ALURA - ALULA
ALUSE - ALUKE
ALVA - ALEWA
ALVARD - ALAWALAKA
ALVARO - ALAWALO
ALVENE - ALAWENE
ALVERNA - ALAWELINA
ALVIA - ALAWIA
ALVIDA - ALAWIKA
ALVIE - ALAWIE
ALVIN - ALEWINA
ALVINO - ALAWINO
ALVIS - ALAWIKE
ALVOLIA - ALAWOLIA
ALWYN - ALAWINE
ALY - ALI
ALYAH - ALIAHA

ALYANNA - ALIANA
ALYCE - ALIKE
ALYCIA - ALIKIA
ALYEEN - ALIENI
ALYNA - ALINA
ALYNN - ALINE
ALYNNAH - ALINAHA
ALYNNE - ALINE
ALYS - ALIKE
ALYSA - ALIKA
ALYSE - ALIKE
ALYSHA - ALIKA
ALYSIA - ALIKIA
ALYSN - ALIKENE
ALYSON - ALIKONU
ALYSSA - ALIKA
ALYSSE - ALIKE
ALYSSIA - ALIKIA
ALYSSUM - ALIKUMO
ALYX - ALIKE
ALYXANDRA - ALIKANAKALA
ALZIRA - ALAKILA
AMA - AMA
AMAAN - AMANA
AMABELLE - AMAPELE
AMADEUS - AMAKEUKO
AMADO - AMAKO
AMAIYA - AMAIIA
AMAL - AMALA
AMALIA - AMALIA

AMALINA - AMALINA

AMAN - AMANA

AMANDA – AMANAKA

AMANDEEP - AMANAKEPI

AMANI - AMANI

AMANITA - AMANIKA

AMANPREET - AMANAPALEKI

AMAR - AMALA

AMARA - AMALA

AMARANTE - AMALANAKE

AMARI - AMALI

AMARIAH - AMALIAHA

AMARIGE - AMALIKE

AMARION - AMALIONU

AMARIS - AMALIKE

AMARISA - AMALIKA

AMARJIT - AMALIIKE

AMASA - AMAKA

AMATTULAH - AMAKULAHA

AMAYA - AMAIA

AMBER - AMAPELE

AMBERLY - AMAPELI

AMBIKA - AMAPIKA

AMBREA - AMAPALEA

AMBREON - AMAPALEONU

AMBRIA - AMAPALIA

AMBROSIA - AMAPALOKIA

AMBYR - AMAPILE

AMEA - AMEA

AMEDEO - AMEKEO

AMEE - EME

AMEEJAY - AMEIAI

AMEENA - AMENA

AMEER - AMELI

AMEERA - AMELA

AMELA - AMELA

AMELAINE - AMELAINE

AMELIA - AMELIA

AMELIE - AMELIE

AMEN - AMENI

AMENDA - AMENIKA

AMERE - AMELE

AMERENZIA - AMELENIKIA

AMERIAH - AMELIAHA

AMERICA - AMELIKA

AMERIE - AMELIE

AMERINTIA - AMELINEKIA

AMERY - AMELI

AMERYN - AMELINE

AMETHYST - AMEKIKE

AMEY - AMEI

AMI -AMI

AMICHAI - AMIKAI

AMIDALA - AMIKALA

AMIE -AMIE

AMIEL - AMIELI

AMILCAR - AMILEKALA

AMILY - AMILI

AMINA - AMINA

AMINDA - AMINEKA

AMINE - AMINE
AMINEH - AMINEHI
AMIR - AMILE
AMIRA - AMILA
AMISH - AMIKE
AMITA - AMIKA
AMIT - AMIKE
AMITA - AMIKA
AMITAB - AMIKAPA
AMITAVA - AMIKAWA
AMITY - AMIKI
AMIYA - AMIIA
AMMIE - AMIE
AMMON - AMONU
AMNESTY - AMANEKI
AMNOUAY - AMANOUAI
AMOLA - AMOLA
AMONI - AMONI
AMOR - AMOLU
AMOREYNA - AMOLEINA
AMORY - AMOLI
AMOS – AMOKA
AMP - AMAPA
AMPARO - AMAPALO
AMRITA - AMALIKA
AMRULLAH - AMALULAHA
AMSYAR - AMAKIALA
AMY – AME
AMYJO - AMIIO
AMYLEY - AMILEI

AN - ANA
ANA - ANA
ANABEL - ANAPELI
ANACELY - ANAKELI
ANADHEL - ANAKAHELI
ANAE - ANAE
ANAHI - ANAHI
ANAIS - ANAIKE
ANAKAREN - ANAKALENI
ANAKIN - ANAKINE
ANALECE - ANALEKE
ANALEE - ANALE
ANALI - ANALI
ANALIA - ANALIA
ANALISE - ANALIKE
ANALISSA - ANALIKA
ANALIZA - ANALIKA
ANALYLA - ANALILA
ANALYN - ANALINE
ANALYSA - ANALIKA
ANAMIKA - ANAMIKA
ANAND - ANANAKA
ANANDA - ANANAKA
ANANI - ANANI
ANANT - ANANAKA
ANANYA - ANANIA
ANAS'A - ANAKA'A
ANASTASIA - ANAKAKIA
ANASTASIOS - ANAKAKIOKU
ANATOLE - ANAKOLE

ANAYA - ANAIA
ANAYELI - ANAIELI
ANAYSE - ANAIKE
ANCA - ANAKA
ANCIL - ANAKILE
ANCORAN - ANAKOLANA
ANDA - ANAKA
ANDELIA - ANAKELIA
ANDER - ANAKELI
ANDERLIS - ANAKELIKE
ANDERS - ANAKELIKI
ANDERSON - ANAKELIKONU
ANDI - ANAKI
ANDIE - ANAKIE
ANDON - ANAKONU
ANDRA - ANAKALA
ANDRE - ANAKELE
ANDREA - ANAKALIA
ANDREANNA - ANAKALEANA
ANDREAS - ANAKALEAKA
ANDREI - ANAKALEI
ANDRELL - ANAKALELI
ANDRES - ANAKALEKI
ANDRESA - ANAKALEKA
ANDRETTI - ANAKALEKI
ANDREUSS - ANAKALEUKO
ANDREW - ANALU
ANDREWINA - ANAKALEWINA
ANDREY - ANAKALEI
ANDRIA - ANAKALIA

ANDRIANNA - ANAKALIANA
ANDRIEN - ANAKALIENI
ANDRIUS - ANAKALIUKO
ANDROMEDA - ANAKALOMEKA
ANDY - ANAKI
ANDYLN - ANAKILINI
ANE - ANE
ANECIA - ANEKIA
ANEL - ANELI
ANELYSE - ANELIKE
ANESHREE - ANEKILE
ANESKA - ANEKIKA
ANESSA - ANEKA
ANETA - ANEKA
ANETTE - ANEKE
ANG - ANA
ANGEL - ANELI
ANGELA - ANELA
ANGELES - ANELEKI
ANGELETTE - ANELEKE
ANGELI - ANELI
ANGELIA - ANELIA
ANGELICA - ANELIKA
ANGELIKA - ANELIKA
ANGELIKI - ANELIKI
ANGELINA - ANELINA
ANGELINE - ANELINE
ANGELIQUE - ANELIKE
ANGELITA - ANELIKA
ANGELITO - ANELIKO

ANGELLA - ANELA
ANGELLE' - ANELE'I
ANGELO - ANELO
ANGIE - ANIE
ANGULIA - ANULIA
ANGUS - ANUKO
ANGY - ANI
ANH - ANAHA
ANI - ANI
ANIA - ANIA
ANIANA - ANIANA
ANIBAL - ANIPALA
ANICES - ANIKEKI
ANICETA - ANIKEKA
ANICKA - ANIKEKA
ANIECEIA - ANIEKEIA
ANIELLA - ANIELA
ANIKA - ANIKA
ANIL - ANILE
ANILA - ANILA
ANINDER - ANINEKELI
ANINDITA - ANINEKIKA
ANINDO - ANINEKO
ANISE - ANIKE
ANISH - ANIKE
ANISHA - ANIKA
ANISSA - ANIKA
ANISTY - ANIKI
ANITRA - ANILA
ANIQUA - ANIKA

ANIS - ANIKE
ANISA - ANIKA
ANISE - ANIKE
ANITA - ANIKA
ANIYA - ANIIA
ANJA - ANIA
ANJALI - ANIALI
ANJEANETTE - ANIEANEKE
ANJELA - ANIELA
ANJIE - ANIIE
ANJOLINE - ANIOLINE
ANJU - ANIU
ANKE - ANAKE
ANYSSA - ANIKA
ANN, ANNE, ANNA - ANA
ANNABEL - ANAPELI
ANNABELLE - ANAPELA
ANNACA - ANAKA
ANNAGRACE - ANAKALAKE
ANNAKAH - ANAKAHA
ANNALEE - ANALE
ANNALEIGH - ANALEIKEHE
ANNALICIA - ANALIKIA
ANNALISA - ANALIKA
ANNALISE - ANALIKE
ANNALOU - ANALOU
ANNAMAE - ANAMAE
ANNAMARIE - ANAMALIE
ANNAT - ANAKA
ANNBRITT - ANAPALIKE

ANNE - ANE   ANOTHEP - ANOKEPI
ANNEKE - ANEKE   ANOTHIP - ANOKIPE
ANNELIESE - ANELIEKE   ANOTHOUNE - ANOKOUNE
ANNELIESSE - ANELIKE   ANOUD - ANOUKO
ANNELIEN - ANELIENI   ANOUSHKA - ANOUKOKA
ANNELLA - ANELA   ANPARO - ANAPALO
ANNETTE - ANEKA   ANROUD - ANALOUKO
ANN GEE - ANA KE   ANSELMO - ANAKELIMO
ANNGEL - ANELI   ANSH - ANAKA
ANNIBAL - ANIPALA   ANSLEE - ANAKALE
ANNICA - ANIKA   ANSLEI - ANAKALEI
ANNICK - ANIKEKE   ANSLEY - ANAKALEI
ANNICE - ANIKE   ANSON – ANEKONA
ANNIE - ANE   ANSUMI - ANAKUMI
ANNIK - ANIKE   ANSUYAH - ANAKUIAHA
ANNIKA - ANIKA   ANTARA - ANAKALA
ANNIKEN - ANIKENI   ANTAYUS - ANAKAIUKO
ANNINA - ANINA   ANTERO - ANAKELO
ANNISA - ANIKA   ANTHEA - ANAKEA
ANNMARIE - ANAMAILE   ANTHONEY - ANAKONEI
ANNORIA - ANOLIA   ANTHONY - AKONI
ANNROSE - ANALOKE   ANTIGONE - ANAKIKONE
ANNUKKA - ANUKA   ANTIKA - ANAKIKA
ANNY - ANI   ANTIONE - ANAKIONE
ANONGLAK - ANONULAKA   ANTISHA - ANAKIKA
ANOOPA - ANOPA   ANTOLIN - ANAKOLINE
ANOOSHA - ANOKA   ANTON - AKONI
ANOPET - ANOPEKI   ANTONELLA - ANAKONELA
ANOPUT - ANOPUKO   ANTONIA - ANAKONIA
ANORY - ANOLI   ANTONIETTA - ANAKONIEKA

ANTONIO - ANAKONIO
ANTOINETTE – ANAKONIA
ANTOLIN - ANAKOLINE
ANTONE – AKONI
ANTONETTE - ANAKONEKE
ANTONIA - ANAKONIA
ANTRANESE - ANALANEKE
ANTRELL - ANALELI
ANTRIKA - ANALIKA
ANTWOINE - ANAKAWOINE
ANTWON - ANAKAWONU
ANU - ANU
ANUAR - ANUALA
ANUJ - ANUI
ANUM - ANUMO
ANUPAMA - ANUPAMA
ANUPINDER - ANUPINEKELI
ANURADHA - ANULAKAHA
ANURANI - ANULANI
ANUSHKA - ANUKOKA
ANUSHREE - ANUKOLE
ANUSUYA - ANUKUIA
ANWAR - ANAWALA
ANYA - ANIA
ANYAH - ANIAHA
ANYELI - ANIELI
AODHAN - AOKUHANA
AOIFE - EPA
APARECIDA - APALEKIKA
APARNA - APALANA

APERNA - APELINA
APHARNAA - APALANA
APIPHANIE - APIPANIE
APO - APO
APOLINAR - APOLINALA
APOLLO - APOLO
APOLONIA - APOLONIA
APOORVA - APOLUWA
APPLE - APALE
APPLEAN - APALEANA
APRECHELLE - APALEKELE
APRIA - APALIA
APRIL – APELILA
APRONIANO - APALONIANO
APRYL - APALILE
APURVA - APULOWA
AQUAMARINE - AKAMALINE
AQUINNAH - AKAINAHA
ARAA - ALA
ARABA - ALAPA
ARABELLA - ALAPELA
ARACELI - ALAKELI
ARACELY - ALAKELI
ARAFNIS - ALAPANIKE
ARAH - ALAHA
ARAIYA - ALAIIA
ARALA - ALALA
ARALYN - ALALINE
ARAME - ALAME
ARAMIS - ALAMIKE

24.

ARAN - ALANA
ARANDA - ALANAKA
ARANIESHA - ALANIEKA
ARASH - ALAKA
ARATHE - ALAKE
ARAXIE - ALAKIE
ARAYLIA - ALAILIA
ARBETHA - ARBETHA
ARCADIO - ALAKAKIO
ARCEIL - ALAKEILE
ARCELIA - ALAKELIA
ARCENIA - ALAKENIA
ARCHANA - ALAKANA
ARCHER - ALAKELI
ARCHIBALD - AKE
ARCHIE – AKE
ARCHITA - ALAKIKA
ARCOLA - ALAKOLA
ARDEECE - ALAKEKE
ARDELL - ALAKELI
ARDEN - ALAKENI
ARDENA - ALAKENA
ARDENE - ALAKENE
ARDIS - ALAKIKA
ARDITH - ALAKIKE
ARDY - ALAKI
AREI - ALEI
AREINA - ALEINA
ARELI - ALELI
ARELIS - ALELIKE

ARETHA - ALEKA
ARETI - ALEKI
AREYNA - ALEINA
AREZOU - ALEKOU
ARGELIA - AKELIA
ARGELL - AKELI
ARGERN - AKELINI
ARGIE - AKIE
ARGUS - AKUKO
ARI - ALI
ARIA - ALIA
ARIADRIA - ALIAKALIA
ARIAN - ALIANA
ARIANA - ALIANA
ARIANNA - ALIANA
ARIANNE - ALIANE
ARIC - ALIKE
ARIEL - ALIELA
ARIELLE - ALIELE
ARIELL - ALIELI
ARIENNE - ALIENE
ARIESSA - ALIEKA
ARIF - ALIPE
ARIJIT - ALIIIKE
ARIN - ALINE
ARIONNE - ALIONE
ARIQUA - ALIKA
ARIS - ALIKE
ARISA - ALIKA
ARISBETH - ALIKEPEKI

ARISTI - ALIKI
ARISTIDIS - ALIKIKIKE
ARIUS - ALIUKO
ARIYANA - ALIIANA
ARIZONA - ALIKONA
ARJELIA - ALIELIA
ARJUN - ALIUNO
ARJUNA - ALIUNA
ARKADY - ALAKAKI
ARKHAM - AKAHAMA
ARLA - ALA
ARLAN - ALANA
ARLANDAR - ALANAKALA
ARLAYNE - ALAINE
ARLECA - ALEKA
ARLECIA - ALEKIA
ARLEEN - ALINA
ARLEN - ALENA
ARLENE - ALENE
ARLETTA - ALEKA
ARLETTE - ALEKE
ARLEVA - ALEWA
ARLI - ALI
ARLIE - ALIE
ARLINA - ALINA
ARLINE - ALINE
ARLO - ALO
ARLYCE - ALIKE
ARMA - ALAMA
ARMAAN - ALAMANA

ARMAND - ALAMANA
ARMANDO - ALAMANAKO
ARMANI - ALAMANI
ARMAVO - ALAMAWO
ARMEL - ALAMELI
ARMENTA - ALAMENIKA
ARMIDA - ALAMIKA
ARMIE - ALAMIE
ARMIN - ALAMINE
ARMINDA - ALAMINEKA
ARMINDO - ALAMINEKO
ARMINE - ALAMINE
ARMOND - ALAMONUKU
ARNA - ALANA
ARNALD - ALANALA
ARNALDO - ALANALO
ARNE - ALANE
ARNEL - ALANELI
ARMELLA - ALAMELA
ARMEN - ALAMENI
ARMEND - ALAMENIKI
ARMENIO - ALAMENIO
ARNET - ALANEKI
ARNETIA - ALANEKIA
ARNETRAS - ALANELAKA
ARNETTA - ALANELA
ARNIE - ALANIE
ARNIECE - ALANIEKE
ARNOLD - ALANOLA
ARNULFO - ALANULOPO

ARON - ALONU
ARONNA - ALONA
AROURA - ALOULA
ARPHA - ALAPA
ARPITA - ALAPIKA
ARRIE - ALIE
ARROYO - ALOIO
ARSELIDA - ALAKELIKA
ARSEN - ALAKENI
ARSENIA - ALAKENIA
ARSENIO - ALAKENIO
ARSHANA - ALAKANA
ARSHNOOR - ALAKANOLU
ARSHPREET - ALAKAPALEKI
ART - AKA
ARTASIA - AKAKIA
ARTEMIO - AKEMIO
ARTICE - AKIKE
ARTIE - AKIE
ARTHEEL - AKELI
ARTHUR – AKA
ARTIA - AKIA
ARTISHA - AKIKA
ARTRAVIA - ALAWIA
ARTURO - AKAO
ARUNA - ALUNA
ARUNDHATI - ALUNOKOHAKI
ARUSHI - ALUKI
ARVIL - ALAWILE
ARVIN - ALAWINE

ARVIND - ALAWINEKE
ARYA - ALIA
ARUNIMA - ALUNIMA
ARVA - ALAWA
ARVID - ALAWIKA
ARWEN - ALAWENI
ARYAN - ALIANA
ASA - AKA
ASANTE - AKANAKE
ASEEMA - AKEMA
ASENA - AKENA
ASENATH - AKENAKA
ARSENIUS - ALAKENIUKO
ASHA - AKALA
ASHAN - AKANA
ASHANTI - AKANAKI
ASHAUNA - AKAUNA
ASHAY - AKAI
ASHEN - AKENI
ASHER - AKELI
ASHFORD - AKAPOLUKU
ASHIA - AKIA
ASHIM - AKIME
ASHIN - AKINE
ASHLEA - AKALEA
ASHLEE - AKALE
ASHLEI - AKALEI
ASHLEIGH - AKALEIKEHE
ASHLEY- AKALEI
ASHLIANN - AKALIANA

ASHIFA - AKIPA

ASHIRA - AKILA

ASHLI - ALALI

ASHLIE - AKALIE

ASHLIN - AKALINE

ASHLLEY - AKALEI

ASHLYN - AKALINE

ASHMERE - AKAMELE

ASHOK - AKOKU

ASHRAF - AKALAPA

ASHTIN - AKAKINE

ASHTON - AKAKONU

ASHTYN - AKAKINE

ASHUTOSH - AKUKOKUHU

ASHWINI - AKAWINI

ASIA - AKIA

ASIALYN - AKIALINE

ASIYAH - AKIIAHA

ASLAM - AKALAMA

ASLI - AKALI

ASLIN - AKALINE

ASMUND - AKAMUNOKO

ASNA - AKANA

ASODAMAH - AKOKAMAHA

ASOVALE - AKOWALE

ASPEN - AKAPENI

ASRUH - AKALUHO

ASSUMPTA - AKUMOPOKA

ASTA - AKA

ASTI - AKI

ASTIN - AKINE

ASTLEY - AKALEI

ASTON - AKONU

ASTREA - AKALEA

ASTRID - AKALIKE

ASUKA - AKUKA

ASWATHY - AKWAKI

ASVE - AKAWE

ASVENORA - AKAWENOLA

ASYA - AKIA

ATANASKA - AKANAKAKA

ATARI - AKALI

ATARIA - AKALIA

ATEF - AKEPI

ATEN - AKENI

ATHAN - AKANA

ATHENA - AKENA

ATHOS - AKOKU

ATIF - AKIPE

ATILICAN - AKILIKANA

ATIYAH - AKIIAHA

ATLANTA - AKALANAKA

ATLANTIS - AKALANAKIKE

ATLAS - AKALAKA

ATLEE - AKALE

ATO - AKO

ATOM - AKOMU

ATRAYA - ALAIA

ATSUKO - AKUKO

ATTIA - AKIA

ATTICUS - AKIKUKO

ATTILAH - AKILAHA

ATTILLIO - AKILIO

ATTYA - AKIA

ATU - AKU

ATUL - AKULO

ATWA - AKAWA

AUALA - AUALA

AUBIE - AUPIE

AUBREE - AUPOLE

AUBREY - AUPOLEI

AUBRIANA - AUPOLIANA

AUBRIANNE - AUPOLIANE

AUBRIE - AUPOLIE

AUBRY - AUPOLI

AUD - AUKO

AUDE - AUKE

AUDHILE - AUKOHILE

AUDIEDRA - AUKIEKILA

AUDILE - AUKILE

AUDRA - AUKOLA

AUDREANNA - AUKOLEANA

AUDREE - AUKELE

AUDRENA - AUKOLENA

AUDREY – AUKELE

AUDREY-ANN - AUKOLEI-ANA

AUDRIE - AUKOLIE

AUDRIELLA - AUKOLIELA

AUDRY - AUKOLI

AUGIE - AUKIE

AUGUST - AUKAKE

AUGUSTINA - AUKUKINA

AUGUSTINE – AUKUKINO

AUGUSTO - AUKUKO

AUGUSTUS - AUKUKUKO

AULANI - AULANI

AULDINE - AULIKINE

AULGAR - AULOKALA

AUNDREA - AUNOKOLEA

AUNI - AUNI

AUNNA - AUNA

AURA - AULA

AURALEE – AULALE

AUREA - AULEA

AURELIA - AULELIA

AURELIO - AULELIO

AURELLA - AULELA

AURIANA - AULIANA

AURICA - AULIKA

AURICE - AULIKE

AURIUS - AULIUKO

AURORA - ALOLA

AURTHUR - AUKULO

AUSKA - AUKOKOA

AUSLINE - AUKOLINE

AUSTEN - AUKENI

AUSTIE - AUKIE

AUSTIN - AUKINA

AUTO - AUKO

AUTREY - AULEI

AUTUMN - AUKUMONO

AVA - AWA

AVALIN - AWALINE

AVANAUGH - AWANAUKOHO

AVANTE - AWANAKE

AVANTIKA = AWANAKIKA

AVELINA - AWELINA

AVEREY - AWELEI

AVERI - AWELI

AVERIE - AWELIE

AVERY - AWELI

AVEY - AWEI

AVIANA - AWIANA

AVIGAYIL - AWIKAIILE

AVILA - AWILA

AVIONCE - AWIONUKE

AVIS - AWIKE

AVIVA - AWIWA

AVNI - AWANI

AVON - AWONU

AVONDA - AWONUKA

AVONELL - AWONELI

AVONLEA - AWONULEA

AVREE - AWALE

AVREY - AWALEI

AVRIL - AWALILE

AVYETTE - AWIEKE

AWILDA - AWILA

AXEL - AKELI

AXTON - AKAKONU

AYA - AIA

AYAHANA - AIAHANA

AYAKA - AIAKA

AYAKO - AIAKO

AYALA - AIALA

AYANA - AIANA

AYANNA - AIANA

AYANO - AIANO

AYAZHIA - AIAKAHIA

AYDA - AIKA

AYDAN - AIKANA

AYDEN - AIKENI

AYDIN - AIKINE

AYESHA - AIEKA

AYETEY - AIEKEI

AYFER - AIPELI

AYIYANA - AIIIANA

AYLA - AILA

AYMERIC - AIMELIKE

AYNA - AINA

AYNSLEE - AINEKELE

AYOMIDE - AIOMIKE

AYONNA - AIONA

AYRES - AILEKI

AYRON - AILONU

AYSHA - AIKA

AYSIA - AIKIA

AYSU - AIKU

AYU - AIU

AYUMI - AIUMI

AYVETTE - AIWEKE
AZALEAH - AKALEAHA
AZAR - AKALA
AZARDOKHT - AKALAKOKUHUKU
AUZARE - AUKALE
AZARIA - AKALIA
AZEEM - AKEMI
AZER - AKELI
AZERBAIJAN - AKELIPAIIANA
AZHAR - AKAHALA
AZI - AKI
AZIE - AKIE
AZILLAH - AKILAHA
AZIMMAH - AKIMAHA
AZIZ - AKIKE
AZIZAH - AKIKAHA
AZLIN - AKALINE
AZRIEL - AKALIELI
AZUCENA - AKUKENA
AZURE - AKULE
AZURDEE - AKULOKE
AZUREEN - AKULENI

B

FIRST NAMES

BABA - PAPA
BABACK - PAPAKAKA
BABEE - PAPE
BABES - PAPEKI
BABETTE - PAPEKE
BABS - PAPAKA
BABUBHAI - PAPUPOHAI
BABY - PAPI
BABYLYN - PAPILINE
BAC - PAKA
BAGHEERA - PAKAHELA
BAGHERIA - PAKAHELIA
BAGHWAN - PAKAHAWANA
BAHIRA - PAHILA
BAILA - PAILA
BAILEE - PAILE
BAILEN - PAILENI
BAILEY - PAILEI
BAILLIE - PAILIE
BAIMEY - PAIMEI
BAKER - PAKELI
BALA - PALA
BALAJI - PALAII
BALAKRISHNA - PALAKALIKENA
BALBIR - PALAPILE
BALDEMAR - PALEMALA
BALDUR - PALULO
BALEIGH - PALEIKEHE
BALENA - PALENA
BALI - PALI

BALJINDER - PALIINEKELI
BALKISU - PALAKIKU
BALLAD - PALAKA
BALOE - PALOE
BALLOO - PALO
BALMORIS - PALAMOLIKE
BALRAJ - PALALAI
BALTAZAR - PALAKAKALA
BALTINEZ - PALAKINEKI
BALTUS - PALAKUKO
BAMBI - PAMAPI
BAMMIE - PAMIE
BANA - PANA
BANCROFT - PANAKALOPUKU
BANE - PANE
BANGTAM - PANAKAMA
BANKS - PANAKAKA
BANKSTON - PANAKAKONU
BANU - PANU
BAO BAI - PAO PAI
BARAKA - PALAKA
BARAT - PALAKA
BARB - PALAPA
BARBARA - PALAPALA
BARBARANN - PALAPALANA
BARBEE - PALAPE
BARBIE - PALAPI
BAREK - PALEKI
BARINDER - PALINEKELI
BARKLEY - PAKALEI

BARNABAS - PALENAPA

BARNARD - PALANALAKA

BARNEY - PALANI

BARON - PALONU

BARR - PALA

BARRETT - PALEKA

BARRIE - PALIE

BARRINGTON - PALINEKONU

BARRY - PALI

BART - PALAKA

BARTH - PAKA

BARTRICIA - PALIKIA

BAS - PAKA

BASCO - PAKAKO

BASIL - PAKILE

BASILIO - PAKILIO

BASKETT - PAKAKEKI

BASMA - PAKAMA

BASS - PAKA

BASSAM - PAKAMA

BASSANT - PAKANAKA

BATEY - PAKEI

BATHILDA - PAKILA

BATRISYIA - PALIKIIA

BATSI - PAKI

BATYA - PAKIA

BAVANDEEP - PAWANAKEPI

BAVIA - PAWIA

BAXTER - PAKAKELI

BAY - PAI

BAYAZID - PAIAKIKE

BAYLA - PAILA

BAYLEE - PAILE

BAYLEIGH - PAILEIKEHE

BAYLIN - PAILINE

BAYLIS - PAILIKE

BAYLOR - PAILOLU

BAYYINAH - PAIINAHA

BEA - PEA

BEAN - PEANA

BEANER - PEANELI

BEAR - PEALA

BEATA - PEAKA

BEATE - PEAKE

BEATRICE - PEAKALIKA

BEATRIX - PEALIKE

BEATRIZ - PEALIKE

BEAU - PEAU

BEAUTY - PEAUKI

BE BE - PE PE

BEBE - PEPE

BECCA - PEKA

BECKETT - PEKIKEKI

BECKHAM - PEKIKIHAMA

BECKI - PEKE

BECKY - PEKE

BEDE - PEKE

BEDELIA - PEKELIA

BEDER - PEKELI

BEE - PE

BEEBO - PEPO

BEEKER - PEKELI

BEETA - PEKA

BEEYT - PEIKE

BEGONIA - PEKONIA

BEHIRA - PEHILA

BEHNAM - PEHINAMA

BEHNAZ - PEHINAKA

BEHRUZE - PEHILUKE

BEILUL - PEILULO

BEKAH - PEKAHA

BEKI - PEKI

BELA - PELA

BELAINE - PELAINE

BELAL - PELALA

BELCAH - PELIKAHA

BELDON - PELONU

BELEL - PELELI

BELEN - PELENI

BELICIA - PELIKIA

BELINDA - PELINEKA

BELITA - PELIKA

BELKUS - PELIKUKO

BELKYS - PELIKIKE

BELLA - PELA

BELLE - PELA

BELMA - PELIMA

BELVA - PELIWA

BEN - PENI

BENDERA - PENIKELA

BENEDICT - PENEKIKO

BENETH - PENEKI

BENETTA - PENEKA

BENG HOON - PENI HONU

BENIAH - PENIAHA

BENICIA - PENIKIA

BENIGNO - PENIKENO

BENILDE - PENILE

BENISSE - PENIKE

BENITA - PENIKA

BENIYAM - PENIIAMA

BENJ - PENI

BENJAMIN - PENIAMINA

BENJIE - PENI'I

BENNETT - PENEKI

BENNIE - KELIWIIE

BENNISE - PENIKE

BENNY - PENI

BENOIT - PENOIKE

BENT - PENIKI

BENTE - PENIKE

BENTLEY - PENIKILEI

BENTON - PENIKONA

BEOWULF - PEOWULOPO

BERENICE - PELENIKE

BERES - PELEKI

BERET - PELEKI

BERGEN - PEKENI

BERGUNDY - PEKUNOKI

BERHANE - PELIHANE

BERIL - PELILE

BERIT - PELIKE

BERJ - PELI

BERKELEY - PEKELEI

BERKLEY - PEKILEI

BERLINDA - PELINEKA

BERN - PELINI

BERNADETTE - PELENAKEKA

BERNADINE - PELINAKINE

BERNAL - PELINALA

BERNARD - PELENALAKO

BERND -PELINIKI

BERNECE - PELINEKE

BERNELL - PELINELI

BERNETTE - PELINEKE

BERNEY - PELINEI

BERNICE - PELENIKA

BERNIE - PELENI

BERNIS - PELINIKE

BERNITA - PELINIKA

BERNY - PELINI

BERRY - PELI

BERT - PELEKA

BERTHA - PELEKA

BERTINA - PEKINA

BERTO - PEKO

BERUK - PELUKO

BERUKA - PELUKA

BERYL - PELULO

BESA - PEKA

BASHEER - PAKELI

BESIM - PEKIME

BESS - PEKA

BESSIE - PUKAKE

BETH - PEKA

BETHANI - PEKANI

BETHANY - PEKANI

BETHEL - PEKELI

BETHESDAA - PEKEKIKA

BETHWYN - PEKIWINE

BERTHIER - PEKIELI

BETO - PEKO

BETSI - PEKI

BETSY - PEKE

BETTE - PEKE

BETTIE - PEKIE

BETTINA - PEKINA

BETTIS - PEKIKE

BETTY - PEKE

BETTYANNE- PEKEANA

BETTYFAY - PEKIPAI

BETTYJANE - PEKIIANE

BETTYJO - PEKIIO

BETTYSUE - PEKIKUE

BETUL - PEKULO

BETZABETH - PEKIKAPEKI

BEULAH - PEULAHA

BEUNA - PEUNA

BEV - PEWI

BEVA -PEWA

BEVERLEE - PEWELE

BEVERLEEN - PEWELENI

BEVERLY - PEWELI

BEVIN - PEWINE

BHAPINDER - PAHAPINEKELI

BHARADWAJ - PAHALAKAWAI

BHARAT - PAHALAKA

BHARATHI - PAHALAKI

BHAVNA - PAHAWANA

BHENG - PAHENI

BHIMER - PAHIMELI

BHROMA - PAHALOMA

BHUPINDER - PAHUPINEKELI

BIA - PIA

BIAGIO - PIAKIO

BIANCA - PIANAKA

BIANCI - PIANAKI

BIANI - PIANI

BIANKA - PIANAKA

BIBEESH - PIPEKI

BIBI - PIPI

BICH - PIKE

BIDDIE - PIKIE

BIE - PIE

BIEGEL - PIEKELI

BIENNA - PIENA

BIFF - PIPE

BIJAN - PIIANA

BILAL - PILALA

BILL - PILA

BILLIE, BILLY - PILI

BILLIE JO - PILI IO

BILLIGAN - PILIKANA

BILLINGSLEY - PILINEKELEI

BINA - PINA

BINDY - PINEKI

BING - PINE

BINH - PINEHE

BINNIE - PINIE

BINNY - PINI

BINYOMIN - PINIOMINE

BIOMIL - PIOMILE

BIPIN - PIPINE

BIRBAL - PILEPALA

BIRDIE - PILEKIE

BIRGIT - PIKIKE

BIRKIN - PIKINE

BIRPAL - PILEPALA

BIRTHE - PIKE

BISHOP - PIKOPU

BISMA - PIKEMA

BIT - PIKE

BITHIA - PIKIA

BITZY - PIKEKI

BJAY - PIAI

BJORN -PIOLUNU

BJORNER - PIOLUNELI

BLA - PALA

BLADE - PALAKE

BLADEMIR - PALAKEMILE

BRAILINN - PALAILINE

BLAINE - PALAINA

BLAIR - PALAILE

BLAISE - PALAIKE

BLAKE - PALIKA

BLAKELY - PALAKELI

BLAKELYN - PALAKELINE

BLANCA - PALANAKA

BLANCHE - PALANEKE

BLANDA - PALANAKA

BLANKA - PALANAKA

BLANTON - PALANAKONU

BLASELI - PALAKELI

BLAZE - PALAKE

BLAZINE - PALAKINE

BLEENE - PALENE

BLESSING - PALEKINE

BLIA - PALIA

BLISS - PALIKE

BLOSSOM - PUA

BLUE - PALUE

BLURRY - PALULI

BLYTHE - PALIKE

BO - PO

BOAZ - POAKA

BOB - LOPAKA

BOBBETTE - POPEKE

BOBBI - POPI

BOBBIE - LOPAKE

BOBBIE JO - POPIEIO

BOBBY - LOPAKE

BOBBYE - POPIE

BOBET - POPEKI

BOBI - POPI

BOBSIE - POPUKIE

BOCIA - POKIA

BODIE - POKIE

BODINE - POKINE

BOGDAN - POKUKANA

BOGIE - POKIE

BOLA - POLA

BOLDIZSAR - POLIKEKALA

BOND - PONUKU

BONG - PONU

BONI - PONI

BONIE - PONIE

BONITA - PONIKA

BONNA - PONA

BONNELL - PONELI

BONNIE - PONI

BONNITA - PONIKA

BONO - PONO

BOO - PO

BOON - PONU

BOONCHOO - PONUKO

BOON HONG - PONU HONU

BOON SENG - PONU KENI

BOON SING - PONU KINE

BOONE - PONE

BOOTIE - POKIE

BOOTS - POKU

BOPHA - POPA

BORGE - POKE

BORIS - POLIKE

BORNWELL - POLUNUWELI

BORRIS - POLIKE

BORY - POLI

BOSS - POKU

BOSTON - POKONU

BOUKE - POUKE

BOWIE - POWIE

BOWMAN - POWUMANA

BOY - POI

BOYA - POIA

BOYANG - POIANA

BOYCE - POIKE

BOYD - POE

BOYET - POIEKI

BOYLE - POILE

BOZENA - POKENA

BRACE - PALAKE

BRACKEN - PALAKAKENI

BRAD - PALAKA

BRADEE - PALAKE

BRADEN - PALAKENI

BRADFORD - PALAKAPOLA

BRADI - PALAKI

BRADLEY - PALAKALEI

BRADUT - PALAKUKO

BRADY - PALAKI

BRADYN - PALAKINE

BRAEDEN - PALAEKENI

BRAEDON - PALAEKONU

BRAELIE - PALAELIE

BRAELYN - PALAELINE

BRAELYNN - PALAELINE

BRAGEN - PALAKENI

BRAIANA - PALAIANA

BRAIDEN - PALAIKENI

BRAISE - PALAIKE

BRAM - PALAMA

BRANA - PALANA

BRANCH - PALANAKA

BRANCO - PALANAKO

BRAND - PALANAKA

BRANDAN - PALANAKANA

BRANDE - PALANAKE

BRANDEN - PALANAKENI

BRANDI - PALANAKI

BRANDICE - PALANAKIKE

BRANDIE - PALANAKEI

BRANDO - PALANAKO

BRANDON - PALANAKONU

BRANDT - PALANAKAKA

BRANDY - PALENAKI

BRANDYE - PALANAKIE

BRANDYN - PALANAKINE

BRANFORD - PALANAPOLUKU

BRANIGAN - PALANIKANA
BRANKO - PALANAKO
BRAN'LYNN - PALANA'ALINE
BRANNIGHAN - PALANIKEHANA
BRANNON - PALANONU
BRANT - PALANAKA
BRANTLEY - PALANAKALEI
BRANSON - PALANAKONU
BRASHA - PALAKA
BASHAAR - PAKALA
BRATTON - PALAKONU
BRAULIO - PALAULIO
BRAVO - PALAWO
BRAXTIN - PALAKAKINE
BRAXTON - PALAKAKONU
BRAXTYN - PALAKAKINE
BRAY - PALAI
BRAYAN - PALAIANA
BRAYDEN - PALAIKENI
BRAYDONN - PALAIKONU
BRAYLEE - PALAILE
BRAYLEN - PALAILENI
BRAYLON - PALAILONU
BRAYOM - PALAIOMU
BRAYTON - PALAIKONU
BRE - PALE
BREA - PALEA
BREAN - PALEANA
BREANN - PALEANA
BREANNA - PALEANA

BREANNE - PALEANE
BREAUNNA - PALEAUNA
BRECHAN - PALEKANA
BRECK - PALEKIKI
BRECKAN - PALEKIKANA
BRECKEN - PALEKIKENI
BRECKLYNN - PALEKIKILINE
BREE - PALE
BREEANN - PALEANA
BREEANNA - PALEANA
BREELYN - PALELINE
BREENA - PALENA
BREEZA - PALEKA
BREEZY - PALEKI
BREIN - PALEINE
BREIYCE - PALEIIKE
BRENA - PALENIA
BRENDA - PALENAKA
BRENDALYN - PALENIKALINE
BRENDAN - PALENIKANA
BRENDEN - PALENIKENI
BRENDLE - PALENIKILE
BRENDOLYN - PALENIKOLINE
BRENDON - PALENIKONU
BRENLEY - PALENILEI
BRENNA - PALENA
BRENNAN - PALENANA
BRENNEN - PALENENI
BRENNER - PALENELI
BRENNON - PALENONU

BREON - PALEONU BRIDDEN - PALIKENI
BRENN - PALENI BRIDE - PALIKE
BRENT - PALENAKA BRIDEY - PALIKEI
BRENTLEY - PALENIKILEI BRIDGER - PALIKEKELI
BRENTON - PALENIKONU BRIDGET - PILIKIKA
BREONNA - PALEONA BRIDGETT - PILIKIKA
BRESHANNA - PALEKANA BRIDGETTE - PALIKEKEKE
BRESLEN - PALEKILENI BRIDGID - PALIKEKIKE
BRET - PALEKI BRIDGITT - PALIKEKIKE
BRETT - PALEKI BRIE - PALIE
BRETTA - PALEKA BRIELLE - PALIELE
BRETTON - PALEKONU BRIGETTE - PALIKEKE
BREVYN - PALEWINE BRIGGS - PALIKEKE
BREWER - PALEWELI BRIGHAM - PALIKEHAMA
BREYAN - PALEIANA BRIGHTON - PALIKEHEKONU
BREYANA - PALEIANA BRIGID - PALIKIKE
BREYDAN - PALEIKANA BRIGITT - PALIKIKE
BREZETTE - PALEKEKE BRIGITTE - PALIKIKE
BRI - PALI BRIGMARY - PALIKEMALI
BRIA - PALIA BRIJIDA - PALIIIKA
BRIAGH - PALIAKAHA BRIKAYLA - PALIKAILA
BRIAN - PALAINA BRILEY - PALILEI
BRIANA - PALIANA BRILI - PALILI
BRIANNA - PALIANA BRINA - PALINA
BRINNAE - PALINAE BRINDY - PALINEKI
BRIANNE - PALIANE BRINK - PALINEKE
BRIANNY - PALIANI BRINLEE - PALINELE
BRIAR - PALIALA BRINN - PALINE
BRICE - PALIKE BRINSTON - PALINEKONU
BRICK - PALIKEKE BRINT - PALINEKE

BRINTON - PALINEKONU

BRIOGHAN - PALIOKUHANA

BRIONNA - PALIONA

BRIONTAE - PALIONUKAE

BRIONY - PALIONI

BRISA - PALIKA

BRISHA - PALIKA

BRISON - PALIKONU

BRISSA - PALIKA

BRISTOL - PALIKOLU

BRISTON - PALIKONU

BRIT - PALI

BRITAIN - PALIKAINE

BRITANIE - PALIKANIE

BRITANY - PALIKANI

BRITENY - PALIKENI

BRITESSIA - PALIKEKIA

BRITNE - PALIKENE

BRITNEE - PALIKENE

BRITNEY - PALIKENEI

BRITNI - PALIKENI

BRITONIE - PALIKONIE

BRITONY -PALIKONI

BRITT - PALI

BRITTA - PALIKA

BRITTAINY - PALIKAINI

BRITTANEY - PALIKANEI

BRITTANI - PALIKANI

BRITTANIE - PALIKANIE

BRITTANY - PALIKANE

BRITTANYE - PALIKANIE

BRITTENY - PALIKENEI

BRITTINEE - PALIKINE

BRITTLEY - PALIKELEI

BRITTNEA - PALIKENEA

BRITTNEE - PALIKENE

BRITTNEY - PALIKENEI

BRITTNI - PALIKENI

BRITTNIE - PALIKENIE

BRITTNY - PALIKENI

BRITTON - PALIKONU

BRITTONIE - PALIKONIE

BRITTONY - PALIKONI

BRIYANA - PALIIANA

BRIYONNA - PALIIONA

BRIZSAY - PALIKEKAI

BROCK - PALOKUKU

BROCKERT - PALOKUKEKI

BRODERICK - PALOKELIKEKE

BRODIE - PALOKIE

BRODY - PALOKI

BROGAN - PALOKANA

BROMLIN - PALOMULINE

BRON - PALONU

BRONCA - PALONUKA

BRONETTE - PALONEKE

BRONLYNN - PALONULINE

BRONNIE - PALONIE

BRONSON - PALONUKONU

BRONTAE - PALONUKAE

BRONTË - PALONUKUËU

BRONWYN - PALONUWINE

BRONYA - PALONIA

BROOK - PALOKU

BROOKE - PALOKE

BROOKEE- PALOKE

BROOKELYN - PALOKULINE

BROOKLYN - PALOKULINE

BROOKNEY - PALOKUNEI

BROOKS - PALOKUKU

BROWN - PALOWUNU

BRUCE – PULUKE

BRUCHA - PALUKA

BRUMLEY - PALUMOLEI

BRUNA - PALUNA

BRUNDABAN - PALUNOKAPANA

BRUNO - PULUNO

BRUNY - PALUNI

BRYA - PALIA

BRYAN - PALIANA

BRYANA - PALIANA

BRYANN - PALIANA

BRYANNA - PALIANA

BRYANT - PALIANAKA

BRYAR - PALIALA

BRYCE - PALIKE

BRYCESON - PALIKEKONU

BRYCLYN - PALIKELINE

BRYDEN - PALIKENI

BRYEN - PALIENI

BRYER - PALIELI

BRYLER - PALILELI

BRYLIE - PALILIE

BRYLIN - PALILINE

BRYNA - PALINA

BRYNDEN - PALINEKENI

BRYNDON - PALINEKONU

BRYNIA - PALINIA

BRYNLAN - PALINELANA

BRYNLEE - PALINELE

BRYNLEIGH - PALINELEIKEHE

BRYNLEY - PALINELEI

BRYNN - PALINE

BRYNNE - PALINE

BRYNZLEY - PALINEKELEI

BRYON - PALIONU

BRYONY - PALIONI

BRYSON - PALIKONU

BRYTAN - PALIKANA

BRYTON - PALIKONU

BRYTTNI - PALIKENI

BUBBA - PUPA

BUBBLES - PUPOLEKI

BUBU - PUPU

BUCK - PUKOKO

BUCKY - PUKOKI

BUD - PUKO

BUDDAH - PUKAHA

BUDDIE – PUKIE

BUDDY - PUKI

BUETTA - PUEKA

BUFFI - PUPI

BUFFY - PUPI

BUFORD - PUPOLUKU

BUGSY - PUKOKI

BUKOLA - PUKOLA

BULBUL - PULOPULO

BUNKY - PUNOKI

BUNNIE, BUNNY - PUNI

BURAK - PULAKA

BURCH - PULOKO

BURDETTE - PULOKEKE

BURKE - PUKE

BURKHARD - PUKOHALAKA

BURKLEY - PUKOLEI

BURL - PULO

BURLEIGH - PULEIKEHE

BURLON - PULONU

BURNELL - PULONELI

BURNETTA - PULONEKA

BURNETTE - PULONEKE

BURNIE - PULONIE

BURROUGHS - PULOUKOHOKO

BURT - PUKO

BURTON - PUKONU

BUSAYO - PUKAIO

BUTCH - PUKOKO

BUTOS - PUKOKU

BUTSKO - PUKOKO

BUZZ - PUKO

BUZZY - PUKI

BYRD - PILEKE

BYRESIA - PILEKIA

BYRL - PILE

BYRON - PAILONA

C

FIRST NAMES

CABATIT - KAPAKIKE
CABELL - KAPELI
CABRINA - KAPALINA
CACEY - KAKEI
CADANCE - KAKANAKE
CADDIE - KAKIE
CADE - KAKE
CADEE - KAKE
CADEN - KAKENI
CADENCE - KAKENIKE
CADIAN - KAKIANA
CADY - KAKI
CAEL - KAELI
CAELI - KAELI
CAESAR – KAIKALA
CAGER - KAKELI
CAGNEY - KAKANEI
CAI - KAI
CAIBREE - KAIPELE
CAIDEE - KAIKE
CAIDEN - KAIKENI
CAIDENCE - KAIKENIKE
CAILEY - KAILEI
CAILIN - KAILINE
CAIN - KAINE
CAINE - KAINE
CAIRDON - KAILEKONU
CAIRO - KAILO
CAITHN - KAIKENE
CAITLIN - KAIKELINE

CAIN - KAINE
CAINE - KAINE
CAIRDON - KAILEKONU
CAIRO - KAILO
CAITHN - KAIKENE
CAITLIN - KAIKELINE
CAITLYN - KAIKELINE
CAITRIN - KAILINE
CAL - KALA
CALABRIA - KALAPALIA
CALAH - KALAHA
CALAHAN - KALAHANA
CALANDRA - KALANAKALA
CALDA - KALA
CALDER - KALELI
CALEB - KALEPA
CALEIGH - KALEIKEHE
CALE - KALE
CALEN - KALENI
CALEY - KALEI
CALI - KALI
CALICO - KALIKO
CALIFORNIA - KALIPOLUNIA
CALILA - KALILA
CALINA - KALINA
CALINTHA - KALINEKA
CALISE - KALIKE
CALISTA - KALIKA
CALIYAH - KALIIAHA
CALL - KALA

CALLA - KALA
CALLAGHAN - KALAKAHANA
CALLAWAY - KALAWAI
CALLE - KALE
CALLEE - KALE
CALLEN - KALENI
CALLI - KALI
CALLIE - KALIE
CALLUM - KALUMO
CALOB - KALOPU
CALUM - KALUMO
CALVARY - KALAWALI
CALVIN - KALAWINA
CALYX - KALIKE
CAM - KAMA
CAMAY - KAMAI
CAMBRIA - KAMAPALIA
CAMBRI - KAMAPALI
CAMBRIA - KAMAPALIA
CAMBRIE - KAMAPALIE
CAMBRY - KAMAPALI
CAMDEN - KAMAKENI
CAMELLIA - KAMELIA
CAMERA - KAMELA
CAMERON -KAMELONU
CAMERYN - KAMELINE
CAMI - KAMI
CAMILA - KAMILIA
CAMILLA - KAMILA
CAMILLE - KAMILE

CAMILLO - KAMILO
CAMILO - KAMILO
CAMMIE - KAMIE
CAMMY - KAMI
CAMPBELL - KAMAPAPELI
CAMRI - KAMALI
CAMRIN - KAMALINE
CAMRYN - KAMALINE
CANAAN - KANANA
CANARIO - KANALIO
CANDACE - KANAKAKE
CANDEN - KANAKENI
CANDI - KANAKE
CANDICE - KANAKIKE
CANDIE - KANAKE
CANDINA - KANAKINA
CANDIS - KANAKIKE
CANDITA - KANAKIKA
CANDY - KANAKE
CANDY-LYNN - KANAKI-ELINE
CANEISHA - KANEIKA
CANON - KANONU
CANTAVE - KANAKAWE
CANTENA - KANAKENA
CANTRELL - KANALELI
CANTU - KANAKU
CANTY - KANAKI
CANUTE - KANUKE
CAOILIN - KAOILINE
CAOIMHE - KAWEWA

CAPRI - KAPALI

CAPRICE - KAPALIKE

CAPTORIA - KAPAKOLIA

CAPY - KAPI

CARA - KALA

CARAH - KALAHA

CARDELLE - KALAKELE

CARDINAL - KALAKINALA

CARELI - KALELI

CAREN - KALENE

CARESSE - KALEKE

CARETH - KALEKI

CAREY - KALEI

CARI - KALI

CARIANNA - KALIANA

CARIDAD - KALIKAKA

CARIE - KALIE

CARIETHA - KALIEKA

CARIM - KALIME

CARINA - KALINA

CARING - KALINE

CARILYN - KALILINE

CARINA - KALINA

CARIS - KALIKE

CARISA - KALIKA

CARISSA - KALIKA

CARITA - KALIKA

CARL - KALA

CARLA - KALA

CARLEE - KALE

CARLEEN - KALENI

CARLEIGH - KALEIKEHE

CARLEIGH-ANN - KALEIKEHE-ANA

CARLEN - KALENI

CARLENA - KALENA

CARLENE - KALENE

CARLETHIA - KALEKIA

CARLETTE - KALEKE

CARLI - KALI

CARLIE - KALIE

CARLIES - KALIEKI

CARLIN - KALINE

CARLIS - KALIKE

CARLISIA - KALIKIA

CARLISLE - KALIKELE

CARLITO - KALIKO

CARLYSSA - KALIKA

CARIN - KALINE

CARITTA - KALIKA

CARLINA - KALINA

CARLLEY - KALEI

CARLO - KALO

CARLOS - KALOKA

CARLOTTA - KALOKA

CARLTON - KAKONU

CARLY - KALI

CARLYLE - KALILE

CARLYNN - KALINE

CARMA - KALAMA

CARMEL - KALAMELI

CARMELA - KALAMELA
CARMELI - KALAMELI
CARMELINA - KALAMELINA
CARMELITA - KALAMELIKA
CARMELYNN - KALAMELINE
CARMELO - KALAMELO
CARMEN - KALAMENI
CARMENCITA - KALAMENIKIKA
CARMENE - KALAMENE
CARMICHAEL - KALAMIKAELI
CARMIE - KALAMIE
CARMINA - KALAMINA
CARMINE - KALAMINE
CARMITA - KALAMIKA
CARMYN - KALAMINE
CARNA - KALANA
CAROL - KALOLA
CAROLANN - KALOLANA
CAROL-ANN - KALOU-ANA
CAROLE - KALOLA
CAROLEE - KALOLE
CAROLIE - KALOLIE
CAROLINA - KALOLINA
CAROLINE - KALOLAINA
CAROLLE - KALOLE
CAROLMAE - KALOLUMAE
CAROLYN - KALOLINE
CARON - KALONU
CARRI - KALI
CARRICK - KALIKEKE

CARRIE - KALIE
CARRINA - KALINA
CARRIANNE - KALIANE
CARRINGTON - KALINEKONU
CARRISSA - KALIKA
CARROLL - KALOLU
CARSEN - KALAKENI
CARSON - KALAKONU
CARSTEN - KALAKENI
CARTER - KAKELI
CARTINA - KAKINA
CARTRELL - KALELI
CARV - KALAWA
CARY - KALI
CARYL - KALILE
CARYN - KALINE
CARYNN - KALINE
CARYS - KALIKE
CAS - KAKA
CASAE - KAKAE
CASE - KAKE
CASEY - KAKEI
CASEYE - KAKEIE
CASH - KAKA
CASHERIE - KAKELIE
CASHMERE - KAKAMELE
CASIE - KAKIE
CASIPHIA - KAKIPIA
CASON - KAKONU
CASPAR - KAKAPALA

CASPER - KAKAPA

CASSANDRA - KAKANAKALA

CASSI - KAKI

CASSIA - KAKIA

CASSIDY - KAKIKI

CASSIDYE - KAKIKIE

CASSIE - KAKIE

CASSIUS - KAKIUKO

CASSONDRA - KAKONUKULA

CASSY - KAKI

CASSYCEL - KAKIKELI

CASTRO - KAKALO

CASULLA - KAKULA

CASY - KAKI

CAT - KAKA

CATALINA - KAKALINA

CATARINA - KAKALINA

CATARRIE - KAKALIE

CATE - KAKE

CATELYN - KAKELINE

CATENA - KAKENA

CATERINA - KAKELINA

CATHERINE - KAKALINA

CATHLEEN - KAKALENI

CATHLYN - KAKALINE

CATHRYN - KALINE

CATHY - KAKI

CATIA - KAKIA

CATIE - KAKIE

CATINA - KAKINA

CATRELL - KALELI

CATRIN - KALINE

CATRINA - KALINA

CATY - KAKI

CAVALYN - KAWALINE

CAVET - KAWEKI

CAVIN - KAWINE

CAVON - KAWONU

CYANI - KIANI

CAYANNE - KAIANE

CAYBRIN - KAIPELINE

CAYCEE - KAIKE

CAYDE - KAIKE

CAYDEN - KAIKENI

CAYE - KAIE

CAYETANO - KAIEKANO

CAYLA - KAILA

CAYLE - KAILE

CAYLEE - KAILE

CAYLEI - KAILEI

CAYLEX - KAILEKI

CAYLOR - KAILOLU

CAYMEN - KAIMENI

CAYNA - KAINA

CAYO - KAIO

CAYSEE - KAIKE

CEANDRYS - KEANAKALIKE

CEANNA - KEANA

CEARA - KEALA

CEARRA - KEALA

CEASAR - KEAKALA

CEATIN - KEAKINE

CECE - KEKE

CECELIA - KEKELIA

CECIL - KEKILIA

CECILE - KEKILE

CECILIA - KEKILIA

CECILIE - KEKILIE

CECILLE - KEKILE

CECILY - KEKILI

CEDAR - KEKALA

CEDRA - KEKILA

CEDRIC - KEKELIKA

CEFERINO - KEPELINO

CEIARA - KEIALA

CEILI - KEILI

CEIRAN - KEILANA

CELE - KELE

CELENA - KELENA

CELENCIA - KELENIKIA

CELENE - KELENE

CELESTE - KELEKE

CELESTINE - KELEKINA

CELESTINO - KELEKINO

CELIA - KELIA

CELICIA - KELIKIA

CELINA - KELINA

CELINDA - KELINEKA

CELINE - KELINE

CELINETTE - KELINEKE

CELLINDRIA - KELINEKELIA

CELSUM - KELIKUMO

CENA - KENA

CENAIDA - KENAIKA

CENCERE - KENIKELE

CENDA - KENIKA

CENOBIA - KENOPIA

CENON - KENONU

CENTRELL - KENILELI

CENZIE - KENIKIE

CERELLA - KELELA

CEREY - KELEI

CERIBET - KELIPEKI

CERIDWEN - KELIKEWENI

CERITA - KELIKA

CESAR - KEKALA

CESARE - KEKALE

CESARIO - KEKALIO

CESELEY - KEKELEI

CESI - KEKI

CESIA - KEKIA

CETA - KEKA

CETERIA - KEKELIA

CETH - KEKI

CEYANNA - KEIANA

CHACEY - KAKEI

CHAD - KAKA

CHADE - KAKE

CHADILAINE - KAKILAINE

CHADWICK - KAKAWIKEKE

CHAELA - KAELA
CHAELEY - KAELEI
CHAELI - KAELI
CHAELIM - KAELIME
CHAGUNBHAI - KAKUNOPOHAI
CHAI - KAI
CHAKA - KAKA
CHAKWIN - KAKAWINE
CHALA - KALA
CHALANA - KALANA
CHALAIN - KALAINE
CHALEE - KALE
CHALET - KALEKI
CHALICE - KALIKE
CHALIPA - KALIPA
CHALIZ - KALIKE
CHALLETTA - KALEKA
CHALLON - KALEONU
CHALYSE - KALIKE
CHAM - KAMA
CHAMAGNE - KAMAKANE
CHAMBERLAIN - KAMAPELAINE
CHAMBREL - KAMAPALELI
CHAMEKA - KAMEKA
CHAMME - KAME
CHAMP - KAMAPA
CHAMRONG - KAMALONU
CHAN - KANA
CHANA - KANA
CHANALL - KANALA

CHANCE - KANAKE
CHANCENI - KANAKENI
CHANCIE - KANAKIE
CHANDA - KANAKA
CHANDANA - KANAKANA
CHANDEN - KANAKENI
CHANDI - KANAKI
CHANDINI - KANAKINI
CHANDLER - KANAKALELI
CHANDLOR - LAMAKALOLU
CHANDRA - KANAKALA
CHANDREL - KANAKALELI
CHANEL - KANELI
CHANELLE - KANELE
CHANEQUA - KANEKA
CHANEY -KANEI
CHANH - KANAHA
CHANI - KANI
CHANIA - KANIA
CHANISE - KANIKE
CHANLEY - KANALEI
CHANNARY - KANALI
CHANNING - KANINE
CHANRITHY - KANALIKI
CHANTAL - KANAKALI
CHANTE - KANAKE
CHANTEL - KANAKELI
CHANTELL - KANAKELI
CHANTELLE - KANAKELE
CHANTENE - KANAKENE

CHANTREY - KANALEI

CHANTAY - KANAKAI

CHAPMAN - KAPAMANA

CHAR - KELA

CHARA - KALA

CHARANVIR - KALANAWILE

CHARAY - KALAI

CHARDON - KALAKONU

CHARDONNAY - KALAKONAI

CHAREEMAE - KALEMAE

CHARELLE - KALELE

CHARENE - KALENE

CHARETTE - KALEKE

CHARI - KALI

CHARINA - KALINA

CHARIS - KALIKE

CHARISC - KALIKEKE

CHARISMA - KALIKEMA

CHARISSA - KALIKA

CHARISSE - KALIKE

CHARITA - KALIKA

CHARITO - KALIKO

CHARITY - MANAWALE'A

CHARL - KALE

CHARLA - KALA

CHARLAINE - KALAINE

CHARLAN - KALANA

CHARLARIA - KALALIA

CHARLEE - KALE

CHARLEEN - KALENI

CHARLEMAGNE - KALEMAKANE

CHARLENE - KALENE

CHARLES - KALE

CHARLETA - KALEKA

CHARLONNIE - KALONIE

CHARLOTT - KALOKU

CHARLOTTE - KALAKI

CHARLIE - KALE

CHARLIZE - KALIKE

CHARLSI - KALAKI

CHARLTON - KAKONU

CHARLY - KALI

CHARMAINE - KALAMAINE

CHARMIAN - KALAMIANA

CHARNA - KALANA

CHARNDIP - KALANAKIPE

CHARNE - KALANE

CHARO - KALO

CHARON - KALONU

CHARREE - KALE

CHARRISSE - KALIKE

CHARTARA - KAKALA

CHARTIIA - KAKIA

CHARU - KALU

CHARULATA - KALULAKA

CHARVETTE - KALAWEKE

CHARYDAN - KALIKANA

CHARYL - KALILE

CHAPIN - KAPINE

CHASE - KAKE

CHASITY - KAKIKI

CHASON - KAKONU

CHASSAH - KAKAHA

CHASTITY - KAKIKI

CHASTON - KAKONU

CHATHAM - KAKAMA

CHAU - KAU

CHAUNCI - KAUNOKI

CHAUNNA - KAUNA

CHAUNTEA - KAUNOKEA

CHAUNTRENIECE - KAUNOLENIEKE

CHAUNTIA - KAUNOKIA

CHAUNTIVIA - KAUNOKIWIA

CHAVI - KAWI

CHAVIS - KAWIKE

CHAW - KAWA

CHAYA - KAIA

CHAYPIN - KAIPINE

CHEVANCE - KEWANAKE

CHAVELA - KAWELA

CHAVELO - KAWELO

CHAYA - KAIA

CHAYCE - KAIKE

CHAYDEN - KAIKENI

CHAYLA - KAILA

CHAZE - KAKE

CHAZELLE - KAKELE

CHAZZ - KAKA

CHE - KE

CHEA - KEA

CHECOTAH - KEKOKAHA

CHEECHING - KEKINE

CHEESHIA - KEKIA

CHEIREE - KEILE

CHELBY - KELIPI

CHELCIE - KELIKIE

CHELE - KELE

CHELENE - KELENE

CHELISE - KELIKE

CHELLE - KELE

CHELO - KELO

CHELSA - KELIKA

CHELSEA - KELIKEA

CHELSEY - KELIKEI

CHELSI - KELIKI

CHELSIE - KELIKIE

CHEMIMA - KEMIMA

CHEN - KENI

CHENAY - KENAI

CH'ENELLE - KA'ENELE

CHENETHA - KENEKA

CHENG - KENI

CHENI - KENI

CHENOA - KENOA

CHENOAH - KENOAHA

CHENOLA - KENOLA

CHENYING - KENIINE

CHEP - KEPI

CHER - KELI

CHERE' - KELE

CHEREE - KELE

CHERESE - KELEKE

CHERI - KELI

CHERIC - KELIKE

CHERICA - KELIKA

CHERIE - KELIE

CHER'IE - KELI'IE

CHERILYN - KELELINA

CHERISE - KELIKE

CHERISH - KELIKE

CHERISTY - KELIKI

CHERITA - KELIKA

CHERITH - KELIKE

CHERLONA - KELONA

CHERLYN - KELINE

CHERMAINE - KELIMAINE

CHERMALETA - KELIMALEKA

CHEROKEE - KELOKE

CHERRA - KELA

CHERRELLE - KELELE

CHERRONE - KELONE

CHERRY - KELI

CHERRYLYN - KELILINE

CHERSTON - KELIKONU

CHERYL - KELELA

CHERYLE - KELILE

CHERYLETTE - KELILEKE

CHERYLYNN - KELILINE

CHERYTH - KELIKE

CHESHANA - KEKANA

CHESLEY - KEKILEI

CHESLI - KEKILI

CHESNEY - KEKINEI

CHESSA - KEKA

CHESTER - KEKELA

CHET - KEKE

CHETTA -KEKA

CHEUNG - KEUNO

CHEUNGWAH - KEUNOWAHA

CHEVIS - KEWIKE

CHEVONNE - KEWONE

CHEVRON - KEWILONU

CHEVY - KEWI

CHEW FERN - KEWI PELINI

CHEYANNA - KEIANA

CHEYANNE - KEIANE

CHEYE - KEIE

CHEYENEA - KEIENEA

CHEYENNA - KEIENA

CHEYENNE - KEIENE

CHEYLENE - KEILENE

CHEYNE - KEINE

CHEYTEN - KEIKENI

CHEZMIN - KEKIMINE

CHHAIL - KAILE

CHI CHI - KI KI

CHIA-EN - KIA-ENI

CHIARA - KIALA

CHICO - KIKO

CHIDI - KIKI

CHIMANE - KIMANE
CHIRAG - KILAKA
CHITO - KIKO
CHIA LIN - KIA LINE
CHIANG - KIANA
CHIBLIE - KIPELIE
CHIEDOZIE - KIEKOKIE
CHIEF - KIEPI
CHIEMI - KIEMI
CHIERRA - KIELA
CHIL - KILE
CHILI - KILI
CHIKA - KIKA
CHIMEA - KIMEA
CHIN - KINE
CHINA - KINA
CHINAMI - KINAMI
CHINARA - KINALA
CHINDA - KINEKA
CHINETHA - KINEKA
CHING - KINE
CHINO - KINO
CHIP - KIPE
CHI'QUAVION - KI'EKAWIONU
CHIQUI - KIKI
CHIQUITA - KIKIKA
CHIRAG - KILAKA
CHIRINA - KILINA
CHISM - KIKEME
CHITRA - KILA

CHIVON - KIWONU
CHIVY - KIWI
CHLOE - KALOE
CHLORY - KALOLI
CHOLE - KOLE
CHOLEE - KOLE
CHOLY - KOLI
CHOMMY - KOMI
CHONA - KONA
CHONG - KONU
CHOOK LING - KOKU LINE
CHOPPER - KOPELI
CHOSEN - KOKENI
CHOW - KOWU
CHOY - KOI
CHRIS - KILIKA
CHISATO - KIKAKO
CHRESTA - KALEKA
CHRISEL - KALIKELI
CHRISHAUN - KALIKAUONO
CHRISHAWNA - KALIKAWANA
CHRISHELLE - KALIKELE
CHRISINA - KALIKINA
CHRISSIA - KALIKIA
CHRISSIE - KALIKIE
CHRISSY - KALIKI
CHRISTA - KILIKIKA
CHRISTABELLA - KALIKAPELA
CHRISTABELLE - KALIKAPELE
CHRISTABELLI - KALIKAPELI

CHRISTABELLO - KALIKAPELO

CHRISTAL - KELIKALA

CHRISTALEE - KALIKALE

CHRISTAN - KALIKANA

CHRISTANOELLE - KALIKANOELE

CHRISTELLE - KALIKELE

CHRISTEN - KALIKENI

CHRISTERPHER - KALIKELIPELI

CHRISTI - KALIKI

CHRISTIA - KALIKIA

CHRISTIAN - KALIKIANA

CHRISTIANA - KALIKIANA

CHRISTIANE - KALIKIANE

CHRISTIE - KALIKIE

CHRISTIN - KALIKINE

CHRISTINA - KILIKINA

CHRISTINE - KILIKINA

CHRISTOF - KALIKOPU

CHRISTOPHER - KILIKOPELA

CHRISTOS - KALIKOKU

CHRISTY - KILIKI

CHRYSTAL - KALIKALA

CHRYSTALIA - KALIKALIA

CHRYSTENE - KALIKENE

CHRYSTIE - KALIKIE

CHU-CHU - KU-OKU

CHUCK, CHUCKY- KUKAKI

CHUCO - KUKO

CHUE - KUE

CHUG - KUKO

CHUMROEN - KUMOLOENI

CHUNG - KUNO

CHUSHEE - KUKE

CHYLAN - KILANA

CHYNA - KINA

CHYOMA - KIOMA

CHYREE' - KILE'I

CHRYS - KALIKE

CHRYSSI - KALIKI

CHRYSSIE - KALIKIE

CHRYSSY - KALIKI

CHRYSTA - KALIKA

CHRYSTALYN - KALIKALINE

CHRYSTELL - KALIKELI

CHYANN - KIANA

CIAN - KIANA

CIANNA - KIANA

CIANTHE - KIANAKE

CIANTHE' - KIANAKE'I

CIARA - KIALA

CIBEIS - KIPEIKE

CICELY - KIKELI

CID - KIKE

CIDALIA - KIKALIA

CIDEL - KIKELI

CIELA - KIELA

CIELLE - KIELE

CIENNA - KIENA

CIERA - KIELA

CIERRA - KIELA

CIGTUM - KIKEKUMO

CILELA - KILELA

CILICIA - KILIKIA

CILISSIA - KILIKIA

CIMARRON - KIMALONU

CINDA - KINEKA

CINDEE - KINEKE

CINDERELLA - KINEKELELA

CINDI - KINEKI

CINDY - KINI

CINNAMON - KINAMONU

CINTIA - KINELIA

CINZIA -KINEKIA

CIPRIAN - KIPELIANA

CIPRIANO - KIPELIANO

CIRO - KILO

CIRCE - KILEKE

CISCO - KIKEKO

CISSIE - KIKIE

CITA - KIKA

CITLALLY - KIKELALI

CJ -KI

CJAVON - KIAWONU

CLAE - KALAE

CLAIR - KALALA

CLAIRE - KALALA

CLANCY - KALANAKI

CLARA - KALALA

CLARE - KALALE

CLAREEN - KALALENI

CLARENCE - KALALENA

CLARENE - KALALENE

CLARICE - KALALIKA

CLARINDA - KALALINEKA

CLARISSA - KALALIKA

CLARISSE - KALALIKE

CLARITY - KALALIKI

CLARK - KALAKA

CLARO - KALALO

CLASSIE - KALAKIE

CLAUDE - KALUKA

CLAUDELL - KALUKALE

CLAUDETTA - KALAUKEKA

CLAUDETTE - KALAUKEKE

CLAUDIA – KALAUKIA

CLAUDIE - KALAUKIE

CLAUDINE - KALAUKAKINE

CLAUDIO - KALAUKIO

CLAUS - KALAUKO

CLAVER - KALAWELI

CLAY - KALAI

CLAYNE - KALAINE

CLAYTARIUS - KALAIKALIUKO

CLAYTON - KALIKONA

CLEAVELAND - KALEAWELANAKA

CLEBURN - KALEPULONE

CLEBURNE - KALEPULONE

CLEISURE - KALEIKULE

CLELIA - KALELIA

CLEM - KALEMA

CLEMENT - KALEMENA
CLEMENTINA - KALEMENIKINA
CLEMIE - KALEMIE
CLEMISHIA - KALEMIKIA
CLEMSON - KALEMIKONU
CLEO - KALEO
CLEOFE - KALEOPE
CLEON - KALEONU
CLEONDRA - KALEONUKULA
CLEONE - KALEONE
CLEOPATRA - KALEOPAKALA
CLEORETTA - KALEOLEKA
CLETA - KALEKA
CLETUS - KALEKUKO
CLEVA - KALEWA
CLEVELAND - KALEWELANAKA
CLEVER - KALEWELI
CLEWIS - KALEWIKE
CLIFF - KALIPA
CLIFFORD - KALIPONA
CLIFTA - KALIPEKA
CLIFTON - KALIPEKONA
CLINT - KALINEKE
CLINTON - KALINAKONA
CLIODNA - KALIOKUNA
CLIONA - KALIONA
CLIVE - KALIWE
CLODAGH - KALOKAKAHA
CLOE - KALOE
CLOETHA - KALOEKA

CLOEY - KALOEI
CLORINDA - KALOLINEKA
CLORISSA - KALOLIKA
CLOUD - KALOUKO
CLOVER - KALOWELI
CLOYCE - KALOIKE
CLYDE - KALAILA
COBE - KOPE
COBURN - KOPULONO
COBY - KOPI
COCO - KOKO
CODI - KOKI
CODY - KOKI
COE - KOE
COETA - KOEKA
COHEN - KOHENI
COHNER - KOHUNELI
COI - KOI
COLANDRA - KOLANAKALA
COLBY - KOLUPI
COLE - KOLE
COLEEN - KOLENI
COLEMAN - KOLEMANA
COLETHIA - KOLEKIA
COLETTE - KOLEKE
COLEY - KOLEI
COLI - KOLI
COLIN, COLLIN - KALINA
COLLEE - KOLE
COLLEEN - KALINA

COLLETTE - KOLEKE

COLM - KOLUMU

COLOMBE - KOLOMUPE

COLONY - KOLONI

COLSON - KOLUKONU

COLT - KOLUKU

COLTEN - KOLUKENI

COLTER - KOLUKELI

COLTON - KOLUKONU

COLUMBUS - KOLUMOPUKO

COMFORT - KOMUPOKU

COMISHA - KOMIKA

COMMANDO - KOMANAKO

CONAGHER - KONAKAHELI

CONAN - KONANA

CONCEPCION - KONUKEPIKIONU

CONCETTA - KONUKEKA

CONCHITA - KONUKIKA

CONERIA - KONELIA

CONLAN - KONULANA

CONLEY - KONULEI

CONNAKA - KONAKA

CONNAL - KONALA

CONNER - KONELI

CONNIE - KANI

CONNOR - KONOLU

CONNY - KONI

CONOR - KONOLU

CONRAD - KONULAKA

CONRADO - KONULAKO

CONRI - KONULI

CONSTANCE - KANAKANAKE

CONSTANTIN - KONUKANAKINE

CONSUELO - KONOKUELO

CONTESSA - KONUKEKA

CONTINA - KONUKINA

CONTRELL - KONULELI

COOKIE - KUKI

COOPER - KOPELI

COPPER - KOPELI

CORA - KALONI

CORAL - KOLALA

CORALIE - KOLALIE

CORAZON – KOLAKONA

CORBAN - KOLUPANA

CORBETT - KOLUPEKI

CORBIN - KOLUPINE

CORBY - KOLUPI

CORD - KOLUKU

CORDAY - KOLUKAI

CORDELIA - KOLUKELIA

CORDELL - KOLUKELI

CORDIA - KOLUKIA

CORDILLA - KOLUKILA

CORDILLO - KOLUKILO

CORE - KOLE

COREEN - KOLENI

CORETTA - KOLEKA

COREY - KOLI

CORI - COLI

CORIA - KOLIA
CORIANDER - KOLIANAKELI
CORIANNE - KOLIANE
CORIN - KOLINE
CORINA - KOLINA
CORINDA - KOLINEKA
CORINN - KOLINE
CORINNA - KOLINA
CORINNE - KOLINA
CORISA - KOLIKA
CORISSA - KOLIKA
CORKIE - KOKIE
CORLETTA - KOLEKA
CORLEY - KOLEI
CORLINDA - KOLINEKA
CORLISS - KOLIKE
CORMA - KOLUMA
CORMAC - KOLMAKA
CORNELIA - KOLUNELIA
CORNELIUS - KOLENELIO
CORNELL - KOLUNELI
CORNET - KOLUNEKI
CORRETHEA - KOLEKEA
CORRIE - KOLIE
CORRIGAN - KOLIKANA
CORRINA - KOLINA
CORRINE - KOLINE
CORRINNE - KOLINE
CORT - KOKU
CORTEZ - KOKEKI

CORTLY - KOKULI
CORTNEY - KOKUNEI
CORTNI - KOKUNI
CORVIN - KOLUWINE
CORY - KOLI
CORYELL - KOLIELI
CORYN - KOLINE
COSETTE - KOKEKE
COSIMA - KOKIMA
COSMO - KOKUMO
COSTA - KOKA
COSTI - KOKI
COTTIA - KOKIA
COTTON - KOKONU
COULTER - KOULOKELI
COURTLAND - KOUKOLANAKA
COURTNEY - KOUKONEI
COURTNI - KOUKONI
COVENTRY - KOWENILI
COVEY - KOWEI
COWELL - KOWELI
COWLEY - KOWULEI
COY - KOI
COYE - KOIE
COYLENE - KOILENE
COZETTE - KOKEKE
COZY - KOKI
CRAIG - KAIKA
CRAISHAN - KALAIKANA
CRANDELL - KALANAKELI

CRAWFORD - KALAWAPOLUKU

CRAYTON - KALAIKONU

CREANNA - KALEANA

CREARY - KALEALI

CREDORA - KALEKOLA

CREED - KALEKI

CREEDENCE - KALEKENIKE

CREIGHTON - KALEIKEHEKONU

CRENA - KALENA

CRESCENCIA - KALEKIKENIKIA

CRESCENT - KALEKIKENIKI

CRESENDA - KALEKENIKA

CRESSIE - KALEKIE

CRESSWELL - KALEKIWELI

CRESTA - KALEKA

CRETIA - KALEKIA

CRICKET - KALIKEKEKI

CRIS - KILIKA

CRISALDO - KALIKALO

CRISANTO - KALIKANAKO

CRISANTEMA - KALIKANAKEMA

CRISELDA - KALIKELA

CRISHELLE - KALIKELE

CRISIANNE - KALIKIANE

CRISJIANA - KALIKIIANA

CRISPIN - KALIKEPINE

CRISSY - KALIKI

CRISTEL - KALIKELI

CRISTIN - KALIKINE

CRISTINA - KALIKINA

CRISTINE - KALIKINE

CRISTIE - KALIKIE

CRISTOBAL - KALIKOPALA

CRISTY - KALIKI

CRIZA - KALIKA

CROSBY - KALOKUPI

CRUZ - KALUKO

CRYSTA - KALIKA

CRYSTAL - KALIKALA

CRYSTEN – KALIKENI

CRYSTIE - KALIKIE

CRYSTINA - KALIKINA

CUBA - KUPA

CUC - KUKO

CULLEN - KULENI

CULLEY - KULEI

CULLUM - KULUMO

CUPIDEAN - KUPIKEANA

CURLEY - KULEI

CURRIE - KULIE

CURSTEN - KULOKENI

CURT - KUKO

CURTIS - KULIKA

CURTNEKA - KUKONEKA

CUSHMEER – KUKOMELI

CUTLER - KUKOLEILI

CUTTER - KUKELI

CUYLER - KUILELI

CYANNE - KIANE
CYBELLE - KIPELE
CYBIL - KIPILE
CYCY - KIKI
CYD - KIKA
CYDNEY - KIKENEI
CYLINTHIA - KILINEKIA
CYMBELINE - KIMEPELINE
CYMIE - KIMIE
CYMONE - KIMONE
CYNDE- KINEKE
CYNDI - KINEKI
CYNDLE - KINEKELE
CYNICA - KINIKA
CYNISE - KINIKE
CYNTHIA - KINIKIA
CYNTIA - KINILIA
CYPRESS - KIPELEKI
CYPRIANO - KIPELIANO
CYRANI - KILANI
CYRE - KILE
CYRIL - KILILE
CYRIS - KILIKE
CYRUS - KULO
CZARINA - KAKALINA

D

FIRST NAMES

DABNEY - KAPANEI
DABREYN - KAPALEINE
DAC - KAKA
DACIA - KAKIA
DACIE - KAKIE
DADEN - KAKENI
DADO - KAKO
DADRE - KAKALE
DAE - KAE
DAEGAN - KAEKANA
DAELYN - KAELINE
DAENA – KAENA
DAENEN - KAENENI
DAETYN - KAEKINE
DAE-VAUN - KAE-IWAUNO
DAF - KAPA
DAG - KAKA
DAGAN - KAKANA
DAGFINN - KAKAPINE
DAGMAR - KAKAMALA
DAGNY - KAKANI
DAGWOOD - KAKAWOKU
DAHL - KAHALA
DAHLIA - KAHALIA
DAHMEER - KAHAMELI
DAHOMEY - KAHOMEI
DAHWEN - KAHAWENI
DAICE - KAIKE
DAIMELYNN – KAIMELINE
DAINA - KAINA

DAINIUS - KAINIUKO
DAIQUAN - KAIKANA
DAIQUIRI - KAIKILI
DAIQUON - KAIKUONU
DAISHA – KAIKA
DAISHEA - KAIKEA
DAI-SUP - KAI-EKUPO
DAISY - KAIKI
DAIVA - KAIWA
DAIZY - KAIKI
DAJAH - KAIAHA
DAJUAN - KAIUANA
DAJOUR - KAIOULO
DAJUNA - KAIUNA
DAKOTA - KAKOKA
DAKOTAH - KAKOKAHA
DAKWAN - KAKAWANA
DALA - KALA
DALALS - KALALAKA
DALAN - KALANA
DALASA - KALAKA
DALE - KAILA
DALENA - KALENA
DALENE - KALENE
DALESSIE - KALEKIE
DALIA - KALIA
DALIAJAH - KALIAIAHA
DALILA - KALILA
DALJIT - KALIIKE
DALLAS - KALAKA

DALLIN - KALINE

DALLIS - KALIKE

DALLON - KALONU

DALPHENA - KALAPENA

DALTEN - KALAKENI

DALTON - KALAKONU

DALVINEY - KALAWINEI

DALYSE - KALIKE

DAM - KAMA

DAMANI - KAMANI

DAMARA - KAMALA

DAMARCUS - KAMALAKUKO

DA'MARCUS - KA'AMALAKUKO

DAMARI - KAMALI

DAMARIS - KAMALIKE

DAMARIUS - KAMALIUKO

DA'MARREYAH - KA'AMALEIAHA

DAMERA - KAMELA

DAMESHIA - KAMEKIA

DAMIA - KAMIA

DAMIAN - KAMIANA

DAMIEN - KAMIENI

DAMIEON - KAMIEONU

DAMIKA - KAMIKA

DAMION - KAMIONU

DAMISHA - KAMIKA

DAMON - KAMONA

DAMOND - KAMONUKU

DAMONTAE - KAMONUKAE

DAMONTRY - KAMONULI

DAMYA - KAMIA

DAN - KANA

DANA - KANA

DANAE - KANAE

DANAKA - KANAKA

DANAN - KANANA

DANCIA - KANAKIA

D'ANDRE - KA'ANAKALE

D'ANGELO - KA'ANELO

DANE - KANE

DANEAN - KANEANA

DANECIA - KANEKIA

DANEEN - KANENI

DANEITA - KANEIKA

DA'NEL - KA'ANELI

DANELLA - KANELA

DANELLE - KANELE

DANERIA - KANELIA

DANETTE - KANEKE

DANI - KANI

DANIA - KANIA

DANICA - KANIKA

DANICE - KANIKE

DANIE - KANIE

DANIEL - KANIELA

DANIELA - KANIELA

DANIELE - KANIELE

DANIELLA - KANIELA

DANIELLE - KANIELE

DANIKA - KANIKA

DANILO - KANILO

DANISHSA - KANIKEKA

DANITA - KANIKA

DANNA - KANA

DANNER - KANELI

DANNI - KANI

DANNNON - KANONU

DANNY - KANI

DAO - KAO

DANRAJH - KANALAIHE

DANTAE - KANAKAE

DANTE - KANAKE

DANTERIA - KANAKELIA

DANTERIOUS - KANAKELIOUKO

DANTRELL - KANALELI

DANUTA - KANUKA

DANUTE - KANUKE

DANYA - KANIA

DANYAL - KANIALA

DANYEA - KANIEA

DANYELLE - KANIELE

DANYL - KANILE

DANYN - KANINE

DANZEL - KANAKELI

DAPHANE - KAPANE

DAPHNE - KAPANE

DAPHINE - KAPINE

DAPHINNE - KAPINE

DAR - KALA

DARA - KALA

DARALYN - KALALINE

DARAN - KALANA

DARANESHIA - KALANEKIA

DARANIQUA - KALANIKA

DARBY - KALAPI

D'ARC - KA'ALAKA

DARCEL - KALAKELI

DARCELL - KALAKELI

DARCI - KALAKI

D'ARCY, DARCY - KALAKI

DARD - KALAKA

DARDENELLA - KALAKENELA

DARE - KALE

DAREN, DARREN - KALENI

DARGAN - KAKANA

DARIA - KALIA

DARIAN - KALIANA

DARICK - KALIKEKE

DARIELLE - KALIELE

DARIEN - KALIENI

DARIENNE - KALIENE

DARIN - KALINA

DARIO - KALIO

DARION - KALIONU

DARIUS - KALIU

DARJA - KALIA

DARLA - KALA

DARLEE - KALE

DARLEEN - KALENI

DARLENE - KALINA

DARLETTA - KALEKA
DARLITH - KALIKE
DARLON - KALONU
DARLYN - KALINE
DARMA - KALAMA
D'ARNE - KA'ALANE
DARNELL - KALANELI
DARNELLE - KALANELE
DARNESHIA - KALANEKIA
DAROLYN - KALOLINE
DARON - KALONU
DARQUISE - KALAKIKE
DARRELL - KALELI
DARRELLYN - KALELINE
DARREN - KALENI
DARRET - KALEKI
DARRIAN - KALIANA
DARRICK - KALIKEKE
DARRICKA - KALIKEKA
DARRIN - KALINE
DARRIONA - KALIONA
DARRIUS - KALIUKO
DARRYL - KALELA
DARRYLYN - KALILINE
DARRYN - KALINE
DARSHAK - KALAKAKA
DARSON - KALAKONU
DART - KAKA
DARTHY - KAKI
DARTRAIL - KALAILE

DARVA - KALAWA
DARVID - KALAWIKA
DARYL - KALELA
DARYLANN - KALILANA
DARYUS - KALIUKO
DARWIN - KALAWINA
DARY - KALI
DARYA - KALIA
DARYN - KALINA
DASCHELE - KAKAKELE
DASEAN - KAKEANA
DASH - KAKA
DASHA - KAKA
DASHANAE - KAKANAE
DASHANNA - KAKANA
DASIA - KAKIA
DASHIELL - KAKIELI
DASMINE - KAKAMINE
DATHAN - KAKANA
DATIE - KAKIE
DATON - KAKONU
DATREONI - KALEONI
DAUD - KAUKO
DAVA - KAWA
DAVALENA - KAWALENA
DAVAN - KAWANA
DARVANY - KALAWANI
DAVE - KAWE
DAVEAT - KAWEAKA
DAVEDDA - KAWEKA

DAVEN - KAWENI

DAVIANNA - KAWIANA

DAVID - KAWIKA

DAVIDA - KAWIKA

DAVIE - KAWIE

DAVIENA - KAWIENA

DAVIN - KAWINE

DAVINA - KAWINA

DAVINDER - KAWINEKELI

DAVION - KAWIONU

DAVIS - KAWIKE

DAVISON - KAWIKONU

DAVON - KAWONU

DAVONTE - KAWONUKE

DAVORN - KAWOLUNU

DAWN - KANA

DAWNA - KAWANA

DAWNALEE - KAWANALE

DAWNDEE - KAWANAKE

DAWNE - KAWANE

DAWNETT - KAWANEKI

DAWNIELLE - KAWANIELE

DAWNTE - KAWANAKE

DAWOOD - KAWOKU

DAWSON - KAWAKONU

DAX - KAKA

DAXTON - KAKAKONU

DAY - KAI

DAYANARA - KAIANALA

DAYETTE - KAIEKE

DAYIA - KAIIA

DAYLA - KAILA

DAYLATWAN - KAILAKAWANA

DAYLE - KAILE

DAYLEN - KAILENI

DAYLEEN - KAILENI

DAYLON - KAILONU

DAYMON - KAIMONU

DAYNA - KAINA

DAYNE - KAINE

DAYSE - KAIKE

DAYSHA - KAIKA

DAYSON - KAIKONU

DAYTON - KAIKONU

DAYVIS - KAIWIKE

DAYZJA - KAIKIA

DAZARREON - KAKALEONU

DAZHON - KAKAHONU

DAZZIEL - KAKIELI

DEAIRIAN - KEAILIANA

DEAMBRA - KEAMAPALA

DEAN - KINI

DEANA - KEANA

DEANDRA - KEANAKALA

DEANDRE' - KEANAKALE'I

DEANDRIA - KEANAKALIA

DEANGELO - KEANELO

DEANICA - KEANIKA

DEANN - KEANA

DEANNA - KIANA

DEANNE - KEANE

DEANNIS - KEANIKE

DEANTE - KEANAKE

DEANO - KEANO

DEARA - KEALA

DEAR - KEALA

DEARBHLA - KEALAWALA

DEARIAS - KEALIAKA

DEARON - KEALONU

DE ASIA - KE AKIA

DEATON - KEAKONU

DEATRA - KEALA

DE'AUNA - KE'AUNA

DEAUNTE' - KEAUNOKE'I

DEAVANNAH - KEAWANAHA

DEB - KEPI

DEBBIE - KEPI

DEBBY - KEPI

DEBORAH - KEPOLA

DEBORLY - KEPOLI

DEBRA - KEPOLA

DEBRALEE - KEPILALE

DEBRONICA - KEPILONIKA

DECE - KEKE

DECEMBER - KEKEMIPELI

DECENTRA - KEKENILA

DECHELLE - KEKELE

DECKLAN - KEKIKILANA

DECKLEN - KEKIKILENI

DECKLIN - KEKIKILINE

DECLAN - KEKILANA

DEDALUS - KEKALUKO

DEDRIC - KEKILIKE

DEDY - KEKI

DEE - KI

DEE ANN - KI ANA

DEE DEE - KI KI

DEEANJO - KEANIO

DEEDEE - KEKE

DEENA - KENA

DEEP - KEPI

DEEPA - KEPA

DEEPAK - KEPAKA

DEEPTI - KEPIKI

DEETTE- KEKE

DE ETTE - KE EKE

DEHMIN - KEHIMINE

DEIARRA - KEIALA

DEIDRA - KEIKELA

DEIDRE - KEIKELE

DEIJIA - KEI'IA

DEIONTE - KEIONUKE

DEIRDRE - KELEKELA

DEITRE - KEILE

DEJA - KEIA

DEJAUN - KEIAUNO

DEJEUNET - KEIEUNEKI

DEJON - KEIONU

DEJONNEE - KEIONE

DEJSHA - KEIKA

DE'JAN'E - KE'IANA'E

DEKESHIA - KEKEKIA

DEKOTA - KEKOKA

DEL - KELI

DELACIE - KELAKIE

DELACRUZ - KELAKALUKO

DELAINA - KELAINA

DELAINE - KELAINE

DELAINEY - KALANEI

DELANIE - KELANIE

DELANA - KELANA

DELANCEY - KELANAKEI

DELANDA - KELANAKA

DELANEE - KELANE

DELANEY - KALANEI

DELANIE - KELANIE

DELANO - KELANO

DELANTA - KELANAKA

DELAYNE - KELAINE

DELBERT - KELIPEKI

DELEASE - KELEAKE

DELEATH - KELEAKA

DELEIGH - KELEIKEHE

DELFA - KELIPA

DELFIDIO - KELIPIKIO

DELFILIO - KELIPILIO

DELFINA - KELIPINA

DELFINO - KELIPINO

DELIA - KELIA

DELICIA - KELIKIA

DELIETA - KELIEKA

DELIGHT - KELIKEHEKE

DELILAH - KELILAHA

DELINA - KELINA

DELINDA - KELINEKA

DELINE - KELINE

DELINSA - KELINEKA

DELISA - KELIKA

DELISHA - KELIKA

DELLA – KELA

DELLENE - KELENE

DELLIE - KELIE

DELMAR - KELIMALA

DELMER - KELIMELI

DELMY - KELIMI

DELNILLA - KELINILA

DELOIS - KELOIKE

DELONA - KELONA

DELONSHA - KELONUKA

DELONYA - KELONIA

DELORA - KELOLA

DELORES - KOLOLEKE

DELOS - KELOKU

DELPHINA - KELIPINA

DELPHINE - KELIPINE

DELROY - KELILOI

DELSA - KELIKA

DELSHUNAE - KELIKUNAE

DELSYN - KELIKINE
DELTA - KELIKA
DELVA - KELIWA
DELVIN - KELIWINE
DELWYN - KELIWINE
DELYN - KELINE
DEMANDRIA - KEMANAKALIA
DEMANI - KEMANI
DEMAR - KEMALA
DEMARCUS - KEMALAKUKO
DEMARIAH - KEMALIAHA
DEMARIAN - KEMALIANA
DEMARION - KEMALIONA
DEMARIE - KEMALIE
DEMARYO - KEMALIO
DE'MARQUEAYLA - KE'IMALAKEAILA
DEMARQUINEZ - KEMALAKINEKA
DEMECIA - KEMEKIA
DEMECO - KEMEKO
DEMERISE - KEMELIKE
DEMESHIA - KEMEKIA
DEMETRI - KEMELI
DEMETRIO - KEMELIO
DEMETRIOUS - KEMELIOUKO
DEMETRIQUE - KEMELIKE
DEMETRUS - KEMELUKO
DEMI - KEMI
DEMIAN - KEMIANA
DEMIKA - KEMIKA
DEMILIA - KEMILIA

DEMINIA - KEMINIA
DEMITRI - KEMILI
DEMITRIA - KEMILIA
DEMITRIUS - KEMIKILIO
DEMOND - KEMONUKU
DEMONICA - KEMONIKA
DEMONSHA - KEMONUKA
DEMONTE - KEMONUKE
DEMPSEY - KEMIPIKEI
DEMY - KEMI
DEN - KENI
DENA - KENA
DENAE - KENAE
DENAI - KENAI
DENAJIA - KENAIIA
DENALI - KENALI
DENBIGH - KENIPIKEHE
DENDRIA - KENIKILIA
DENEA - KENEA
DENEANE - KENEANE
DENEBE - KENEPE
DENECE - KENEKE
DENEE - KENE
DENEEN - KENENI
DENEI - KENEI
DENELLE - KENELE
DENETRA - KENELA
DENETTE - KENEKE
DENHAM - KENIHAMA
DENIA - KENIA

DENICO - KENIKO

DENIE - KENIE

DENIELLE - KENIELE

DENIM - KENIME

DENISE - KENIKI

DENISHA - KENIKA

DENITA - KENIKA

DENIZ - KENIKE

DENNEA - KENEA

DENNI - KENI

DENNICA - KENIKA

DENNIELL - KENIELI

DENNINE - KENINE

DENNIS - KENIKE

DENNY - KENI

DENSSEY - KENIKEI

DENTON - KENIKONU

DENVA - KENIWA

DENVER - KENIWELI

DENZAL - KENIKALA

DENZELL - KENIKELI

DEO - KEO

DEON - KEONU

DEONDRA - KEONUKULA

DEONICA - KEONIKA

DEONNA - KEONA

DEONT'A - KEONUKU'A

DEONTAE - KEONUKAE

DEORA - KEOLA

DEPRI - KEPILI

DEQUARIUS - KEKALIUKO

DEQUATTA - KEKAKA

DERALD - KELALA

DARELD - KALELI

DERAY - KELAI

DEREE - KELE

DEREK - KELEKA

DERETH - KELEKI

DERICKA - KELIKEKA

DERIUS - KELIUKO

DERMAN - KELIMANA

DERMOT - KELIMOKU

DERNA - KELINA

DERREL - KELELI

DERREN - KELENI

DERRIAN - KELIANA

DERRICK - KELIKEKE

DERRILL - KELILE

DERRILLYNN - KELILINE

DERRINGTON - KELINEKONU

DERRON - KELONU

DERRY - KELI

DER SHENG - KELI KENI

DERUNTA - KELUNOKA

DERWIN - KELIWINE

DERWOOD - KELIWOKU

DERYL - KELILE

DESARAE - KEKALAE

DESARAY - KEKALAI

DESERIE - KEKELIE

DESHA - KEKA
DESHANASTY - KEKANAKI
DESHAWN - KEKAWANA
DESHAYLA - KEKAILA
DESHEENA - KEKENA
DESHENI - KEKENI
DESHOUNN - KEKOUNO
DESI -KEKI
DESIANN - KEKIANA
DESIKA - KEKIKA
DESIRAE - KEKILAE
DESIREE - KEKILI
DESMAN - KEKIMANA
DESMINDA - KEKIMINEKA
DESMOND - KEKIMONUKU
DESORI - KEKOLI
DESPINA - KEKIPINA
DESSA - KEKA
DESSIE - KEKIE
DESTENY - KEKENI
DESTIN - KEKINE
DESTINEE - KEKINE
DESTINY - KEKINI
DETLEV - KEKILEWI
DETREL - KELELI
DETTYE - KEKIE
DETYET - KEKIEKI
DEUCE - KEUKE
DEVAN - KEWANA

DEVANTE - KEWANAKE
DEVANY - KEWANI
DEVAUGHN - KEWAUKONO
DEVELYA - KEWELIA
DEVEN - KEWENI
DEVENDRI- KEWENIKILI
DEVENN - KEWENI
DEVER - KEWELI
DEVEREAUX - KEWELEAUKO
DEVERL - KEWELI
DEVIA - KEWIA
DEVIN - KEWINE
DEVINA - KEWINA
DEVINE - KEWINE
DEVLYN - KEWILINE
DEVON - KEWONU
DEVONA - KEWONA
DEVONDA - KEWONUKA
DEVONE - KEWONE
DEVONNA – KEWONA
DEVONNE - KEWONE
DEVONTE - KEWONUKE
DEVORA - KEWOLA
DEVRIE - KEWILIE
DEVYANI - KEWIANI
DEVYN - KEWINE
DEWAN - KEWANA
DEWANN - KEWANA
DEWAYNE - KEWAINE

DEWEY - KEWEI

DEWI - KEWI

DEWITT - KEWIKE

DEXTER - KEKELA

DEYANIRA - KEIANILA

DEYCI - KEIKI

DEYETTE - KEIEKE

DEYSI - KEIKI

DEZ - KEKI

DEZEREY - KEKELEI

DEZHIANNA - KEKIHIANA

DEZMINE - KEKIMINE

DEZMON - KEKIMONU

DHALIA - KAHALIA

DHANI - KAHANI

DHANYA - KAHANIA

DHARMA - KAHALAMA

DHARMESH - KAHALAMEKI

DHASHNIE - KAHAKANIE

DHIRAJ - KAHILAI

DHRITI - KAHALIKI

DHRUV - KAHALUWO

DI - KI

DIA - KIA

DIAHNE - KIAHANE

DIALLO - KIALO

DIAMINE - KIAMINE

DIAMOND - KIAMONUKU

DIAMONIQUE - KIAMONIKUE

DIAN - KIANA

DIANA - KIANA

DIANE - KIANE

DIANEKA - KIANEKA

DIANET - KIANEKI

DIANN - KIANA

DIANNA- KIANA

DIANNE - KIANE

DIANTWON - KIANAKAWONU

DIARRA - KIALA

DIAVIANNE - KIAWIANE

DIB - KIPE

DICHINE - KIKINE

DICK - LIKEKE

DICKIE - KIKEKIE

DICKRAN - KIKEKELANA

DICKSON - KIKEKEKONU

DIDAY - KIKAI

DIDI - KIKI

DIDIEL - KIKIELI

DIDIER - KIKIELI

DIDIMIO - KIKIMIO

DIEGO - KIEKO

DIEP - KIEPI

DIETER - KIEKELI

DIETRICH - KIELIKE

DIJENAE - KIIENAE

DIJON - KIIONU

DIKSHA - KIKEKA

DILAN - KILANA

DILEEPA - KILEPA

DILENIA - KILENIA

DILIA - KILIA

DILINI - KILINI

DILLARD - KILALAKA

DILLINGER - KILINELI

DILLON - KILONU

DILRAJ - KILELAI

DILYARA - KILIALA

DIME - KIME

DIMITRE - KIMILE

DIMITRI - KIMILI

DIMITRIE - KIMILIE

DIMITRY - KIMILI

DIMITY - KIMIKI

DIMPLE - KIMEPELE

DINA - KINA

DINAH - KINA

DINE - KINE

DINEL - KINELI

DINESH - KINEKI

DING - KINE

DINITA - KINIKA

DINKA - KINEKA

DINO - KINO

DINORAH - KINOLAHA

DIOGENES - KIOKENEKI

DIOLINDA - KIOLINEKA

DIOMARIE - KIOMALIE

DION - KIONU

DIONDRE - KIONUKULE

DIONISIA - KIONIKIA

DIONNE - KIONA

DIONTEYA - KIONUKEIA

DIONYSE - KIONIKE

DIOR - KIOLU

DIOSDADO - KIOKUKAKO

DIPAK - KIPAKA

DIPTI - KIPEKI

DIRACE - KILAKE

DIRK - KIKE

DIRON - KILONU

DISA - KIKA

DISHA - KIKA

DISNEY - KIKENEI

DITA - KIKA

DITAS - KIKAKA

DIVA - KIWA

DIVINE - KIWINE

DIVINIA - KIWINIA

DIVINO - KIWINO

DIVYA - KIWIA

DIXIE - KIKI

DIXON - KIKONU

DIZAHAB - KIKAHAPA

DJALMA - KIALAMA

DJANILYN - KIANILINE

DJOBI - KIOPI

D'LYNN - KA'ALINE

D'MARQUIS - KA'AMALAKIKE

D'MILE - KA'AMILE

DMITRI - KAMILI

DMITRIY - KAMILII

DOANE - KOANE

DOBBY - KOPI

DOC - KOKU

DOCIA - KOKIA

DODDIE - KOKIE

DODETTE - KOKEKE

DODGE - KOKUKE

DODIE - KOKIE

DODY - KOKI

DOINA - KOINA

DOLAN - KOLANA

DOLEZA - KOLEKA

DOLJAI - KOLIAI

DOLLENA - KOLENA

DOLLIE - KOLIE

DOLLY - KOLI

DOLLYE - KOLIE

DOLORES – KOLOLELE

DOLTON - KOLUKONU

DOMANIC - KOMANIKE

DOMENIC - KOMENIKE

DOMENICO - KOMENIKO

DOMENIQUE - KOMENIKE

DOMINAY - KOMINAI

DOMINIC - KOMINIKO

DOMINICK - KOMINIKEKE

DOMINIK - KOMINIKE

DOMING - KOMINE

DOMINGO - KOMINIKO

DOMINIQUE - KOMINIKE

DOMINO - KOMINO

DOMINUS - KOMINUKO

DOMISTY - KOMIKI

DOMNY - KOMUNI

DOMONIQUE - KOMONIKUE

DON - KONA

DONA - KONA

DONALD - KONALA

DONALYN - KONALINE

DONATO - KONAKO

DONAVAN - KONAWANA

DONAVIN - KONAWINE

DONDI - KONUKI

DONDII - KONUKI

DONDRA - KONUKULA

DONELL - KONELI

DONELLA - KONELA

DONETTA - KONEKA

DONG - KONU

DONIELLE - KONIELE

DONILDA - KONILA

DONISHA - KONIKA

DONITA - KONIKA

DONNA - KONA

DONNAE' - KONAE'I

DONNA JO - KONA IO

DONNAMARIE - KONAMALIE

DONNECIA - KONEKIA

DONNELL - KONELI

DONNIE – KONIE

DONNIS - KONIKE

DONNY - KONI

DONNYA - KONIA

DONOVA - KONOWA

DONOVAN - KONOWANA

DONTAE - KONUKAE

DONTAVIUS - KONUKAWIUKO

DONTAYE - KONUKAIE

DONTE - KONUKE

DONTERRIS - KONUKELIKE

DONTIE - KONUKIE

DONTRAIL - KONULAILE

DONYA - KONIA

DONYAE - KONIAE

DONZAVIEN - KONUKAWIENI

DONZELLE - KONUKELE

DOONEY - KONEI

DORA - KOLA

DORANNA - KOLANA

DORCAS - KOLUKAKA

DORDIA - KOLUKIA

DORE - KOLE

DOREEN - KOLINA

DORELLE - KOLELE

DOREN - KOLENI

DORENDA - KOLENIKA

DORESSA - KOLEKA

DORETHA - KOLEKA

DORETTA - KOLEKA

DORI - KOLI

DORIAN - KOLIANA

DORIE - KOLIE

DORINDA - KOLINEKA

DORINE - KOLINE

DORINO - KOLINO

DORIS - KOLIKA

DORMA - KOLUMA

DORNE - KOLUNE

DOROTEO - KOLOKEO

DOROTHEA - KOLOKEA

DOROTHY - KOLOKEA

DORRAN - KOLANA

DORRIT - KOLIKE

DORSEY - KOLUKEI

DORTHA - KOKA

DORTHE - KOKE

DORTHEA - KOKEA

DORTHI - KOKI

DORY - KOLI

DORYAN - KOLIANA

DOS - KOKU

DOSHA - KOKA

DOT - KOKU

DOTTIE - KOKIE

DOUA - KOUA

DOUG - KOUKO

DRES - KALEKI
DRESDEN - KALEKIKENI
DREW - KALEWI
DREWRY - KALEWILI
DREXTER - KALEKIKELI
DREY - KALEI
DREYSON - KALEIKONU
DRINA - KALINA
DRINAN - KALINANA
DRINDA - KALINEKA
DRISANA - KALIKANA
DRIZELLE - KALIKELE
DRU - KALU
DRUE - KALUE
DRUSCILLA - KALUKOKILA
DRUSHELL - KALUKELI
DRUV - KALUWO
DUANA - KUANA
DUANE - KUANE
DUBBIEL - KUPIELI
DUC - KUKO
DUCHESS - KUKEKI
DUDLEY - KUKALI
DUEHL - KUEHILI
DUFF - KUPO
DUGALD - KUKALA
DUGAN - KUKANA
DUJUAN - KUIUANA
DUKE - KUKE
DULCE - KUKE

DULCET - KULOKEKI
DULCILIA - KULOKILIA
DUNCAN - KUNAKANA
DUNG - KUNO
DUNN - KUNO
DUNSTIN - KUNOKINE
DUNYA - KUNIA
DUPRE - KUPOLE
DUQUESNE - KUKEKINE
DURAN - KULANA
DURAND - KULANAKA
DURANDA - KULANAKA
DURBIN - KULOPINE
DURELL - KULELI4
DURIM - KULIME
DURINDA - KULINEKA
DURK - KUKO
DURLYN - KULINE
DURNIAN - KULONIANA
DURVAL - KULOWALA
DURWIN - KULOWINE
DURWOOD - KULOWOKU
DUSAN - KUKANA
DUSANA - KUKANA
DUSIT - KUKIKE
DUSKY - KUKOKI
DUSTIN - KUKINE
DUSTY - KUKI
DUSTYN - KUKINE
DUTCH - KUKOKO

DUTCHESS - KUKOKEKI

DUTTON - KUKONU

DUTTRELL - KULELI

DUVONDA - KUWONUKA

DUY - KUI

D' VANTE - KA'A WANAKE

DWAIN - KAWAINE

DWANA - KAWANA

DWAYLA - KAWAILA

DWAYNE - KAWAINE

DWEEZIL - KAWEKILE

DWIGHT - KUAIKA

DYAHNEE - KIAHANE

DYANA - KIANA

DYANN - KIANA

DYESS - KIEKI

DYETTE - KIEKE

DYMOND - KIMONUKU

DYLA - KILA

DYLAN - KILANA

DYLEAH - KILEAHA

DYLON - KILONU

DYMIN - KIMINE

DYMPLE - KIMEPELE

DYNA - KINA

DYNASTY - KINAKI

DYNE - KINE

DYRISE - KILIKE

DYRK - KIKE

DYSHAUNN - KIKAUNO

E

FIRST NAMES

EADAOINE - EAKAOINE
EAGLE - EAKELE
EAMONN - EAMONU
EAN - EANA
EARL - EALA
EARLE - EALE
EARLENE - EALENE
EARLINE - EALINE
EARNEST - EALANEKI
EARNESTINE - EALANEKINE
EARNIE - EALANIE
EARON - EALONU
EARTHA - EAKA
EASHWAR - EAKAWALA
EASON - EAKONU
EASTER - EAKELI
EASTON - EAKONU
EATHAN - EAKANA
EATHERLENE - EAKELENE
EARTHIE - EAKIE
EAVEN - EAWENI
EBBIE - EPIE
EBEN - EPENI
EBENEY - EPENEI
EBERTO - EPEKO
EBLISH - EPILIKE
EBONIE - EPONIE
EBONY - EPONI
EBONYANNE - EPONIANE
EBRU - EPILU

ECHLAN - EKILANA
ECHO - EKO
ECKARD - EKIKALAKA
ED - EKI
EDA - EKA
EDAN - EKANA
EDDA - EKA
EDDE - EKE
EDDI - EKI
EDDIE - EKIE
EDDY - EKI
EDDYMIE - EKIMIE
EDEE - EKE
EDELINE - EKELINE
EDEN - EKENI
EDGAR - EKEKA
EDGARDO - EKEKAKO
EDGARY - EKIKALI
EDIBERTO - EKIPEKO
EDIE - EKIE
EDILBERTO - EKILEPEKO
EDILIA - EKILIA
EDISON - EKIKONU
EDITH - EKIKA
EDITHA - EKIKA
EDLA - EKILA
EDLE - EKILE
EDLYN - EKILINE
EDMAR - EKIMALA
EDME - EKIME

EDMOND - EKEMONA
EDMUND - EKIMUNOKO
EDNA - EKENA
EDON - EKONU
EDOTHIA - EKOKIA
EDRIAN - EKILIANA
EDRIC - EKILIKE
EDRICA - EKILIKA
EDRONDA - EKILONUKA
EDSEL - EKIKELI
EDSON - EKIKONU
EDUARD - EKUALAKA
EDUARDO - EKUALO
EDWARD - EKEWAKA
EDWIGE - EKIWIKE
EDWIN - ELUENE
EDWINA - EKIWINA
EDYTA - EKIKA
EDYTHE - EKIKE
EDZEL - EKIKELI
EEBEE - EPE
EEF - EPI
EERIK - ELIKE
EESA - EKA
EETA - EKA
EFFAT - EPAKA
EFFIE - EPIE
EFIM - EPIME
EFLEDA - EPILEKA

EFRAIM - EPILAIME
EFRAIN - EPILAINE
EFRAT - EPILAKE
EFREN - EPILENI
EFROM - EPILOMU
EFTHIMIA - EPIKIMIA
EGAN - EKANA
EGIL - EKILE
EGON - EKONU
EGYPT - EKIPEKE
EHAB - EHAPA
EILA - EILA
EILEEN - AILINA
EILIDH - EILIKEHE
EILISH - EILIKE
EILIYA - EILIIA
EINAR - EINALA
EINI - EINI
EION - EIONU
EIREEN - EILENI
EISEN - EIKENI
EISLEY - EIKELEI
EITHAN - EIKANA
EJAY - EIAI
EKATERINA - EKAKELINA
EKTA - EKIKA
EL - ELI
ELAINA - ELAINA
ELAINE - ILEINA

ELAIRA - ELAILA

ELAM - ELAMA

ELAN - ELANA

ELANA - ELANA

ELAYNA - ELAINA

ELBA - ELIPA

ELBER - ELIPELI

ELBERT - ELIPEKI

ELBONY - ELIPONI

ELDA - ELA

ELDAR - ELALA

ELDENE - ELENE

ELDON - ELONU

ELDORIS - ELOLIKE

ELDRED - ELILEKI

ELEA - ELEA

ELEANOR - ELENOLA

ELENORA - ELENOLA

ELE - ELE

ELEESA - ELEKA

ELENA – ELENA

ELENER - ELENELI

ELENG - ELENI

ELENI - ELENI

ELEUTERIA - ELEUKELIA

ELEUTERIO - ELEUKELIO

ELEXIS - ELEKIKE

ELFRIEDA - ELIPILIEKA

ELGA - ELIKA

ELGIN - ELIKINE

ELHAM - ELIHAMA

ELHASSANE - ELIHAKANE

ELI - ELI

ELIAMAR - ELIAMARA

ELIANA - ELIANA

ELIANE - ELIANE

ELIANY - ELIANI

ELIAS - ELIAKA

ELICA - ELIKA

ELICELDA - ELIKELA

ELICIA - ELIKIA

ELIDA - ELIKA

ELIDI - ELIKI

ELIHU - ELIHU

ELIJA, ELIJAH – ELIA

ELIKA - ELIKA

ELIN - ELINE

ELINA - ELINA

ELIO - ELIO

ELIROSE - ELILOKE

ELISA - ELIKA

ELISABET - ELIKAPEKI

ELISABETH - ELIKAPEKI

ELISAPETA - ELIKAPEKA

ELISE - ELIKE

ELISEAUNA - ELIKEAUNA

ELISEO - ELIKEO

ELISET - ELIKEKI

ELISHEVA - ELIKEWA

ELISNA - ELIKENA

ELISSA - ELIKA

ELITA - ELIKA

ELIYAH - ELIIAHA

ELIZA - ELAIKA

ELIZABETH – ELIKAPEKA

ELIZAR - ELIKALA

ELIZBETH - ELIKEPEKI

ELIZEBETH - ELIKEPEKI

ELIZEN - ELIKENI

ELKE - ELIKE

ELKEER - ELIKELI

ELLA - ELA

ELLAINE - ELAINE

ELLE - ELE

ELLEN, ELENA - ELENA

ELLAREE - ELALE

ELLERY - ELELI

ELLESE - ELEKE

ELLI - ELI

ELLIANA - ELIANA

ELLIE - ELIE

ELLIOT - ELIOKA

ELLIS - ELIKE

ELLISON - ELIKONU

ELLISSA - ELIKA

ELLISTON - ELIKONU

ELLSWORTH - ELIKIWOKU

ELLYANA - EILANA

ELLYSE - ELIKE

ELKE - ELIKE

ELKIN - ELIKINE

ELMA - ELIMA

ELMAR - ELIMALA

ELMARI - ELIMALI

ELMER - ELEMA

ELMETA - ELIMEKA

ELMINA - ELIMINA

ELMIRA - ELIMILA

ELMO - ELIMO

ELNA - ELINA

ELNORA - ELINOLA

ELNORE - ELINOLE

ELODIE - ELOKIE

ELOIS - ELOIKE

ELOISE - ELOIKA

ELONNA - ELONA

ELORA - ELOLA

ELOY - ELOI

ELPHA - ELIPA

ELREE - ELILE

ELROSS - ELILOKU

ELROY - ELELOE

ELSA - ELIKA

ELSABET - ELIKAPEKI

ELSE - ELIKE

ELSIE - ELEKI

ELSILANI - ELIKILANI

ELSJIE - ELIKIIE

ELSPETH - ELIKIPEKI

ELSY - ELIKI

ELTA - ELIKA

ELTHORA - EIKOLA

ELTON - ELEKONA

ELVA - ELIWA

ELVERA - ELIWELA

ELVIA - ELIWIA

ELVIE - ELIWIE

ELVIN - ELEWINA

ELVIRA - ELEWIA

ELVIS - ELEWIKA

ELVWRYN - ELIWIWILINE

ELWANDA - ELIWANAKA

ELWIN - ELIWINE

ELWOOD - ELIWOKU

ELY - ELI

ELYNAEA - ELINAEA

ELYNORA - ELINOLA

ELYSE - ELEKI

ELYSSA - ELIKA

ELYTE - ELIKE

ELZIE - ELIKIE

EMALISE - EMALIKE

EMAN - EMANA

EMANUEL - EMANUELI

EMARI - EMALI

EMAY - EMAI

EMBER - EMIPELI

EMBERLYNN - EMIPELINE

EMBOR - EMIPOLU

EMBRY - EMIPILI

EME - EME

EMEILIEYA - EMEILIEIA

EMELIE - EMELIE

EMELYN - EMELINE

EMER - EMELI

EMERA - EMELA

EMERAL - EMELALA

EMERALD - EMELALA

EMERIC - EMELIKE

EMERICO - EMELIKO

EMERIE - EMELIE

EMERITA - EMELIKA

EMERSON - EMELIKONU

EMERSYN - EMELIKINE

EMERY - EMELI

EMESE - EMEKE

EMESIS - EMEKIKE

EMETH - EMEKI

EMI - EMI

EMIDIO - EMIKIO

EMIKO - EMIKO

EMIL - EMELA

EMILA - EMILA

EMILEE - EMILE

EMILEIGH - EMILEIKEHE

EMILEY - EMILEI

EMILI - EMILI

EMILIA - EMILIA

EMILEE - EMILE

EMILEIGH - EMILEIKEHE

EMILEY - EMILEI

EMILI - EMILI

EMILIA - EMILIA

EMILIANO - EMILIANO

EMILIE - EMILIE

EMILINNA - EMILINA

EMILIO - EMILIO

EMILY - EMELE

EMILYANNE - EMILIANE

EMILYROSE - EMILILOKE

EMINA - EMINA

EMLER - EMILELI

EMMA - EMA

EMMAJEN - EMAIENI

EMMALEE - EMALE

EMMALINE - EMALINE

EMMA LUNA - EMA LUNA

EMMANUEL - EMANUELI

EMMANUELA - EMANUELA

EMMARIE - EMALIE

EMMARYN - EMALINE

EMME - EME

EMMELINE - EMELINE

EMMELYNN - EMELINE

EMME-MARIE - EME-IMALIE

EMMERSON - EMELIKONU

EMMETT - EMEKI

EMMITT - EMIKE

EMMY - EMI

EMORY - EMOLI

EMPRESS - EMIPILEKI

ENAN - ENANA

ENCORE - ENIKOLE

ENDA - ENIKA

ENDDI - ENIKI

ENDYA - ENIKIA

ENE - ENE

ENELIO - ENELIO

ENELVIA - ENELIWIA

ENELYSE - ENELIKE

ENESSA - ENEKA

ENGCHIN - ENIKINE

ENGLAND - ENILANAKA

ENG SENG - ENI KENI

ENG TSE - ENI KE

ENG TZE - ENI KAKE

ENID - ENIKE

ENIKO - ENIKO

ENILDA - ENILA

ENJOLI - ENIOLI

ENNIE - ENIE

ENOC - ENOKU

ENOCH - ENOKU

ENOIS - ENOIKE

ENRICA - ENILIKA

ENRICK - ENILIKEKE

ENRIQUE - ENILIKE

ENRIQUETA - ENILIKEKA

ENSLEY - ENIKILEI

ENTELA - ENIKELA

ENZA - ENIKA

ENZO - ENIKO

EOGHAN - EOKUHANA

EPATI - EPAKI

EPHRAIM - EPILAIME

EPHREM - EPILEMI

EPIMENIO - EPIMENIO

EPIPHANY - EPIPANI

EPPI - EPI

EPPIFANIO - EPIPANIO

EQUANA - EKANA

EQUET - EKEKI

ERA - ELA

ERALYN - ELALINE

ERAN - ELANA

ERANDI - ELANAKI

ERARD - ELALAKA

ERASMUS - ELAKAMUKO

ERB - ELIPI

ERCIDIO - ELIKIKIO

EREK - ELEKI

ERENDIRA - ELENIKILA

ERHARD - ELIHALAKA

ERHARDT - ELIHALAKAKA

ERI - ELI

ERIBERTO - ELIPEKO

ERIC - ELIKA

ERICA - ELIKA

ERICH - ELIKE

ERICK - ELIKEKE

ERICKA - ELIKEKA

ERICKSON - ELIKEKEKONU

ERIDA - ELIKA

ERIK - ELIKE

ERIKA - ELIKA

ERIKAH - ELIKAHA

ERIMAR - ELIMALA

ERIN - ELINA

ERINA - ELINA

ERINN - ELINA

ERIQ - ELIKE

ERISA - ELIKA

ERLENE - ELENE

ERLIE - ELIE

ERLINDA - ELINEKA

ERLON - ELONU

ERLYN - ELINE

ERMA - ELIMA

ERMALINE - ELIMALINE

ERMILO - ELIMILO

ERMINA - ELIMINA

ERNA - ELINA

ERNAL - ELINALA

ERNANI - ELINANI

ERNEST - ELENEKI

ERNESTINE - ELENEKINA

ERNESTO - ELINEKO

ERNETTE - ELINEKE

ERNIE - ELINIE

ERRALYN - ELALINE

ERROL - ELOLU

ERRYN - ELINE

ERSKINE - ELIKIKINE

ERUNDINO - ELUNOKINO

ERVIN - ELEWINA

ERWIN - ELIWINE

ERYKAH - ELIKAHA

ERYN - ELINE

ESA - EKA

E'SAUN - E'IKAUNO

ESCALONA - EKIKALONA

ESCHANIA - EKIKANIA

ESELLA - EKELA

ESEQUIEL - EKEKIELI

ESHAWN - EKAWANA

ESHEN - EKENI

ESKIL - EKIKILE

ESMAEL - EKIMAELI

ESME - EKIME

ESMEE - EKIME

ESMERALDA - EKIMELALA

ESMINE - EKIMINE

ESPEN - EKIPENI

ESPERANZA - EKIPELANAKA

ESPERIDA - EKIPELIKA

ESPIRIDION - EKIPILIKIONU

ESSA - EKA

ESSAIE - EKAIE

ESSAM - EKAMA

ESSCEL - EKIKELI

ESSENCE - EKENIKE

ESSIE - EKIE

ESTACIA - EKAKIA

ESTALE - EKALE

ESTEBAN - EKEPANA

ESTEFANIA - EKEPANIA

ESTELLA - EKELA

ESTELLE - EKELE

ESTER - EKELI

ESTEVAN - EKEWANA

ESTHER - EKEKELA

ESTIME - EKIME

ESTINA - EKINA

ESTON - EKONU

ESTRELLITA - EKILELIKA

ESTREYA - EKILEIA

ESTY - EKI

ESYNCE - EKINEKE

ETAB - EKAPA

ETANA - EKANA

ETERNITY - EKELINIKI

ETEVISE - EKEWIKE

ETHAN - EKANA

ETHEL - EKELA

ETHELYN - PALAKONU

ETHON - EKONU

ÉTIENNE - ÉAKIENE

ETEKA - EKEKA

ETSIE - EKIE

ETSUKO - EKUKO

ETTA - EKA

ETTY - EKI

EUCLIDE - EUKOLIKE

EUDEIA - EUKOEIA

EUDORA - EUKOLA

EUEL - EUELI

EUFRONIO - EUPOLONIO

EUGEL - EUKELI

EUGENE - LUKINI

EUGENIA - LUKINIA

EULA - EULA

EULENE - EULENE

EULINDA - EULINEKA

EULY - EULI

EUNICE - EUNIKE

EUNSUNG - EUNOKUNO

EUPHEMIA - EUPEMIA

EURA - EULA

EURIDES - EULIKEKI

EUSEBIO - EUKEPIO

EUSTACE - EUKAKE

EUSTOLIA - EUKOLIA

EVA - IWA

EVALLYN - EWALINE

EVAN - EWANA

EVANGELINA - EWANELINA

EVANGELINE - EWANELINA

EVANGELISTA - EWANELIKA

EVANI - EWANI

EVANJELYN - EWANIELINE

EVARISTA - EWALIKA

EVE - EWA

EVEGAIL - EWEKAILE

EVELINE - EWALINA

EVELYN - EWALINA

EVENCE - EWENIKE

EVER - EWELI

EVEREST - EWELEKI

EVERETT - EWELEKI

EVERETTE - EWELEKE

EVERIC - EWELIKE

EVERLIE - EWELIE

EVERSON - EWELIKONU

EVERLYN - EWELINE

EVERYLEE - EWELILE

EVETTE - IWEKE

EVI - EWI

EVIE - EWIE

EVONNA - EWONA

EVONNE - EWONE

EVORIA - EWOLIA

EVY - EWI

EWALDE - EWALE

EWAN - EWANA

EWEN - EWENI

EWILL - EWILE

EXIE - EKIE

EXIQUIO - EKIKIO

EXLYN - EKILINE

EYAN - EIANA

EYDIE - EIKIE

EZEKIEL - EKEKIELI

EZEQUIEL - EKEKIELI

EZHIL - EKIHILE

EZIO - EKIO

EZRA - EKELA

EZRI - EKILI

EZZLEE - EKILE

F

FIRST NAMES

FAAFE - PAPE

FABI - PAPI

FABIAN - PAPIANO

FABIANA - PAPIANA

FABIO - PAPIO

FABIOLA - PAPIOLA

FABRE'ANTE - PAPALE'ANAKE

FABRICE - PAPALIKE

FABRIZIO - PAPALIKIO

FADI - PAKI

FADILLAH - PAKILAHA

FADRA - PAKALA

FAELYNN - PAELINE

FAGAN - PAKANA

FAHAMIDA - PAHAMIKA

FAIRUZA - PAILUKA

FAIRY - PAILI

FAITH -MANAOIO

FAIZ - PAIKE

FAIZA - PAIKA

FAIZAH - PAIKAHA

FALANDA - PALANAKA

FALCON - PALAKONU

FALIA - PALIA

FALISHA - PALIKA

FALLAN - PALANA

FALLON - PALONU

FALLYN - PALINE

FANCY - PANAKI

FANE - PANE

FANG - PANA

FANI - PANI

FANNIE - PANIE

FANNY - PANE

FANON - PANONU

FANYA - PANIA

FAPIMA - PAPIMA

FARAZ - PALAKA

FAREE - PALE

FAREN - PALENI

FARID - PALIKE

FARIDA - PALIKA

FARIHA - PALIHA

FARINA - PALINA

FARIS - PALIKE

FARLEY - PALEI

FARNAZ - PALANAKA

FARNSWORTH - PALANAKAWOKU

FARRAH - PALAHA

FARREN - PALENI

FARRIZ - PALIKE

FARROL - PALOLU

FARRON - PALONU

FARROS - PALOKU

FARRY - PALI

FARUQ - PALUKO

FARY - PALI

FASIL - PAKILE

FATIMA - PAKIMA

FAUN - PAUNO

FAUSTINA - PAUKINA

FAUSTINO - PAUKINO

FAUSTO - PAUKO

FAWAD - PAWAKA

FAWN - PAWANA

FAWZIA - PAWAKIA

FAY - PEI

FAYANN - PAIANA

FAYDRE - PAIKELE

FAYE - PAIE

FAYETTA - PAIEKA

FAZEICA - PAKEIKA

FE - PE

FEATHER - PEAKELI

FEBELYN - PEPELINE

FEBIE - PEPIE

FEDAK - PEKAKA

FEDELMIA - PEKELIMIA

FEDERICO - PEKELIKO

FEDIE - PEKIE

FEDRO - PEKILO

FEERMAN - PELIMANA

FEJI - PEII

FEL - PELI

FELECIA - PELEKIA

FELICE - PELIKE

FELICHI - PELIKI

FELICIA - PELIKIA

FELICIANA - PELIKIANA

FELICIDAD - PELIKIKAKA

FELICITY - PELIKIKI

FELILA - PELILA

FELINO - PELINO

FELIPE - PELIPE

FELITA - PELIKA

FELIX - PELIKE

FELIZ - PELIKE

FELLY - PELI

FELTON - PELIKONU

FEMI - PEMI

FENADY - PENAKI

FENG QI - PENI KI

FENIA - PENIA

FENN - PENI

FENNELLEY - PELELEI

FENSTERMACHER - PENIKELIMAKELI

FERALLYN - PELALINE

FERDIE - PELIKIE

FERDINAND - PELIKINANAKA

FERENCE - PELENIKE

FERESHTEH - PELEKIKEHI

FERG - PEKI

FERGAL - PEKALA

FERGUS - PEKUKO

FERJENEL - PELIENELI

FERMIN - PELIMINE

FERN - PELENA

FERNANDA - PELINANAKA

FERNANDO - PELINANAKO

FERNELL - PELINELI

FERNIECE - PELINIEKE

FEROL - PELOLU

FEROZE - PELOKE

FERRELL - PELELI

FERREN - PELENI

FERRISSA - PELIKA

FERROL - PELOLU

FERYL - PELILE

FESILAFAI - PEKILAPAI

FEYGEL - PEIKELI

FEZA - PEKA

FIANA - PIANA

FIDEL - PIKELI

FIDELIA - PIKELIA

FIELDER - PIELELI

FIELDING - PIELINE

FIENA - PIENA

FIFAH - PIPAHA

FIFER - PIPELI

FIFI - PIPI

FILIMON - PILIMONU

FILIPE - PILIPE

FILIPINAS - PILIPINAKA

FILJOSH - PILIOKU

FILMON - PILEMONU

FILOMENA - PILOMENA

FINBAR - PINEPALA

FINE - PINE

FINEST - PINEKI

FINLEY - PINELEI

FINN - PINE

FINTAN - PINEKANA

FINUALLAH - PINUALAHA

FIONA - PIONA

FIONN - PIONU

FIORA - PIOLA

FIORELLA - PIOLELA

FIRAT - PILAKA

FIRIND - PILINEKE

FIRMANN - PILEMANA

FISHER - PIKELI

FITZ - PIKEKE

FITZGERALD - PIKEKEKELALA

FITZROY - PIKEKELOI

FIZZ - PIKE

FLAMUR - PALAMULO

FLAVEL - PALAWELI

FLAVEO - PALAWEO

FLAVIA - PALAWIA

FLAVIO - PALAWIO

FLEADIA - PALEAKIA

FLECHA - PALEKA

FLETCHER - PALEKIKELI

FLEUR - PALEULO

FLEURETTE - PALEULEKE

FLINT - PALINEKE

FLIPPER - PALIPELI

FLO - PALO

FLOANN - PALOANA

FLONNESE - PALONEKE

FLOR - PALOLU
FLORA - POLOLA
FLORALEE - PALOLALE
FLORENCE - POLOLENA
FLORENTINA - PALOLENIKINA
FLORETTE - PALOLEKE
FLORIAN - PALOLIANA
FLORIDA - PALOLIKA
FLORIN - PALOLINE
FLORINDA - PALOLINEKA
FLORIDALMA - PALOLIKALAMA
FLORIEDAINE - PALOLIEKAINE
FLORINE - PALOLINE
FLORISBALDO - PALOLIKEPALO
FLORITA - PALOLIKA
FLOSSIE - PALOKIE
FLOYD - POLOLIKA
FLUVIA - PALUWIA
FLYNN - PALINE
FOGG - POKU
FOLASSHADE - POLAKAKE
FONDA - PONUKA
FONDRIETA - PONUKULIEKA
FONJA - PONIA
FONTAYNE - PONUKAINE
FONZIE - PONUKIE
FOOL - POLU
FORAM - POLAMA
FORD - POLUKU
FORMEKA - POLUMEKA

FORREST - POLEKI
FORTUNATE - POKUNAKE
FORTUNE - POKUNE
FOSTER - POKELI
FOTINI - POKINI
FOUA - POUA
FOX - POKU
FOY - POI
FRALEY - PALALEI
FRAN - PALANA
FRANCE - PALANAKE
FRANCELIA - PALANAKELIA
FRANCES - PALAKIKA
FRANCESCA - PALANAKEKIKA
FRANCESCO - PALANAKEKIKO
FRANCHELLE - PALANAKELE
FRANCIA - PALANAKIA
FRANCIE - PALANAKIE
FRANCINE - PALAKINE
FRANCIS - PALAKIKO
FRANCISCA - PALANAKIKEKA
FRANCISCO - PALAKIKO
FRANCO - PALANAKO
FRANCOIS - PALANAKOIKE
FRANK – PALANI
FRANKETA - PALANAKEKA
FRANKIE - PALANAKIE
FRANKLIN - PELANEKELINA
FRANKLYN - PALANAKALINE
FRANKUS - PALANAKUKO

FRANSICO - PALANAKIKO

FRANSONNA - PALANAKONA

FRANTEENA - PALANAKENA

FRANZ - PALANAKA

FRASER - PALAKELI

FRECKLES - PALEKIKILEKI

FRED - PELEKE

FREDA - PALIKA

FREDDIE - PALEKIE

FREDERICA - PALEKELIKA

FREDERICK - PELEKE

FREDLYN - PALEKILINE

FREDNA - PALEKINA

FREDRIK - PALEKILIKE

FREDRIKA - PALEKILIKA

FREEDOM - PALEKOMU

FREEMAN - PALEMANA

FREEMONT - PALEMONUKU

FREIDA - PELIKA

FRESIA - PALEKIA

FREYA - PALEIA

FRIDA - PALI

FRIDAY - PALIKAI

FRIEDA - PELIKA

FRIEDERIKE - PALIEKELIKE

FRIEL - PALIELI

FRIK - PALIKE

FRISCO - PALIKEKO

FRITZ - PALIKEKE

FROILAN - PALOILANA

FRONIA - PALONIA

FRONIE - PALONIE

FROY - PALOI

FU - PU

FUAB - PUAPA

FUAMATALA - PUAMAKALA

FUATINO - PUAKINO

FUE - PUE

FUENTES - PUENIKEKI

FULTON - PULOKONU

FULVIO - PULOWIO

FUMIKO - PUMIKO

FURANA - PULANA

FURNEY - PULONEI

FURY - PULI

FYNN - PINE

FYRE - PILE

FYSE - PIKE

G

FIRST NAMES

GAAL - KALA

GABA - KAPA

GABBY - KAPI

GABE - KAPE

GABI - KAPI

GABIELLE - KAPIELE

GABINO - KAPINO

GABRIEL - KAPELIELA

GABRIELA - KAPALIELA

GABRIELLA - KAPALIELA

GABRIELLE - KAPALIELE

GABRYEL - KAPALIELI

GABY - KAPI

GADIEL - KAKIELI

GAE - KAE

GAELYNN - KAELINE

GAERVYN - KAELIWINE

GAETANNE - KAEKANE

GAETANO - KAEKANO

GAGE - KAKE

GAGIK - KAKIKI

GAIL - KAILA

GAINES - KAINEKI

GAJENDRA - KAIENIKILA

GAL - KALA

GALADRIEL - KALAKALIELI

GALE - KALE

GALEN - KALENI

GALIA - KALIA

GALILEO - KALILEO

GALINA - KALINA

GAMBLE - KAMAPALE

GAMILAH - KAMILAHA

GAMINI - KAMINI

GAMMON - KAMONU

GAMORRO - KAMOLO

GANI - KANI

GANIU - KANIU

GANKA - KANAKA

GANNON - KANONU

GAOCHENG - KAOKENI

GARDNER - KALAKANELI

GAREK - KALEKI

GARETH - KALEKI

GAREY - KALEI

GARIFALIA - KALIPALIA

GARFIELD - KALAPIELI

GARILYNN - KALILINE

GARIMA - KALIMA

GARION - KALIONU

GARJUHAN - KALIUHANA

GARLAND - KALANAKA

GARNER - KALANELI

GARNESHA - KALANEKA

GARNETTE - KALANEKE

GARRA - KALA

GARREN - KALENI

GARRETH - KALEKI

GARRETT - KALEKI

GARRI - KALI

GARRICK - KALIKA

GARRIE - KALIE

GARRIETTE - KALIEKE

GARRISON - KALIKONU

GARRON - KALONU

GARRY - KALI

GARTH - KAKA

GARVEY - KALAWEI

GARVIN - KALAWINE

GARY - KALI

GASPER - KAKAPELI

GASTON - KAKONU

GATHA - KAKA

GATLIN - KAKALINE

GATSBY - KAKAPI

GAUDE-LYNE - KAUKE-ILINE

GAURAR - KAULALA

GAURAV - KAULAWA

GAVEN - KAWENI

GAVIN - KAWINE

GAVRIEL - KAWALIELI

GAWAIN - KAWAINE

GAXIN - KAKINE

GAY - KAI

GAYATHRI - KAIALI

GAYDRE - KAIKELE

GAYE - KAIE

GAYLA - KAILA

GAYLAN - KAILANA

GAYLAND - KAILANAKA

GAYLE - KAILA

GAYLEN - KAILENI

GAYLENE - KAILENE

GAYLORD - KAILOLA

GAYLYN - KAILINA

GAYNA - KAINA

GAYNELL - KAINELI

GAYNOR - KAINOLU

GAYTHREESA - KAILEKA

GAZELLE – KAKELE

GBEMISOLA - KAPEMIKOLA

GEANETTE - KEANEKE

GEANNIE - KEANIE

GEARLINE - KEALINE

GECKO - KEKIKO

GEDDES - KEKEKI

GEDELL - KEKELI

GEDIMINAS - KEKIMINAKA

GEENA - KENA

GEETA - KEKA

GEHAN - KEHANA

GEHRIG - KEHILIKE

GEILESA - KEILEKA

GEINA - KEINA

GEIR - KEILE

GEISELA - KEIKELA

GEK HONG - KEKI HONU

GELILA - KELILA

GELO - KELO
GELSOMIN - KELIKOMINE
GELSON - KELIKONU
GELYN - KELINE
GEMA - KEMA
GEMBERLING - KEMIPELINE
GEMDALIN - KEMIKALINE
GEMINI - KEMINI
GEMMA - KEMA
GEMMABELE - KEMAPELE
GEMRAE - KEMILAE
GENA - KENA
GENARO - KENALO
GENE - KINI
GENEA - KENEA
GENEAL - KENEALA
GENEEN - KENENI
GENEISKA - KENEIKEKA
GENELLE - KENELE
GENEROSO - KENELOKO
GENESEE - KENEKE
GENESHIA - KENEKIA
GENESIS - KENEKIKE
GENEVA - KENEWA
GENEVIE - KENEWIE
GENEVIEVE - KENEWIWE
GENI - KENI
GENIA - KENIA
GENIE - KENIE
GENIECE - KENIEKE

GENILA - KENILA
GENNA - KENA
GENNADIY - KENAKII
GENNARA - KENALA
GENNIELYNN - KENIELINE
GENNIFER - KENIPELI
GENNINE - KENINE
GENNY - KENI
GENOA - KENOA
GENOLA - KENOLA
GENTI - KENIKI
GENTRY - KENILI
GEOFF - KEOPU
GEOFFREY - KEOPELE
GEOMAR - KEOMALA
GEONETTE - KEONEKE
GEORDAN - KEOLUKANA
GEORGANNA - KEOKANA
GEORGE – KEOKI
GEORGENE - KEOKENA
GEORGETTA - KEOKEKA
GEORGETTE - KEOKEKE
GEORGIA - KEOKIA
GEORGIANA - KEOKIANA
GEORGIAREE - KEOKIALE
GEORGIE - KEOKIE
GEORGINA - KEOKINA
GEORGINE - KEOKINE
GEORGIO - KEOKIO
GEORGONNA - KEOKONA

GEORGY - KEOKI
GEQUANAINA - KEKANAINA
GERAD - KELAKA
GERALD - KELALA
GERALDINE - KALELAKINE
GERALYN - KELALINE
GERALYNN - KELALINE
GERARD - KELALAKA
GERARDO - KELALAKO
GERBER - KELIPELI
GERGANA - KEKANA
GERHARD - KELIHALAKA
GERI - KELI
GERLINA - KELINA
GERLINDE - KELINEKE
GERMAIN - KELIMAINE
GERMANI - KELIMANI
GERONIMO - KELONIMO
GERRA - KELA
GERREN - KELENI
GERRI - KELI
GERRICK - KELIKEKE
GERRIT - KELIKE
GERRY - KELI
GERSHON - KELIKONU
GERSON - KELIKONU
GERT - KEKI
GERTA - KEKA
GERTRUDE - KELEKUKE
GERUSA - KELUKA

GERVEY - KELIWEI
GERVON - KELIWONU
GESHAUN - KEKAUNO
GESINA - KEKINA
GESSNER - KEKINELI
GEURIN - KEULINE
GEVENA - KEWENA
GEVON - KEWONU
GEVORG - KEWOKU
GEWEL - KEWELI
GEYCEL - KEIKELI
GEZELE - KEKELE
GHAGE - KAHAKE
GHAZALEIGH - KAHAKALEIKEHE
GHEE - KAHE
GHIDI - KAHIKI
GHILDA - KAHILA
GHISLAIN - KAHIKELAINE
GHOUTHAM - KAHOUKAMA
GI UN - KI UNO
GIA - KIA
GIACCHINO - KIAKINO
GIADA - KIAKA
GIADDA - KIAKA
GIAN - KIANA
GIANA - KIANA
GIANCARLO - KIANAKALO
GIANELLE - KIANELE
GIANLUCA - KIANALUKA
GIANMARCO - KIANAMALAKO

GIANNA - KIANA

GIANNE - KIANE

GIANNI - KIANI

GIANNINA - KIANINA

GIATANNA - KIAKANA

GIBI - KIPI

GIBSON - KIPEKONU

GICELLIS - KIKELIKE

GICELY - KIKELI

GIDEON - KILEONA

GIDGET - KIKEKEKI

GIETA - KIEKA

GIG - KIKE

GIGI - KIKI

GIJO - KIIO

GIL - KILI

GILA - KILA

GILBERT – KILIPAKI

GILBERTO - KILIPAKO

GILDA - KILA

GILDARDO- GILDARDO

GILES - KILE

GILFORD - KEKOA

GILLES - KILEKI

GILLIAN - KILIANA

GILLIGAN - KILIKANA

GILLYAN - KILIANA

GILMORE - KILEMOA

GILNA - KILENA

GIM CHUAN - KIME KUANA

GINA - KINA

GINELE - KINELE

GINETTE - KINEKE

GINGER - AWAPUHI

GINNY – KINI

GINO - KINO

GIO - KIO

GIONNI - KIONI

GIORGIE - KIOKIE

GIOVANNA - KIOWANA

GIOVANNI - KIOWANI

GIRASOL - KILAKOLU

GIRDEN - KILEKENI

GIRESA - KILEKA

GISELA - KIKELA

GISELE, GISELLE - KIKELE

GITHA - KIKA

GITTE - KIKE

GIULI - KIULI

GIULIA - KIULIA

GIULIANNA - KIULIANA

GIULIETTA - KIULIEKA

GIUSEPPE - KIUKEPE

GIVANA - KIWANA

GIVERNY - KIWELINI

GIZELLE - KIKELE

GJORN - KIOLUNU

GLACIA - KALAKIA

GLADA - KALAKA

GLADDIE - KALAKIE

GLADSTONE - KALAKAKONE

GLADYES - KALAKIEKI

GLADYS - KALAKEKE

GLAIZA - KALAIKA

GLAN - KALANA

GLANCY - KALANAKI

GLASSELL - KALAKELI

GLAYLEE - KALAILE

GLAYN - KALAINE

GLEMA - KALEMA

GLEN - KALENI

GLENDA - KELENEKA

GLENDON - KALENIKONU

GLENDORA - KALENIKOLA

GLENMORY - KALENIMOLI

GLENN - KELENA

GLENNA - KALENA

GLENNIS - KALENIKE

GLENNON - KALENONU

GLENORA - KALENOLA

GLENYS - KALENIKE

GLO - KALO

GLORIA - KOLOLIA

GLORIANN - KALOLIANA

GLORIE - KALOLIE

GLORIELLE - KALOLIELE

GLORY - KALOLI

GLYNDA - KALINEKA

GLYNESE - KALINEKE

GLYNN - KALINE

GOWAN - KOWANA

GODFREY - KOKAPELI

GOD'ISS - KOKU'IKE

GOGDUE - KOKUKUE

GOIST - KOIKE

GOKNUR - KOKUNULO

GOLA - KOLA

GOLDA - KOLA

GOLDIE - KOLIE

GOLIE - KOLIE

GOMER - KOMELI

GOMERZINDA - KOMELIKINEKA

GOMEZ - KOMEKI

GONZAGA - KONUKAKA

GONZALO - KONUKALO

GONZALOS - KONUKALOKU

GOPAL - KOPALA

GORAN - KOLANA

GORBY - KOLUPI

GORDO - KOLUKO

GORDON - KOLEKONA

GORDY - KOLUKI

GOTHER - KOKELI

GOVAN - KOWANA

GOVERNOR - KOWELINOLU

GOVIND - KOWINEKE

GRACE - KALAKE

GRACEN - KALAKENI

GRACHA - KALAKA

GRACIANO - KALAKIANO

GRACIE - KALAKIE

GRACIELA - KALAKIELA

GRACITA - KALAKIKA

GRACYN - KALAKINE

GRADA - KALAKA

GRADON - KALAKONU

GRADY - KALAKI

GRAEME - KALAEME

GRAFTON - KALAPAKONU

GRAHAM - KALAHAMA

GRAMS - KALAMAKA

GRANDON - KALANAKONU

GRANT - KALANAKA

GRANTHAM - KALANAKAMA

GRANVILLE - KALANAWILE

GRASHINA - KALAKINA

GRAY - KALAI

GRAYDON - KALAIKONU

GRAYLON - KALAILONU

GRAYSON - KALAIKONU

GRAZIELLA - KALAKIELA

GRAZYNA - KALAKINA

GREATNECK - KALEAKANEKIKI

GRECEL - KALEKELI

GRECIA - KALEKIA

GREENIE - KALENIE

GREER - KALELI

GREG - KELEKO

GREGG – KALEKI

GREGGREY - KALEKILEI

GREGOR - KALEKOLU

GREGORIA - KALEKOLIA

GREGORY - KELEKOLIO

GREIG - KALEIKE

GREILEN - KALEILENI

GREN - KALENI

GRET - KALEKI

GRETA - KALEKA

GRETCHEN – KELEKENA

GRETEL - KALEKELI

GRETHE - KALEKE

GREVERA - KALEWELA

GREY - KALEI

GREYSON - KALEIKONU

GRIEVOUS - KALIEWOUKO

GRIFFIN - KALIPINE

GRIFFING - KALIPINE

GRIFFITH -KALIPIKE

GRIN - KALINE

GRISELDA - KALIKELA

GRISSEL - KALIKELI

GRIT - KALIKE

GROGAN - KALOKANA

GROVER - KALOWELI

GRYTA - KALIKA

GRYTHA - KALIKA

GUADALUPANA - KUAKALUPANA

GUADALUPE - KUAKALUPE

GUARACY - KUALAKI

GUAROV - KUALOWU

GUDRUN - KUKOLUNO

GUENEVERE - KUENEWELE

GUENIVERE - KUENIWELE

GUENTER - KUENIKELI

GUIDO - KUIKO

GUIERMO - KUIELIMO

GUILHERME - KUILEHELIME

GUILA - KUILA

GUILIANA - KUILIANA

GUILLERMINA - KUILELIMINA

GUILLERMO - KUILELIMO

GUINNESS - KUINEKI

GUIZAR - KUIKALA

GULIANO - KULIANO

GUMECINDO - KUMEKINEKO

GUNDI - KUNOKI

GUNDULA - KUNOKULA

GUNILLA - KUNILA

GUNNAR - KUNALA

GUNNER - KUNELI

GUNNY - KUNI

GÜNTER - KAÜANAKELI

GUNTHER - KUNOKELI

GURI - KULI

GURJIT - KULIIKO

GURPREET - KULOPOLEKI

GURPRIT - KULOPOLIKE

GURSTAR - KULOKALA

GURTHA - KUKA

GURURAJ - KULULAI

GUS - KUKO

GUSTAVO - KUKAWO

GUTHRIE - KULIE

GUY - KAI

GUYNETH - KUINEKI

GWEN - KAWENA

GWENDA - KAWENIKA

GWENDALEE - KAWENIKALE

GWENDOLYN - KAWENAKOLINA

GWENN - KAWENA

GWYDOTTA - KAWIKOKA

GWYN - KAWINE

GWYNNERA - KAWINELA

GWYNETH - KAWINEKI

GYASI - KIAKI

GYPSY - KIPEKI

GYTIS - KIKIKE

GYULA - KIULA

H

FIRST NAMES

HA - HA
HAAKON - HAKONU
HAASHIM - HAKIME
HABIB - HAPIPE
HACKETTE - HAKAKEKE
HADANYA - HAKANIA
HADDEN - HAKENI
HADLEE - HAKALE
HADLEY - HAKALEI
HADRIAN - HAKALIANA
HADYN - HAKINE
HAELEN - HAELENI
HAELI - HAELI
HAFID - HAPIKE
HAGAN - HAKANA
HAGEN - HAKENI
HAGER - HAKELI
HAHNAHMIE - HAHANAHAMIE
HAI - HAI
HAIA - HAIA
HAIDE - HAIKE
HAIDEN - HAIKENE
HAIDYN - HAIKINE
HAIFA - HAIPA
HAIG - HAIKE
HAILEE- HAILE
HAILEIGH - HAILEIKEHE
HAILEY - HAILEI
HAILIE - HAILIE
HAILLE - HAILE

HAIWEN - HAIWENI
HAJAR - HAIALA
HAJRAH - HAILAHA
HAKIM - HAKIME
HAL - HALA
HALAH - HALAHA
HALBERT - HALAPEKI
HALCY - HALAKI
HALDEN - HALENI
HALEH - HALEHI
HALEIGH - HALEIKEHE
HALEMA - HALEMA
HALEN - HALENI
HALEY - HALEI
HALIM - HALIME
HALL - HALA
HALLE - HALE
HALLEY -HALEI
HALI - HALI
HALIDA - HALIKA
HALIE - HALIE
HALINA - HALINA
HALLA - HALA
HALLEE - HALE
HALLIE - HALIE
HALO - HALO
HALSEY - HALAKEI
HALYNA - HALINA
HAMDA - HAMAKA
HAMID - HAMIKE

HAMIL - HAMILE

HAMILTON - HAMILEKONU

HAMIN - HAMINE

HAMISH - HAMIKE

HAMLET - HAMALEKI

HAMP - HAMAPA

HAMPTON - HAMAPAKONU

HAMSITHA - HAMAKIKA

HAMZA - HAMAKA

HAN - HANA

HANA - HANA

HANAH - HANAHA

HANAHLEI - HANAHALEI

HANAKO - HANAKO

HANDE - HANAKE

HANG - HANA

HANH - HANAHA

HANILLA - HANILA

HANK - KANEKE

HANNA - HANA

HANNAH - KANA

HANNAHMIE - HANAHAMIE

HANNE - HANE

HANNELORE - HANELOLE

HANNIBAL - HANIPALA

HANS - KANEKE

HANSA - HANAKA

HANSEN - HANAKENI

HANSIKA - HANAKIKA

HANZEL - HANAKELI

HAPPY - HAPI

HARALIN - HALALINE

HARDY - HALAKI

HARE - HALE

HARI – HALI

HARINDER - HALINEKELI

HARIS - HALIKE

HARITH - HALIKE

HARJ - HALI

HARJWINDER - HALIWINEKELI

HARL - HALA

HARLA - HALA

HARLAN - HALANA

HARLEE - HALE

HARLEIGH - HALEIKEHE

HARLENE - HALENE

HARLEY - HALEI

HARLIE - HALIE

HARLON - HALONU

HARMIK - HALAMIKE

HARMON - HALAMONU

HARMONY - HALAMONI

HARNAYA - HALANAIA

HARNISH - HALANIKE

HAROLD - HALOLA

HARPAL - HALAPALA

HARPER - HALAPELI

HARPREET - HALAPALEKI

HARPYE - HALAPIE

HARRELL - HALELI

HARRIAN - HALIANA

HARRIET - HALIKAKA

HARRINGTON - HALINEKONU

HARRIS - HALIKE

HARRISON - HALIKONU

HARRY - HALE

HARRYETTE - HALIEKE

HARSHBIR - HALAKAPILE

HARSHIL - HALAKILE

HARSHITA - HALAKIKA

HART - HAKA

HARTLEY - HAKALEI

HARUKO -HALUKO

HARVEY - KALEWE

HARVIR - HALAWILE

HASANAH - HAKANAHA

HASHIMOTO - HAKIMOKO

HASIA - HAKIA

HASSAN - HAKANA

HASSIAN - HAKIANA

HASSIE - HAKIE

HASTI - HAKI

HASTINGS - HAKINEKE

HASTON - HAKONU

HATTIE - HAKIE

HAVEN - HAWENI

HAVIER - HAWIELI

HAWKEN - HAWAKENI

HAWKEYE - HAWAKEIE

HAWTHORNE - HAWAKOLUNE

HAYDEE - HAIKE

HAYDEN - HAIKENI

HAYES - HAIEKI

HAYLA - HAILA

HAYLEE - HAILE

HAYLEI - HAILEI

HAYLEIGH - HAILEIKEHE

HAYLEY - HAILEI

HAYLI - HAILI

HAYLIE - HAILIE

HAYNE - HAINE

HAYWOOD - HAIWOKU

HAZEL - HAIKELA

HAZELYN - HAKELINE

HAZEN - HAKENI

HAZZA - HAKA

HEARIE - HEALIE

HEATH - HEAKA

HEATHER – HEKELE

HEATHRLYN - HEKELEINI

HEAVEN - HEAWENI

HEBER - HEPELI

HECTOR – KEKEKA

HECTORINE - HEKOLINE

HEDI - HEKI

HEDWIG - HEKEWIKA

HEDY – HEKI

HEE - HE

HEENA - HENA

HEENAM - HENAMA

HEESUN - HEKUNO

HEE YOUNG - HE IOUNO

HEGE - HEKE

HEIDI - HEIKI

HEIDKE - HEIKEKE

HEIDRUN - HEIKELUNO

HEIDY - HEIKI

HEIKE - HEIKE

HEIKO - HEIKO

HEINRICH - HEINELIKE

HEINZ - HEINEKE

HEKTOR - HEKIKOLU

HELANA - HELANA

HELEEN - HELENI

HELEN - HELENA

HELENA - HELENA

HELENE - HELENE

HELGA - HELIKA

HELIA - HELIA

HELLE - HELE

HELMA - HELIMA

HEMANG - HEMANA

HEMELYN - HEMELIN

HELMER - HELIMELI

HELMUT - HELIMUKO

HENDRI - HENIKILI

HENDRIK - HENIKILIKE

HENG CHEUN - HENI KEUNO

HENGYI - HENII

HENHAN - HENIHANA

HENLE - HENILE

HENNA - HENA

HENNER - HENELI

HENNESSEY - HENEKEI

HENRIK - HENILIKE

HENRIKAS - HENILIKAKA

HENRIETTA - HENELIAKA

HENRIETTE - HENELIEKE

HENRY - HENELE

HENRYDAVID - HENILIKAWIKE

HENRYETTA - HENILIEKA

HENSA - HENIKA

HENSLEY - HENIKILEI

HENTIE - HENIKIE

HERACLIO - HELAKALIO

HERB - HAPA

HERBERT - HAPAKI

HERBERTH - HELIPEKI

HERCULANO - HELIKULANO

HERIEANN - HELIEANA

HERIBERTO - HELIPEKO

HERK - HEKI

HERKY - HEKI

HERLON - HELONU

HERMAN - HALEMANO

HERMES - HELIMEKI

HERMIK - HELIMIKE

HERMILA - HELIMILA

HERMINDA - HELIMINEKA

HERMINIA - HELIMINIA

HERMIONE - HELIMIONE

HERNAN - HELINANA

HERNANDO - HELINANAKO

HERNIE - HELINIE

HERRYAN - HELIANA

HERSCHEL - HELIKIKELI

HERSHELL - HELIKELI

HERSHO - HELIKO

HERTHA - HEKA

HERVE - HELIWE

HERWIN - HELIWINE

HESH - HEKI

HESTAND - HEKANAKA

HESTER – KEKALA

HESTRIE - HEKILIE

HEYWARD - HEIWALAKA

HEZEKIAH - HEKEKIAHA

HICKORY - HIKEKOLI

HICKS - HIKEKEKE

HIDAYAT - HIKAIAKA

HIDEKO - HIKEKO

HIEDI - HIEKI

HIEN - HIENI

HIEU - HIEU

HIFSA - HIPEKA

HIKOYAT - HIKOIAKA

HILARIA - HILALIA

HILARIO - HILALIO

HILARY – HILALIO

HILBERT - HILEPEKI

HILCIAS - HILEKIAKA

HILDA – KELEKA

HILDEBRANDO - HILEPILANAKO

HILDEGARDE - HILEKALAKE

HILDEN - HILENI

HILLAR - HILALA

HILLARD - HILALAKA

HILLARI - HILALI

HILLARY - HILALI

HILLIS - HILIKE

HILMO - HILEMO

HILOLA - HILOLA

HILSA - HILEKA

HILTON - HILEKONU

HIMANISH - HIMANIKE

HIMIE - HIMIE

HING - HINE

HIOLLIS - HIOLIKE

HIPOLITO - HIPOLIKO

HIRAANI - HILANI

HIRAM – HAILAMA

HIRO - HILO

HIROKO - HILOKO

HISAYO - HIKAIO

HITA - HIKA

HITESH - HIKEKI

HITOMI - HIKOMI

HJORDES - HIOLUKEKI

HLI - HALI
HO - HO
HOA - HOA
HOANCA - HOANAKA
HOANG - HOANA
HOBBS - HOPUKU
HOBERT - HOPELEKA
HOBIE - HOPIE
HODA - HOKA
HODGES - HOKUKEKI
HOGAN - HOKANA
HOISOOK - HOIKOKU
HO JUNG - HO IUNO
HOKE - HOKE
HOLAM - HOLAMA
HOLBERT - HOLUPEKI
HOLBIEN - HOLUPIENI
HOLDEN - HOLENI
HOLGER - HOLUKELI
HOLIDAY - HOLIKAI
HOLLAND - HOLANAKA
HOLLEE - HOLE
HOLLI - HOLI
HOLLIE - HOLIE
HOLLIS - HOLIKE
HOLLISTER - HOLIKELI
HOLLY - HALI
HOLT - HOLUKU
HOMER - HOMELA
HONESTY - HONEKI

HONEY - KELE
HONEYLYN - HONEILINE
HONG - HONU
HONORA - HONOLA
HOOMAN - HOMANA
HOPE - MANA'OLANA
HORACE - KOLEKA
HORATIO - HOLAKIO
HORNE - HOLUNE
HORSLEY - HOLUKULEI
HORST - HOLUKU
HORTENCIA - HOKENIKIA
HOSANNA - HOKANA
HOSEA - HOKEA
HOSEIN - HOKEINE
HOSS - HOKU
HOSSLEY - HOKULEI
HOUSTON - HOUKONU
HOWARD - HAOA
HOWELL - HOWELI
HOWIE - HOWIE
HOYT - HOIKE
HOZZAIN - HOKAINE
HRISHIKESH - HALIKIKEKIHI
HUANNE - HUANE
HUBERT - KUPEKA
HUBERTA - HUPEKA
HUDES - HUKEKI
HUDIYATI - HUKIIAKI
HUDSON - HUKOKONU

HUEY - HUEI
HUFF - HUPO
HUGH – HIU
HUGHE - HUKOHE
HUGO - HUKO
HUGUETTE - HUKUEKE
HUI JUN - HUI IUNO
HUILING - HUILINE
HUMAIR - HUMAILE
HUMBERTO - HUMOPEKO
HUMNA - HUMONA
HUMSINI - HUMOKINI
HUNDLEY - HUNOKOLEI
HUNER - HUNELI
HUNG - HUNO
HUNT - HUNOKO
HUNTER - HUNOKELI
HUONG - HUONU
HUSAINA - HUKAINA
HUSTON - HUKONU
HUTCH - HUKOKO
HUTT - HUKO
HUY - HUI
HWAI - HAWAI
HWAI-CHYI - HAWAI-EKII
HWAI-LIN - HAWAI-ELINE
HYACINTH - HIAKINEKE
HYATT - HIAKA
HYDY - HIKI
HYEJU - HIEIU

HYKE - HIKE
HYKEME - HIKEME
HYO - HIO
HYOUGO - HIOUKO
HYRIA - HILIA
HYRUM - HILUMO
HYTHUM - HIKUMO
HYUNG - HIUNO
HYUNJOO - HIUNIO

I

FIRST NAMES

IAH - IAHA

IAN – IANA

IANNA - IANA

IARA - IALA

IARI - IALI

IBEN - IPENI

IBI - IPI

IBRAHIM - IPELAHIME

IBTIHAL - IPEKIHALA

ICA - IKA

ICEL - IKELI

ICHABOD - IKAPOKA

ICLAL - IKELALA

IDA - AIKA

IDAH - IKAHA

IDALESIA - IKALEKIA

IDALIA - IKALIA

IDALINA - IKALINA

IDALIS - IKALIKE

IDALYS - IKALIKE

IDAN - IKAKA

IDEA - IKEA

IDEL - IKELI

IDELLA - IKELA

IDENA - IKENA

IDOLINA - IKOLINA

IDOY - IKOI

IDRIS - IKELIKE

IENA - IENA

IESHA - IEKA

IEYASU - IEIAKU

IFEOMAN - IPEOMANA

IGGY - IKI

IGNACIO - IKENAKIO

IGNAS - IKENAKA

IGOR - IKOLU

IHOR - IHOLU

IJAHALA - IIAHALA

IKE - IKE

IKEL - IKELI

IKENNA - IKENA

IKHYUN - IKEHIUNO

IKIRA - IKILA

IKRAM - IKELAMA

ILA - ILA

ILAM - ILAMA

ILAN - ILANA

ILANA - ILANA

ILARIA - ILALIA

ILDA - ILA

ILDIKO - ILIKO

ILEAN -ILEANA

ILEANA - ILEANA

ILEEN - ILENI

ILENE - ILENE

ILIA - ILIA

ILIAN - ILIANA

ILIANA - ILIANA

ILIE - ILIE

ILLADELLA - ILAKELA

ILLEANA - ILEANA

ILLIANA - ILIANA

ILLINOIS - ILINOIKE

ILLISA - ILIKA

ILLYANA - ILIANA

ILONA - ILONA

ILONKA - ILONUKA

ILOO - ILO

ILSA - ILEKA

ILSE - ILEKE

ILSHAR - ILEKALA

ILUMINADA - ILUMINAKA

ILY - ILI

ILYA - ILIA

ILYNCA - ILINEKA

ILYSE - ILIKE

IMA - IMA

IMAGINE - IMAKINE

IMAN - IMANA

IMANI - IMANI

IMANUELLE - IMANUELE

IMARI - IMALI

IMEE - IME

IMELDA - IMELA

IMKE - IMEKE

IMLA - IMELA

IMMANUEL - IMANUELI

IMOGEN - IMOKENI

IMOGENE - IMOKENE

IMRAN - IMELANA

IMRE - IMELE

INA - INA

INAARA - INALA

INAAYAT - INAIAKA

INAKI - INAKI

INAY - INAI

INDALECIO - INEKALEKIO

INDERPAL - INEKELIPALA

INDIA - INEKIA

INDIANA - INEKIANA

INDIE - INEKIE

INDIGO - INEKIKO

INDIRA - INEKILA

INDRA - INEKELA

INDRE - INEKELE

INDY - INEKI

INEIDA - INEIKA

INES - INEKI

INESS - INEKI

INETTA - INEKA

INEZ - AINEKI

INFINITY - INEPINIKI

INGA - INA

INGE - INE

INGER - INELI

INGI - INI

INGRID - INAKIKA

INGVAR - INEWALA

INIE JEAN - INIE IEANA

INILI - INILI

INMACULADA - INEMAKULAKA

INYSE - INIKE

INO - INO

INOEL - INOELI

IOLA - IOLA

IONA - IONA

IONE - IONE

IONEL - IONELI

IOTA - IOKA

IPSHITA - IPEKIKA

IQVINDER - IKEWINEKELI

IRA - ILA

IRACEMA - ILAKEMA

IRAIACE - ILAIAKE

IRAIS - ILAIKE

IRANETTA - ILANEKA

IRBY - ILEPI

IREESE - ILEKE

IRELAND - ILELANAKA

IRENE - AILINA

IRETA - ILEKA

IRIA - ILIA

IRIC - ILIKE

IRIDIAN - ILIKIANA

IRINA - ILINA

IRIS - AILIKA

IRSULA - ILEKULA

IRMA - AIMA

IRVAN - ILEWANA

IRVING - IWINI

IRWIN - IWINI

ISAAC – IKA'AKA

ISAAK – IKA'AKA

ISABEAU - IKAPEAU

ISABEL - IKEPELA

ISABELLA - IKEPELA

ISABELLE - IKEPELA

ISCAH - IKEKAHA

ISADORA - IKAKOLA

ISAI - IKAI

ISAIAH – IKAIA

ISAIAS - IKAIAKA

ISELA - IKELA

ISELLA - IKELA

ISH - IKE

ISHA - IKA

ISHAAN - IKANA

ISHARA - IKALA

ISHBEL - IKEPELI

ISIACC - IKIAKA

ISIDORE - IKIKOLO

ISIDRO - IKIKELO

ISIS - IKIKE

ISLEY - IKELEI

ISMAEL - IKEMAELI

ISMA'IL - IKEMA'ILE

ISMARA - IKEMALA

ISMENE - IKEMENE

ISNELLA - IKENELA
ISRAEL - IKELAELI
ISSENIA - IKENIA
ISSIAH - IKIAHA
ISSRAA - IKELA
ISTAR - IKALA
ITA - IKA
ITALINA - IKALINA
ITALY - IKALI
ITHACA - IKAKA
ITZEL - IKEKELI
ITZIA - IKEKIA
IVA - IWA
IVAN - IWANA
IVANA - IWANA
IVANNAH - IWANAHA
IVAR - IWALA
IVELISSE - IWELIKE
IVETTE - IWEKE
IVONNE - IWONE
IVORY - IWOLI
IVY - IWI
IWAN - IWANA
IWANDA - IWANAKA
IWONA - IWONA
IXCHEL - IKEKELI
IYA - IIA
IYANNA - IIANA
IYENDA - IIENIKA
IYLEEN - IILENI

IZAAC - IKAKA
IZABELLA - IKAPELA
IZAIAH - IKAIAHA
IZANDRA - IZANDRA
IZEL - IKELI
IZIKA - IKIKA
I'ZSHAE - I'EKEKAE
IZUMI - IKUMI
IZYBEL - IKIPELI
IZZIE - IKIE
IZZY - IKI

J

FIRST NAMES

JAA - IA

JAACK - IAKAKA

JAALA - IALA

JAALAM - IALAMA

JAANN - IANA

JABARI - IAPALI

JABE - IAPE

JABEZ - IAPEKI

JABIN - IAPINE

JABRIEL - IAPALIELI

JACAN - IAKANA

JACE - IAKE

JACEE - IAKE

JACELYN - IAKELINE

JACENTA - IAKENIKA

JACEY - IAKEI

JACHELLE - IAKELE

JACI - IAKI

JACIE - IAKIE

JACINDA - IAKINEKA

JACINE - IAKINE

JACINTA - IAKINEKA

JACK – KEAKA

JACKE - IAKAKE

JACKIE - KEAKUKI

JACKILYN - IAKAKILINE

JACKLYN - IAKAKALINE

JACKLYNN - IAKAKALINE

JOCKO - IOKUKO

JACKSEN - IAKAKAKENI

JACKSON - KEAKAKONA

JACKY - IAKAKI

JACLYN - IAKALINE

JACO - IAKO

JACOB – IAKOPA

JACOBI - IAKOPI

JACOLBI - IAKOLUPI

JACOREE - IAKOLE

JACORI - IAKOLI

JA'COURI - IA'AKOULI

JACQIE - IAKIE

JACQLYN - IAKALINE

JACQUANTA - IAKAKANAKA

JACQUE – IAKAKE

JACQUELINE - KEAKULINA

JACQUELYN - IAKAKELINE

JACQUES - IAKAKEKI

JACQUI - IAKAKI

JACQUIE - IAKAKAI

JACQUIS - IAKAKIKE

JACQULYNN - IAKAKULINE

JACY - IAKI

JADA - IAKA

JADAH - IAKAHA

JADAYA - IAKAIA

JADE - KEIKE

JADEN - IAKENI

JADENE - IAKENE

JADINE - IAKINE

JADON - IAKONU

JADYN - IAKINE

JADZIA - IAKAKIA

JAE - IAE

JAEDA - IAEKA

JAEDEN - IAEKENI

JAEDON - IAEKONU

JAEDYN - IAEKINE

JAEGER - IAEKELI

JAEL - IAELI

JAELA - IAELA

JAELEE - IAELE

JAELI - IAELI

JAELYN - IAELINE

JAEMYN - IAEMINE

JAESON - IAEKONU

JAETTA - IAEKA

JAEWON - IAEWONU

JAFFAR - IAPALA

JAFRAH - IAPALAHA

JAGEL - IAKELI

JAGGER - IAKELI

JAHALA - IAHALA

JAHARYA - IAHALIA

JAHAY - IAHAI

JAHDIEL - IAHAKIELI

JAHEIM - IAHEIME

JAHIRA - IAHILA

JAH'LIL - IAHA'ALILE

JAHKIER - IAHAKIELI

JAHMAINE - IAHAMAINE

JAHMAL - IAHAMALA

JAHMELIA - IAHAMELIA

JAHNA - IAHANA

JAHNN - IAHANA

JAHNYL - IAHANILE

JAHRED - IAHALEKI

JAHVEL - IAHAWELI

JAI - IAI

JAICEE - IAIKE

JAICEPH - IAIKEPI

JAICYEA - IAIKIEA

JAID - IAIKE

JAIDA - IAIKA

JAIDAN - IAIKANA

JAIDEN - IAIKENI

JAIDYN - IAIKINE

JAIKOB - IAIKOPU

JAIME - IAIME

JAIMEE - IAIME

JAIMELLE - IAIMELE

JAIMIE - IAIMIE

JAIMSEY - IAIMEKEI

JAIR - IAILE

JAIRH - IAILEHE

JAIRUS - IAILUKO

JAITHEN - IAIKENI

JAJUAN - IAIUANA

JAKARLA - IAKALA

JAKAYLA - IAKAILA

JAKE - IAKE

JAKEB - IAKEPI

JAKELIN - IAKELINE

JAKIA - IAKIA

JAKIERRA - IAKIELA

JAKIM - IAKIME

JAKIN - IAKINE

JAKISHA - IAKIKA

JAKOB - IAKOPU

JAKSON - IAKAKONU

JALA - IALA

JALAINE - IALAINE

JALAIR - IALAILE

JALEAH - IALEAHA

JALEEL - IALELI

JALEESA - IALEKA

JALEN - IALENI

JALENE - IALENE

JALIK - IALIKE

JALISA - IALIKA

JALIYAH - IALIIAHA

JALONDA - IALONUKA

JALYN - IALINE

JALYSA - IALIKA

JAM - IAMA

JAMA - IAMA

JAMAI - IAMAI

JAMAAL - IAMALA

JAMAICA - IAMAIKA

JAMAL - IMALA

JAMALLIAH - IAMALIAHA

JAMANI - IAMANI

JAMANILA - IAMANILA

JAMAR - IAMALA

JAMARI - IAMALI

JAMARIUS - IAMALIUKO

JAMARK - IAMAKA

JAMECA - IAMEKA

JAMEE - IAME

JAMEL - IAMELI

JAMELIN - IAMELINE

JAMELLIA - IAMELIA

JAMERE - IAMELE

JAMES - KIMO

JAMESCY - IAMEKIKI

JAMESETTE - IAMEKEKE

JAMESHA - IAMEKA

JAMESON - IAMEKONU

JAMEY - IAMEI

JAMI - IAMI

JAMIA - IAMIA

JAMIE - KIMI

JAMIEJO - IAMIEIO

JAMIELYNN - IAMIELINE

JAMIKA - IAMIKA

JAMIL - IAMILE

JAMILA - IAMILA

JAMILLAH - IAMILAHA

JAMIMA - IAMIMA

JAMINI - IAMINI

JAMISON - IAMIKONU

JAMIYAH - IAMIIAHA

JAMNA - IAMANA

JAMO - IAMO

JAMON - IAMONU

JAMYCHEAL - IAMIKEALA

JAMYRA - IAMILA

JAMZIE - IAMAKIE

JAN - IANA

JANA - IANA

JANAE - IANAE

JANAEA - IANAEA

JANAI - IANAI

JANAIJA - IANAIIA

JANAINA - IANAINA

JARAMIE - IALAMIE

JANAY - IANAI

JANAYA - IANAIA

JANCEE - IANAKE

JANCELLE - IANAKELE

JANCI - IANAKI

JANDALE - IANAKALE

JANDI - IANAKI

JANE - IANE

JANEAN - IANEANA

JANEE - IANE

JANEEN - IANENI

JANEECE - IANEKE

JANEICE - IANEIKE

JANEIVE - IANEIWE

JANEL - IANELI

JANELL - IANELI

JANELLA - IANELA

JANELLE - IANELE

JANENE - IANENE

JANER - IANELI

JANERYL - IANELILE

JANESSA - IANEKA

JANET - IANEKI

JANETTA - IANEKA

JANETTE - IANEKE

JANEXY - IANEKI

JANEY - IANEI

JANI - IANI

JANIA - IANIA

JA'NIAH - IA'ANIAHA

JANIAH - IANIAHA

JANICA - IANIKA

JANICE - KANIKE

JANIE - IANIE

JANIECE - IANIEKE

JANIEL - IANIELI

JANIFER - IANIPELI

JANIKA - IANIKA

JANILLE - IANILE

JANINA - IANINA

JANINE – IANINI

JANIS - IANIKE

JANIYA - IANIIA

JANIYAH - IANIIAHA

JANNA - IANA

JANNAH - IANAHA

JANNE - IANE

JANNEKE - IANEKE

JANNEST - IANEKI

JANNET - IANEKI

JANNIFFER - IANIPELI

JANOT' - IANOKU'U

JANSON - IANAKONU

JANTHA - IANAKA

JANTHINA - IANAKINA

JANYIA - IANIIA

JAPHETH - IAPEKI

JAPI - IAPI

JA'QAI - IA'AKAI

JAQUAN - IAKUANA

JAQUARIUS - IAKALIUKO

JAQUELINE - IAKELINE

JAQUESHA - IAKEKA

JAQUETTA - IAKEKA

JAQUINA - IAKINA

JARA - IALA

JARAD - IALAKA

JARDEN - IALAKENI

JARED – IALEKA

JAREK - IALEKI

JAREL - IALELI

JAREN - IALENI

JARETT - IALEKI

JARICA - IALIKA

JARIEN - IALIENI

JARI-MATTI - IALI-EMAKI

JARINE - IALINE

JARKA - IAKA

JAROD - IALOKU

JAROM- IALOMU

JAROMY - IALOMI

JARON - IALONU

JARRAH - IALAHA

JARRED - IALEKI

JARRELL - IALELI

JARRETT - IALEKI

JARROD - IALOKU

JARRYD - IALIKE

JARVIS - IALAWIKE

JARYN - IALINE

JAS - IAKA

JASALYNN - IAKALINE

JASAN - IAKANA

JASANALIN - IAKANALINE

JASANALYN - IAKANALINE

JASCINTH - IAKAKINEKE

JASEER - IAKELI

JASEN - IAKENI

JASFER - IAKAPELI

JASHA - IAKA

JASHAUN - IAKAUNO

JASHAWN - IAKAWANA

JASHUIA - IAKUIA

JASKARAN - IAKAKALANA

JASMERE - IAKAMELE

JASMIN - IAKAMINE

JASMINA - IAKAMINA

JASMINE – PIKAKE

JASMYN - IAKAMINE

JASNA - IAKANA

JASON – IAKONA

JASEAN - IAKEANA

JASINIA - IAKINIA

JASPER - IAKEPA

JASPREET - IAKAPALEKI

JASSIDY - IAKIKI

JASSIEL - IAKIELI

JASSY - IAKI

JATAYLA - IAKAILA

JATERRIA - IAKELIA

JATHAN - IAKANA

JATIA - IAKIA

JATIN - IAKINE

JATINDER - IAKINEKELI

JATRAVIS - IALAWIKE

JAUCELYN - IAUKELINE

JAUNXAQUE - IAUNOKAKE

JAVAN - IAWANA

JAVANNAH - IAWANAHA

JAVAUGHN - IAWAUKOHONO

JAVAYLEN - IAWAILENI

JAVELL - IAWELI

JAVIEN - IAWIENI

JAVIER - IAWIELI

JAVIN - IAWINE

JAVON - IAWONU

JAVONDA - IAWONUKA

JAVONI - IAWONI

JAVORIS - IAWOLIKE

JAWANNA - IAWANA

JAX - IAKA

JAXON - IAKONU

JAXSON - IAKAKONU

JAY – KEI

JAY-ARE - IAI-ALE

JAYA - IAIA

JAYADI - IAIAKI

JAYANALYN - IAIANALINE

JAYANTA - IAIANAKA

JAYANTI - IAIANAKI

JAYASHREE - IAIAKALE

JAYASHREE - IAIAKALE

JAYATRI - IAIALI

JAYCEE - IAIKE

JAYCENE - IAIKENE

JAYCIE - IAIKIE

JAYDA - IAIKA

JAYDAIN - IAIKAINE

JAYDE - IAIKE

JAYDEE - IAIKE

JAYDEN - IAIKENI

JAYDON - IAIKONU

JAYE - IAIE

JAYESH - IAIEKI

JAYKEEL - IAIKELI

JAYLA - IAILA

JAYLEEN - IAILENI

JAYLEN - IAILENI

JAYLENE - IAILENE

JAYLIN - IAILINE

JAYLINE - IAILINE

JAYLON - IAILONU

JAYME - IAIME

JAYMEE - IAIME

JAYMESON - IAIMEKONU

JAYMIE - IAIMIE

JAYMIN - IAIMINE

JAYMYSS - IAMIKE

JAYNA - IAINA

JAYNAY - IAINAI

JAYNE - IAINE

JAYNELL - IAINELI

JAY-R - IAI-ELE

JAYSON - IAIKONU

JAYVON - IAIWONU

JAZAMINE - IAKAMINE

JAZAREA - IAKALEA

JAZELLE - IAKELE

JAZMIN - IAKAMINE

JAZMINN - IAKAMINE

JAZMON - IAKAMONU

JAZMINE - IAKAMINE

JAZMUN - IAKAMUNO

JAZMYNE - IAKAMINE

JAZZ - IAKA

JAZZLIAN - IAKALIANA

JAZZLYN - IAKALINE

JAZZMAND - IAKAMANAKA

JAZZMINE - IAKAMINE

J'DEE - I'EKE

JEADENE - IEAKENE

JEAN – KINI

JEANA - IEANA

JEANATHAN - IEANAKANA

JEAN-CLAUDE - IEANA-AKALAUKE

JEANEEN - IEANENI

JEANELLE - IEANELE

JEANETTE – KENEKE

JEAN-GUY - IEANA-AKUI

JEANIE - IEANIE

JEANINE - KININI

JEAN-LUC - IEANA-ALUKO

JEANKEE - IEANAKE

JEANMARC - IEANAMALAKA

JEANNA - IEANA

JEANNE - KIANE

JEANNEN - IEANENI

JEANNENE - IEANENE

JEANNIE - IEANIE

JEANNINE - IEANINE

JEANPAUL - IEANAPAULO

JEAN-PHILLIPE - IEANA- APILIPE

JEAN-YVES - IEANA-IWEKI

JEAVEN - IEAWENI

JEB - IEPI

JEBEDIAH - IEPEKIAHA

JECOLIAH - IEKOLIAHA

JED - IEKI

JEDARIUS - IEKALIUKO

JEDIDIAH - IEKIKIAHA

JEENA - IENA

JEENY - IENI

JEEPS - IEPIKI

JEEVAN - IEWANA

JEFF - IEPI

JEFFAWN - IEPAWANA

JEFFEREY - IEPELEI

JEFFERSON - IEPELIKONU

JEFFERY - IEPELI

JEFFIE - IEPIE

JEFFNEY - IEPINEI

JEFFREY – IEPELI

JEFFRIES - IEPILIEKI

JEFRI - IEPILI

JEHAN - IEHANA

JEILEN - IEILENI

JEIMY - IEIMI

JEJUAN - IEIUANA

JELANI - IELANI

JELENA - IELENA

JE'LIN - IE'ILINE

JELLEKE - IELEKE

JEMAYA - IEMAIA

JEMEILA - IEMEILA

JEMIMAH - IEMIMAHA

JEMMA - IEMA

JEMMIE - IEMIE

JEMUEL - IEMUELI

JEN - IENI

JENA - IENA

JENACA - IENAKA

JENADE - IENAKE

JENAE - IENAE

JENAH - IENAHA

JENAFER - IENAPELI

JENALA - IENALA

JENAN - IENANA

JENAPHER - IENAPELI

JENARO - IENALO

JENASIS - IENAKIKE

JENAVIEVE - IENAWIEWE

JENDA - IENIKA

JENEASE - IENEAKE

JENEE - IENE

JENEFEL - IENEPELI

JENELDA - IENELA

JENELLE - IENELE

JENENE - IENENE

JENERRA - IENELA

JENESSA - IENEKA

JENESSE - IENEKE

JENEVA - IENEWA

JENI - IENI

JENICA - IENIKA

JENIECE - IENIEKE

JENIK - IENIKE

JENILL - IENILE

JENILYN - IENILINE

JENINA - IENINA

JENINE - IENINE

JANIQUE - IANIKE

JENISE - IENIKE

JENITA - IENIKA

JENITHA - IENIKA

JENN - IENI

JENNA - IENA

JENNAE - IENAE

JENNAFER - IENAPELI

JENNAH - IENAHA

JENNAPHER - IENAPELI

JENNAY - IENAI

JENNE - IENE

JENNEAL - IENEALA

JENNER - IENELI

JENNETE - IENEKE

JENNEY - IENEI

JENNI - IENI

JENNIANNE - IENIANE

JENNICA - IENIKA

JENNIE - KINI

JENNIFER – KINIPELA

JENNILYN - IENILINE

JENNIN - IENINE

JENNINGS - IENINEKE

JENNISA - IENIKA

JENNY - KINI

JENORA - IENOLA

JENS - IENIKI

JENSEEN - IENIKENI

JENSEN - IENIKENI

JENSON - IENIKONU

JENTRY - IENILI

JENWA - IENIWA

JENYA - IENIA

JEOVANNA - IEOWANA

JERA - IELA

JERALD - IELALA

JERALEE - IELALE

JERALYNN - IELALINE

JERAMIE - IELAMIE

JERAPHEL - IELAPELI

JERARD - IELALAKA

JERARDO - IELALAKO

JERE - IELE

JERED - IELEKI

JEREDINE - IELEKINE

JEREEN - IELENI

JEREKAIAH - IELEKAIAHA

JERELL - IELELI

JEREMIAH - IELEMIA

JEREMY - KELEMI

JERENE - IELENE

JERET - IELEKI

JERI - KELI

JERIANN - IELIANA

JERICA - IELIKA

JERICHA - IELIKA

JERICO - IELIKO

JERIECE - IELIEKE

JERIEL - IELIELI

JERILYN - IELILINE

JERIZA - IELIKA

JERLEY - IELEI

JERLIN - IELINE

JERMAINE - IELIMAINE

JERMANEE - IELIMANE

JERMAUL - IELIMAULO

JERMELLE - IELIMELE

JERMIA - IELIMIA

JERNELL - IELINELI

JENILL - IENILE

JEROD - IELOKU

JEROME - KELOME

JERON - IELONU

JERONDA - IELONUKA

JERONIMO - IELONIMO

JERONY - IELONI

JERRA - IELA

JERRAD - IELAKA

JERRALY - IELALI

JERRI - IELI

JERRIANNE - IELIANE

JERRICA - IELIKA

JERRICK - IELIKEKE

JERRILYN - IELILINE

JERROD - IELOKU

JERROLD - KELOLA

JERRY - KELI

JERRY-LYN - IELI-ELINE

JERSEY - IELIKEI

JERUEL - IELUELI

JERUSHA - IELUKA

JERVELYN - IELIWELINE

JERVY - IELIWI

JERWAIN - IELIWAINE

JERWANDA - IELIWANAKA

JESENIA - IEKENIA

JESIAH - IEKIAHA

JESIKA - IEKIKA

JESPER - IEKIPELI

JESS - IEKI

JESSA - IEKA

JESSALYNN - IEKALINE

JESSAMINE - IEKAMINE

JESSAMY - IEKAMI

JESSE – IEKE

JESSED - IEKEKI

JESSEIM - IEKEIME

JESSENIA - IEKENIA

JESSI - IEKI

JESSICA - IEKIKA

JESSIE – IEKE

JESSIELYNN - IEKIELINE

JESSIKA - IEKIKA

JESSINA - IEKINA

JESSINY - IEKINI

JESSLYN - IEKILINE

JESSUP - IEKUPO

JESSYTA - IEKIKA

JESTINA - IEKINA

JESUS - IESU

JESY - IEKI

JETHA - IEKA

JETT- IEKI

JETTA - IEKA

JETTIE - IEKIE

JEVAUN - IEWAUNO

JEVNE - IEWINE

JEWEL - IEWELI

JEWELL - IEWELI

JEZANDRA - IEKANAKALA

JEZEBEL - IEKEPELI

JEZIEL - IEKIELI

JEZREEL - IEKILELI

JEZZICA - IEKIKA

JHA'MHYRIA - IHA'AMAHILIA

JHANE - IHANE

JHAVARIAH - IHAWALIAHA

JHELYN - IHELINE

JHINKEE - IHINEKE

JHISELLE - IHIKELE

JHON - IHONU

JHOVANNY - IHOWANI

JIA - IIA

JIANNI - IIANI

JIHAD - I'IHAKA

JIHANA - IIHANA

JIHANN - IIHANA

JIIN - IINE

JILAINE - IILAINE

JILES - IILEKI

JILL - KILA

JILLAYNE - IILAINE

JILLIAN - IILIANA

JIM - KIMO

JIMALEE - IIMALE

JIMBO - IIMEPO

JIMENA - IIMENA

JIMI - IIMI

JIMICA - IIMIKA

JIMMEQUIA - IIMEQUIA

JIMMIE - IEMIE

JIMMY - KIME

JINA - IINA

JINCE - IINEKE

JINELL - IINELI

JING - IINE

JINGJING - IINIINE

JINHA - IINEHA

JINJER - IINIELI

JINN - IINE

JINNY - IINI

JINU - IINU

JIONTEL - IIONUKELI
JIORJIO - IIOLIIO
JIOVANNNI - IIOWANI
JIREH - IILEHI
JIRO - IILO
JISELLE - IIKELE
JITEN - IIKENI
JITHENDER - IIKENIKELI
JITHMI - IIKEMI
JITKA - IIKEKA
JIWANA - IIWANA
JI-WOONG - II-EWONU
JNANA - INANA
JO - IO
JO-JO - IO-IO
JOAB - IOAPA
JOACHIM - IOAKIME
JOAN - IO'ANA
JOANA - IOANA
JOANALYN - IOANALINE
JOANIE - IOANIE
JOANITA - IOANIKA
JO ANN - IO ANA
JOANN - IOANA
JOANNA - IOANA
JOANNE - IOANE
JOANNY - IOANNI
JOÃO - IOÃO
JOAQUIN - WAKINA
JOARO - IOALO

JOASH - IOAKA
JOB - IOPU
JOBELLE - IOPELE
JOBETH - IOPEKI
JOBY - IOPI
JOCE - IOKE
JOCELYN - IOKELINE
JOCHEN - IOKENI
JODECY - IOKEKI
JODEE - IOKE
JODECY - IOKEKI
JODENE - IOKENE
JODI - IOKI
JODIE - IOKIE
JODY - KOKI
JOE - IOE, KEO
JOEANN - IOEANA
JOEANNE - IOEANE
JOEBILL - IOEPILE
JOEHN - IOEHINI
JOEI - IOEI
JOEL - IOELA
JOELENCIA - IOELENIKIA
JOELLA - IOELA
JOELLE - IOELE
JOELLEN - IOELENI
JOELY - IOELI
JOELYNN - IOELINE
JOENE - IOENE
JOENELL - IOENELI

JOEP - IOEPI

JOESPH - IOEKIPI

JOESWANDI - IOEKIWANAKI

JOETTA - IOEKA

JOETTE - IOEKE

JOEY - IOEI

JOFELYN - IOPELINE

JOFFREY - IOPULEI

JOHAB - IOHAPA

JOHAN - IOHANA

JOHANNA - IOHANA

JOHANNE - IOHANE

JOHANNES - IOHANEKI

JOHANNY - IOHANI

JOHANSEN - IOHANAKENI

JOHARI - IOHALI

JOHN - KEONI

JOHNATHAN - IOHUNAKANA

JOHN-DAVID - KEONI-KAWIKA

JOHNEA - IOHUNEA

JOHNELL - IOHUNELI

JOHNENE - IOHUNENE

JOHNETTE - IOHUNEKE

JOHNIKA - IOHUNIKA

JOHNNA - IOHUNA

JOHNNE - IOHUNE

JOHNNIE - IOHUNIE

JOHNNIFER - IOHUNIPELI

JOHNNY - IOHUNI

JOHNS - IOHUNUKO

JOHNSIE - IOHUNUKIE

JOHNSON - IOHUNUKONU

JOHNSTON - IOHUNUKONU

JOHONNA - IOHONA

JOI - IOI

JOIE - IOIE

JOIS - IOIKE

JOJEAN - IOIEANA

JOJI - IOII

JOJO - IOIO

JOKESHA - IOKEKA

JOLANDA - IOLANAKA

JOLEEN - IOLENI

JOLENA - IOLENA

JOLENE - IOLENE

JOLETTA - IOLEKA

JOLI - IOLI

JOLIE - IOLIE

JOLIFFER - IOLIPELI

JOLINE - IOLINE

JOLLY - IOLI

JOLONDA - IOLONUKA

JOLYN - IOLINA

JOLYNN - IOLINE

JOLYNNE - IOLINE

JOMARIE - IOMALIE

JOMER - IOMELI

JON – IONA

JONAH - IONA

JONALYN - IONALINE

JONAS - IONAKA
JONATHAN - IONAKANA
JONATHEN - IONAKENI
JONATHON - IONAKANA
JONAVAN - IONAWANA
JONAY - IONAI
JONE - IONE
JONELLA - IONELA
JONELLE - IONELE
JONENE - IONENE
JONES - IONEKI
JONEZIE - IONEKIE
JONI - IONI
JONICA - IONIKA
JONILYN - IONILINA
JONIQUE - IONIKE
JONG - IONU
JONNA - IONA
JONNEL - IONELI
JONNI - IONI
JONO - IONO
JONQUIL - IONUKILE
JONTANE - IONUKANE
JONTY - IONUKI
JONYA - IONIA
JONYECE - IONIEKE
JOO YEON - IO IEONU
JOPET - IOPEKI
JORAM - IOLAMA
JORAN - IOLANA

JORAND - IOLANAKA
JORASSE - IOLAKE
JORCHA - IOLUKA
JORDAN - IOLAKANA
JORDANA - IOLUKANA
JORDANNA - IOLUKANA
JORDANNE - IOLUKANE
JORDEE - IOLUKE
JORDEL - IOLUKELI
JORDEN - IOLUKENI
JORDI - IOLUKI
JORDIE - IOLUKIE
JORDIN - IOLUKINE
JORDON - IOLUKONU
JORDY - IOLUKI
JORDYN -IOLUKINE
JORELL - IOLELI
JORETTA - IOLEKA
JORGE - IOKE
JORGEN - IOKENI
JORGINA - IOKINA
JORGO - IOKO
JORI - IOLI
JORJA - IOLIA
JORN - IOLUNU
JORRYN - IOLINE
JORY - IOLI
JOSAH - IOKAHA
JOSANNE - IOKANE
JOSE - KOKE

JOSEE - IOKE

JOSEFA - IOKEPA

JOSELEE - IOKELE

JOSELIN - IOKELINE

JOSELMA - IOKELIMA

JOSELYN - IOKELINE

JOSEPH - IOKEPA

JOSEPHINA - IOKEPINA

JOSEPHINE - IOKEPINE

JOSETTE - IOKEKE

JOSIAH - IOKIAHA

JOSIE - IOKIE

JOSH - IOKU

JOSHALYN - IOKALINE

JOSHMYR - IOKUMILE

JOSH'SHEA - IOKU'UKUHEA

JOSHUA - IOKUA

JOSHUWA - IOKUWA

JOSIAH - IOKIAHA

JOSKO - IOKUKO

JOSLYN - IOKULINE

JOSTAN - IOKANA

JOSUÉ - IOKUÉO

JOTHAM - IOKAMA

JOTHAN - IOKANA

JETHERENE - IEKELENE

JOTHI - IOKI

JOTINA - IOKINA

JOTTI - IOKI

JOURNAE - IOULONAE

JOURAN - IOULANA

JOURNEE - IOULONE

JOURNEY - IOULONEI

JOVANI - IOWANI

JOVANIQUE - IOWANIKE

JOVANA - IOWANA

JOVETTA - IOWEKA

JOVI - IOWI

JOVIT -IOWIKE

JOVITA - IOWIKA

JOVON - IOWONU

JOWANNA - IOWANA

JOY - IOI

JOYANNE - IOIANE

JOYCE - IOKE

JOYCELYN - IOIKELINE

JOYEL - IOIELI

JOYETTE - IOIEKE

JOYLYNN - IOILINE

JOYOUS - IOIOUKO

JOZAN - IOKANA

JOZEE - IOKE

JOZLYNN - IOKULINE

JOZSEF - IOKUKEPI

J'SON - I'EKONU

JUAL - IUALA

JUAN - KUANU

JUANA - IUANA

JUANALINE - IUANALINE

JUANALYN - IUANALINE

JUANCHO - IUANAKO

JUANDERA - IUANAKELA

JUANELLA - IUANELA

JUANETTA - IUANEKA

JUANITA - WANIKA

JUBIEL - IUPIELI

JUCA - IUKA

JUD - IUKO

JUDAH - IUKAHA

JUDD - IUKO

JUDE - IUKE

JUDEE - IUKE

JUDENE - IUKENE

JUDGE - IUKOKE

JUDI - IUKI

JUDIE - IUKIE

JUDINE - IUKINE

JUDITH - IUKIKA

JUDSON - IUKOKONU

JUDY - IUKI

JUEL - IUELI

JUENE - IUENE

JUERGEN - IUEKENI

JUHEE - IUHE

JUILI - IUILI

JUJUN - IUIUNO

JULANE - IULANE

JULENE - IULENE

JULES - KIULE

JULI - IULI

JULIA - IULIA

JULIAN - KULIANO

JULIANA - IULIANA

JULIANNA - IULIANA

JULIANNE - IULIANE

JULIE - KULI

JULIELLE -IULIELE

JULIEN - IULIENI

JULIENNE - IULIENE

JULIET - IULIEKI

JULIETA - IULIEKA

JULIETTE – KULIANA

JULINA - IULINA

JULIO - IULIO

JULION - IULIONU

JULIS - IULIKE

JULISSA - IULIKA

JULITA - IULIKA

JULIUS - IULIO

JULLIAN - IULIANA

JULY - IULI

JULYN - IULINE

JULYNE - IULINE

JUMAH - IUMAHA

JUMAINE - IUMAINE

JUN - IUNO

JUNAID - IUNAIKE

JUNAIDAH - IUNAIKAHA

JUNE - IUNE

JUNED - IUNEKI

JUNG - IUNO

JUNIE - IUNIE

JUNILHO - IUNILEHO

JUNILITA - IUNILIKA

JUNIOR - IUNIOLU

JUNIUS - IUNIUKO

JUNG-AH - IUNO- AHA

JUNKO - IUNOKO

JUNNEIL - IUNEILE

JUNO - IUNO

JUNON - IUNONU

JUNYWATI - IUNIWAKI

JUOZAS - IUOKAKA

JUPITER - IUPIKELI

JURAL - IULALA

JURATE - IULAKE

JURNEE - IULONE

JURONE - IULONE

JUSTEEN - IUKENI

JUSTICE - IUKIKE

JUSTIN - IUKEKINI

JUSTINA - IUKINA

JUSTINE - IUKINE

JUSTINIANO - IUKINIANO

JUSTIS - IUKIKI

JUSTISE - IUKIKE

JUSTON - IUKONU

JUSTYNA - IUKINA

JUTHIKA - IUKIKA

JUTTA - IUKA

JUVENAL - IUWENALA

JUVIEL - IUWIELI

JUWAN - IUWANA

JYOT - IIOKU

JYOTHI - IIOKI

JYOTHIPRIYA - IIOKIPELIIA

JY'QUAE - II'EKAE

JYTTE - IIKE

K

FIRST NAMES

KAA - KA

KAANA - KANA

KAARI - KALI

KABRINA - KAPALINA

KACEY - KAKEI

KACHING - KAKINE

KACI - KAKI

KACIA - KAKIA

KACIE - KAKIE

KACPER - KAKAPELI

KACTUS - KAKUKO

KADAN - KAKANI

KADE - KAKE

KADEEM - KAKEMI

KADELYNN - KAKELINE

KADEN - KAKENI

KADENCE - KAKENIKE

KADESHA - KAKEKA

KADI - KAKI

KADIN - KAKINE

KADIR - KAKILE

KADISH - KAKIKE

KADY - KAKI

KAE - KAE

KAEGAN - KAWKANA

KAELA - KAELA

KAELEE - KAELE

KAELEIGH - KAELEIKEHE

KAELENE - KAELENE

KAELER - KAELELI

KAELIN - KAELINE

KAELINE - KAELINE

KAELYNNE - KAELINE

KAFY - KAPI

KAHLIA - KAHALIA

KAHLIL - KAHALILE

KAHLUN - KAHALUNO

KAHO - KAHO

KAI- KAI

KAIA - KAIA

KAIDANCE - KAIKANAKE

KAIHIOLA - KAIHIOLA

KAIHOU - KAIHOU

KAILA - KAILA

KAILAH - KAILAHA

KAILANI - KAILANI

KAILE - KAILE

KAILEE - KAILE

KAILEEN - KAILENI

KAILEIGH - KAILEIKEHE

KAILEY - KAILEI

KAILI - KAILI

KAILY - KAILI

KAILYN - KAILINE

KAINA - KAINA

KAINALU - KAINALU

KAIONDRAIRE - KAIONUKULAILE

KAIPO - KAIPO

KAIRA - KAILA

KAISA - KAIKA

KAISEE - KAIKE
KAISHA - KAIKA
KAISON - KAIKONU
KAITLAND - KAIKELANAKA
KAITLIN - KAIKELINE
KAITLYN - KAIKELINE
KAITO - KAIKO
KAITY - KAIKI
KAIYA - KAIIA
KAIZAN - KAIKANA
KAIZER - KAIKELI
KAJ - KAI
KALA - KALA
KALAH - KALAHA
KALAHAN - KALAHANA
KALAI - KALAI
KALAISHA - KALIAIKA
KALAN - KALANA
KALDEN - KALENI
KALE - KALE
KALEB - KALEPI
KALEE - KALE
KALEENA - KALENA
KALEIGH - KALEIKEHE
KALELA - KALELA
KALEN - KALENI
KALENA - KALENA
KALENE - KALENE
KALEO - KALEO
KALERA - KALELA

KALEY - KALEI
KALFRED - KALAPALEKI
KALI - KALI
KALIA - KALIA
KALIANNA - KALIANA
KALIE - KALIE
KALIEGH - KALIEKIHI
KALIMAH - KALIMAHA
KA YING - KA IINE
KALLE - KALE
KALLEE - KALE
KALLEM - KALEMI
KALLEN - KALENI
KALLIE - KALIE
KALLIOPI - KALIOPI
KALLISTER - KALIKELI
KALMAN - KALAMANA
KALON - KALONU
KALUMBRIA - KALUMOPOLIA
KALVERT - KALAWEKI
KALYANN - KALIANA
KALYB - KALIPE
KALYN - KALINE
KALYSSA - KALIKA
KAM - KAMA
KAMAILE - KAMAILE
KAMAKSHYA - KAMAKAKIA
KAMALEN - KAMALENI
KAMALU - KAMALU
KAMANI - KAMANI

KAMARIA - KAMALIA

KAMAS - KAMAKA

KAMBER - KAMAPELI

KAMBERLYN - KAMAPELINE

KAMBRIA - KAMAPALIA

KAMBRY - KAMAPALI

KAMDYN - KAMAKINE

KAMEKO - KAMEKO

KAMELA - KAMELA

KAMELISH - KAMELIKE

KAMEN - KAMENI

KAMERAN - KAMELANA

KAMERON - KAMELONU

KAMETRA - KAMELA

KAMI - KAMI

KAMIKA - KAMIKA

KAMIL - KAMILE

KAMILA - KAMILA

KAMILAH - KAMILAHA

KAMILLA - KAMILA

KAMIYAH - KAMIIAHA

KAMLIN - KAMALINE

KAMREEH - KAMALEHI

KAMREN - KAMALENI

KAMRIE - KAMALIE

KAMRON - KAMALONU

KAMRY - KAMALI

KAMRYN - KAMALINE

KANANI - KANANI

KANCHANA - KANAKANA

KANDA - KANAKA

KANDACE - KANAKAKE

KANDES - KANAKEKI

KANDI - KANAKI

KANDICE - KANAKIKE

KANDIS - KANAKIKE

KANDRA - KANAKALA

KANE - KANE

KANEESHIA - KANEKIA

KANEYA - KANEIA

KANISA - KANIKA

KANIYAH - KANIIAHA

KANNA - KANA

KANTIN - KANAKINE

KANTRELL - KANALELI

KANYO - KANIO

KAOHINANI - KAOHINANI

KAOMON - KAOMONU

KAOMOO - KAOMO

KAOMUDI - KAOMUKI

KAORI - KAOLI

KAOS - KAOKU

KAPIL - KAPILE

KAPLAN - KAPALANA

KAPREECE - KAPALEKE

KAPSUN - KAPAKUNO

KAPUSTA - KAPUKA

KARA - KALA

KARAH - KALAHA

KARALINE - KALALINE

KARAMI - KALAMI

KARL - KALE

KAREE' - KALE'I

KARLA - KALALA

KAREL - KALELI

KARLENE - KALENE

KAREM, KAREEM - KALEMI

KARL-HEINZ - KALA-AHEINEKE

KAREN - KALENA

KARLEE - KALE

KARENNA - KALENA

KARLEIGH - KALEIKEHE

KARESS - KALEKI

KARLI - KALI

KARESSA - KALEKA

KARLIE - KALIE

KAREWI - KALEWI

KARLING - KALINE

KARI - KALI

KARLITA - KALIKA

KARIANN - KALIANA

KARLTON - KAKONU

KARIANNA - KALIANA

KARLY - KALI

KARIE - KALIE

KARLYN - KALINE

KARILAYNE - KALILAINE

KARMA - KALAMA

KARILEE - KALILE

KARMEN - KALAMELA

KARIMA - KALIMA

KARMINA - KALAMINA

KARIME - KALIME

KARN - KALANA

KARIN - KALINA

KARNA - KALANA

KARINA - KALINA

KARO - KALO

KARINE - KALINE

KARODY - KALOKI

KARINI - KALINI

KAROL - KALOLU

KARININA - KALININA

KAROLEE - KALOLE

KARIS - KALIKE

KAROLEEN - KALOLENI

KARISHMA - KALIKEMA

KAROLINE - KALOLINE

KARISMA - KALIKEMA

KAROLYN - KALOLINE

KARISSA - KALIKA

KARON - KALONU

KARISTA - KALIKA

KARONJA - KALONIA

KARIYAH - KALIIAHA

KARRA - KALA

KARIZMA - KALIKEMA

KARRABI - KALAPI

KARJA - KALIA

KARRIE - KALIE

KARRIEANN - KALIEANA

KARRINGTON - KALINEKONU

KARRIS - KALIKE

KARRYNE - KALINE

KARSEN - KALAKENI

KARSTEN - KALAKENI

KARSTON - KALAKONU

KARSYN - KALAKINE

KARTARA - KAKALA

KARTHIK - KAKIKE

KARTHIKEYA - KAKIKEIA

KARYL - KALILE

KARYN - KALINE

KAS - KAKA

KASANDRA - KAKANAKALA

KASAUNDRA - KAKAUNOKOLA

KASEY - KAKEI

KASHA - KAKA

KASHAN - KAKANA

KASHELLE - KAKELE

KASHIF - KAKIPE

KASHIRA - KAKILA

KASI - KAKI

KASIA - KAKIA

KASIANI - KAKIANI

KASIE - KAKIE

KASIMIR - KAKIMILE

KASON - KAKONU

KASONDRA - KAKONUKULA

KASS - KAKA

KASSANDRA - KAKANAKALA

KASSI - KAKI

KASSIDY - KAKIKI

KASSIE - KAKIE

KASSITY - KAKIKI

KASSY - KAKI

KAT - KEKA

KATALINA - KAKALINA

KATANA - KAKANA

KATANYA - KAKANIA

KATARINA - KAKALINA

KATARINE - KAKALINE

KATARZYNA - KAKALAKINA

KATASHIA - KAKAKIA

KATAYAH - KAKAIAHA

KATE, KATIE - KEKE

KATEISHA - KAKEIKA

KATELIN - KAKELINE

KATELYN - KAKELINE

KATERI - KAKELI

KATERINA - KAKELINA

KATERRA - KAKELA

KATEY - KAKEI

KATHA - KAKA

KATHARINE - KAKALINE

KATHEE - KAKE

KATHERINE - KAKALINA

KATHERN - KAKELINI

KATHERYN - KAKELINE

KATHERYNE - KAKELINE

KATHI - KAKI

KATHIE - KAKIE

KATHLEEN - KAKALINA

KATHLYN - KAKALINE

KATHRINE - KAKALINA

KATHRYN - KALINE

KATHYRINA - KAKILINA

KATHY - KAKI

KATHYA - KAKIA

KATI - KAKI

KATIA - KAKIA

KATIANA - KAKIANA

KATIE - KEKE

KATIE-JO - KAKIE-IO

KATINA - KAKINA

KATJIA - KAKIIA

KATLIN - KAKALINE

KATLYN - KAKALINE

KATO - KAKO

KATRICE - KALIKE

KATRINA - KALINA

KATRYN - KALINE

KATURAH - KAKULAHA

KATY - KAKI

KATYA - KAKIA

KAUJJA - KAUIA

KAUNTEYA - KAUNOKEIA

KAUR - KAULO

KAUSHIK - KAUKIKE

KAVI - KAWI

KAVOCEYA - KAWOKEIA

KAVON - KAWONU

KAWAN - KAWANA

KAWINA - KAWINA

KAY - KEI

KAYA - KAIA

KAYANN - KAIANA

KAYCE - KAIKE

KAYCEE - KAIKE

KAYCIE - KAIKIE

KAYDAWN - KAIKAWANA

KAYDEE - KAIKE

KAYDEN - KAIKENI

KAYDENCE - KAIKENIKE

KAYDRIE - KAIKELIE

KAYDYNNE - KAIKINE

KAYE - KAIE

KYRIE - KILIE

KYRON - KILONU

KYRSTEN - KILEKENI

KYRSTI - KILEKI

KAYE-ANN - KAIE-ANA

KAYENATH - KAIENAKA

KAYHAN - KAIHANA

KAYLA - KAILA

KAYLAN - KAILANA

KAYLANA - KAILANA

KAYLANI - KAILANI

KAYLEE- KAILE

KAYLEEN - KAILENI

KAYLEENA - KAILENA	KEALY - KEALI
KAYLEIGH - KAILEIKEHE	KEAN - KEANA
KAYLEN - KAILENI	KEANA - KEANA
KAYLENE - KAILENE	KEANDRA - KEANAKALA
KAYLEY - KAILEI	KEANE - KEANE
KAYLI - KAILI	KEANU - KEANU
KAYLIA - KAILIA	KEARA - KEALA
KAYLIE - KAILIE	KEARCY - KEALAKI
KAYLIN - KAILINE	KEARRA - KEALA
KAYLIPH - KAILIPE	KEARY - KEALI
KAYLON - KAILONU	KEARNEY - KEALANEI
KAYLYN - KAILINE	KEASHA - KEAKA
KAYLYNN - KAILINE	KEATON - KEAKONU
KAYNE - KAINE	KEATYN - KEAKINE
KAYRON - KAILONU	KEARTONYA - KEAKONIA
KAYSEE - KAIKE	KECK - KEKIKI
KAYSHA - KAIKA	KEDAR - KEKALA
KAYSIE - KAIKIE	KEDO - KEKO
KAYT - KAIKE	KEDRIA - KEKILIA
KAYTLYN - KAIKELINE	KEDZIE - KEKIKIE
KAYVIA - KAIWIA	KEE - KE
KAYVON - KAIWONU	KEEANA - KEANA
KAYWANDA - KAIWANAKA	KEEGAN - KEKANA
KAZDAN - KAKAKANA	KEELAN - KELANA
KAZUMI - KAKUMI	KEELEE - KELE
KAZZA - KAKA	KEELI - KELI
KE - KE	KEELIN - KELINE
KEACH - KEAKA	KEELY - KELI
KEAGAN - KEAKANA	KEEMIA - KEMIA
KEAIRA - KEAILA	KEENAN - KENANA

KEEVIS - KEWIKE
KEETA - KEKA
KEE TIONG - KE KIONU
KEGAN - KEKANA
KEHARI - KEHALI
KEHAU - KEHAU
KEHL - KEHILI
KEIANA - KEIANA
KEIDRA - KEIKELA
KEIDY - KEIKI
KEIGHT - KEIKEHEKE
KEIGHTLYNN - KEIKEHEKELINE
KEIGHVIN - KEIKEHEWINE
KEIGN - KEIKENE
KEIKO - KEIKO
KEILA - KEILA
KEILEIGH - KEILEIKEHE
KEILI - KEILI
KEILINN - KEILINE
KEILY - KEILI
KEIO - KEIO
KEION - KEIONU
KEIR - KEILE
KEIRA - KEILA
KEIRAN - KEILANA
KEIROL - KEILOLU
KEIRON - KEILONU
KEIRSTAN - KEILEKANA
KEIRSTY - KEILEKI
KEISHA - KEIKA

KEISHANNA - KEIKANA
KEISHLA - KEIKELA
KEISTEN - KEIKENI
KEISTER - KEIKELI
KEISUKE - KEIKUKE
KEITA - KEIKA
KEITH - KIKA
KEITHA - KEIKA
KEITOUNDA - KEIKONUOKA
KEIYON - KEIIONU
KEJIH- KEIIHE
KEJUAN - KEIUANA
KELAN - KELANA
KELBY - KELIPI
KELCEE - KELIKE
KELCEY - KELIKEI
KELCI - KELIKI
KELCIE - KELIKIE
KELD - KELI
KELDA - KELA
KELDON - KELONU
KELE - KELE
KELECHI - KELEKI
KELI - KELI
KELIA - KELIA
KELINA - KELINA
KELL - KELI
KELLA - KELA
KELLAN - KELANA
KELLARI - KELALI

KELLEE - KELE
KELLEN - KELENI
KELLENE - KELENE
KELLER - KELELI
KELLEY - KELI
KELLI - KELI
KELLIANNE - KELIANE
KELLIE - KELIE
KELLINA - KELINA
KELLON - KELONU
KELLY - KELI
KELMETRIUS - KELIMELIUKO
KELSEA - KELIKEA
KELSEY - KELIKEI
KELSHA - KELIKA
KELSI - KELIKI
KELSIE - KELIKIE
KELSO - KELIKO
KELSON - KELIKONU
KELSY - KELIKEI
|KELTI - KELIKI
KELTON - KELIKONU
KELTRICE - KELILIKE
KELVIN - KELEWINA
KELYNN - KELINE
KEMA - KEMA
KEMARIA - KEMALIA
KEMBERLE - KEMIPELE
KEMBOLYN - KEMIPOLINE
KEMI - KEMI

KEMO - KEMO
KEMPER - KEMIPELI
KEN – KENI
KENADEE - KENAKE
KENAN - KENANA
KENANDRA - KENANAKALA
KENAZ - KENAKA
KENDA - KENIKA
KENDAL - KENIKALA
KENDALL - KENIKALA
KENDALLYN - KENIKALINE
KENDEL - KENIKELI
KENDELIA- KENIKELIA
KENDON - KENIKONU
KENDRA - KENIKILA
KENDREANNA - KENIKILEANA
KENDRICK - KENEKIKI
KENDRON - KENIKILONU
KENDYE - KENIKIE
KENESAW - KENEKAWA
KENESHA - KENEKA
KENETHA - KENEKA
KENICE - KENIKE
KENIS - KENIKE
KENISON - KENIKONU
KENJI - KENII
KENLEE - KENILE
KENLEY - KENILEI
KENNA - KENA
KENNARD - KENALAKA

KENNDA - KENIKA

KENNEDI - KENEKI

KENNEDY - KENEKI

KENNETH - KENEKE

KENNI - KENI

KENNITH - KENIKE

KENNTRY - KENILI

KENNY- KENI

KENOLY - KENOLI

KENSEY - KENIKEI

KENSINGTON - KENIKINEKONU

KENSLEY - KENIKILEI

KENSON - KENIKONU

KENT - KENEKA

KENTA - KENIKA

KENTON - KENIKONU

KENYA - KENIA

KENYAINA - KENIAINA

KENYAN - KENIANA

KENYATTA - KENIAKA

KENYETTA - KENIEKA

KENYON - KENIONU

KENZIE - KENIKIE

KEO - KEO

KEOKAH - KEOKAHA

KEOMI - KEOMI

KERA - KELA

KEREM - KELEMI

KEREN - KELENI

KERENSA - KELENIKA

KERI - KELI

KERIAN - KELIANA

KERILYN - KELILINE

KERMINE - KELIMINE

KERMIT - KELIMIKE

KERN - KELINI

KERNST - KELINIKI

KERRI - KELI

KERRICK - KELIKEKE

KERRIE - KELIE

KERRIGAN - KELIKANA

KERRIN - KELINE

KERRY - KELI

KERSEY - KELIKEI

KERSTEIN - KELIKEINE

KERSTI - KELIKI

KERSTIN - KELIKINE

KERWIN - KELIWINE

KERYES - KELIEKI

KERYNNE - KELINE

KESA - KEKA

KESARA - KEKALA

KESCHMIRA - KEKIKIMILA

KESHA - KEKA

KESHANA - KEKANA

KESHAWN - KEKAWANA

KESHLA - KEKILA

KESHRIE - KEKILIE

KESIA - KEKIA

KESLEY - KEKILEI

KESSLA - KEKILA

KESTER - KEKELI

KESTUTIS - KEKUKIKE

KETA - KEKA

KETAN - KEKANA

KETCHEM - KEKIKEMI

KETHMANY - KEKIMANI

KETI - KEKI

KETRA - KELA

KETURAH - KEKULAHA

KETYN - KEKINE

KEVAL - KEWALA

KEVAN - KEWANA

KEVIN - KEWINA

KEVINA - KEWINA

KEVLYNN - KEWILINE

KEVYN - KEWINE

KEWANNA - KEWANA

KE XIN - KE KINE

KEYA - KEIA

KEYANTE - KEIANAKE

KEYARA - KEIALA

KEYDRA - KEIKELA

KEYGEN - KEIKENI

KEYIA - KEIIA

KEYIRA - KEIILA

KEYLEEN - KEILENI

KEYLLE - KEILE

KEYNA - KEINA

KEYNI - KEINI

KEYONA - KEIONA

KEYONNA - KEIONA

KEYOSHA - KEIOKA

KEYSHA - KEIKA

KEYSHAUN - KEIKAUNO

KEYSHAWN - KEIKAWANA

KEYTON - KEIKONU

KEZIA - KEKIA

KEZIN - KEKINE

KHADEEJA - KAHAKEIA

KHADIJA - KAHAKIIA

KHADYA - KAHAKIA

KHAI - KHAI

KHAIA - KAHAIA

KHALED - KAHALEKI

KHALEN - KAHALENI

KHALID - KAHALIKE

KHALIECE - KAHALIEKE

KHALIF - KAHALIPE

KHALIL - KAHALILE

KHALILA - KAHALILA

KHAMARI - KAHAMALI

KHAMFONG - KAHAMAPONU

KHAMVAY - KAHAMAWAI

KHANH - KAHANAHA

KHANIM - KAHANIME

KHAREEM - KAHALEMI

KHARIS - KAHALIKE

KHAYMAN - KAHAIMANA

KHEPERA - KAHEPELA

KHIELA - KAHIELA

KHIEM - KAHIEMI

KHIRY - KAHILI

KHOA - KAHOA

KHOI - KAHOI

KHOLE - KAHOLE

KHOU - KAHOU

KHRISLYN - KAHALIKELINE

KHRYSTALIAH - KAHALIKALIAHA

KHUSHI - KAHUKI

KHWAGA - KAHAWAKA

KHYLA - KAHILA

KHYLEE - KAHILE

KIAH - KIAHA

KIAHINI - KIAHINI

KIAHNI - KIAHANI

KIAJUANA - KIAIUANA

KIAM - KIAMA

KIAMESHA - KIAMEKA

KIANA - KIANA

KIANDRA - KIANAKALA

KIANI - KIANI

KIANNA - KIANA

KIANTE - KIANAKE

KIARA - KIALA

KIARIA - KIALIA

KIA WEE - KIA WE

KIAYA - KIAIA

KIBBIE - KIPIE

KICK - KIKEKE

KIDD - KIKE

KIDRON - KIKELONU

KIEFER - KIEPELI

KIEL - KIELI

KIELY - KIELI

KIEMERA - KIEMELA

KIEONNA - KIEONA

KIER - KIELI

KIERA - KIELA

KIERAN - KIELANA

KIERRA - KIELA

KIERSTEN - KIELIKENI

KIERSTIE - KIELIKIE

KIERSTON - KIELIKONI

KIERSTYN - KIELIKINE

KIETH - KIEKI

KIEUYANA - KIEUIANA

KIHOMI - KIHOMI

KIIYANNI - KIIANI

KIKI - KIKI

KIKO - KIKO

KILANY - KILANI

KILEEN - KILENI

KILEY - KILEI

KILLIAN - KILIANA

KILYN - KILINE

KIM – KIMO, KIMI

KIMA - KIMA

KIMALISA - KIMALIKA

KIMANI - KIMANI

KIMARIE - KIMALIE

KIMBALL - KIMEPALA

KIMBER - KIMEPELI

KIMBERLEE - KIMEPELE

KIMBERLEY - KIMEPELEI

KIMBERLIE - KIMEPELIE

KIMBERLIN - KIMEPELINE

KIMBERLY - KIMIPELE

KIMBERLYNE - KIMEPELINE

KIMBLE - KIMEPELE

KIMBRA - KIMEPELA

KIMBRIANE - KIMEPELIANE

KIMELA - KIMELA

KIMERY - KIMELI

KIMETRA - KIMELA

KIM HOCK - KIMO HOKUKU

KIMIKO - KIMIKO

KIMMER - KIMELI

KIMMERS - KIMELIKE

KIMMY - KIMI

KIMNING - KIMENINE

KIMORA - KIMOLA

KIMSAY - KIMEKAI

KIMYATTA - KIMIAKA

KINA - KINA

KINCAID - KINEKAIKE

KINDAL - KINEKALA

KINDEL - KINEKELI

KINDLE - KINEKELE

KINDRA - KINEKELA

KINDREA - KINEKELEA

KINDREY - KINEKELEI

KING - KINE

KINGSLEY - KINEKELEI

KINGSTON - KINEKONU

KINLEA - KINELEA

KINLEY - KINELEI

KINNEY - KINEI

KINSEY - KINEKEI

KINSLEY - KINEKELEI

KINSON - KINEKONU

KINTAN - KINEKANA

KINUYO - KINUIO

KINWA - KINEWA

KINZY - KINEKI

KIO - KIO

KIOJA - KIOIA

KIOWA - KIOWA

KIP - KIPE

KIPLEE - KIPELE

KIPRA - KIPELA

KIPRAS - KIPELAKA

KIRA - KILA

KIRAN - KILANA

KIRANDEEP - KILANAKEPI

KIRANJIT - KILANIIKE

KIRANJOT - KILANIOKU

KIRANPREET - KILANAPALEKI

KIRBY - KILEPE

KIRCHELLE - KILEKELE

KIRILEE - KILILE

KIRIN - KILINE

KIRK - KELEKA

KIRPAL - KILEPALA

KIRSTEN - KILEKENI

KIRSTI - KILEKI

KIRSTIE - KILEKIE

KIRSTIN - KILEKINE

KIRSTY - KILEKI

KIRSTYN - KILEKINE

KIRT - KIKE

KIRTINA - KIKINA

KIRUTHIGA -KILUKIKA

KISHA - KIKA

KISHIN - KIKINE

KISHORI - KIKOLI

KISHOTE - KIKOKE

KISNE - KIKENE

KISO - KIKO

KISTY - KIKI

KIT - KIKE

KITA - KIKA

KITSON - KIKONU

KITTY - KIKI

KIVELA - KIWELA

KIWANNDA - KIWANAKA

KIYANA - KIIANA

KIYATTA - KIIAKA

KIYOKO - KIIOKO

KIZZY - KIKI

KJOL - KJOL

KLARA - KALALA

KLARISSA - KALALIKA

KLAUDIA - KALAUKIA

KLAUS - KALAUKO

KLEBBER - KALEPELI

KLEBER - KALEPELI

KLEMENTYNA- KALEMENIKINA

KLINT - KALINEKE

KLOE - KALOE

KLOE' - KALOE'I

KNOLYN - KANOLINE

KNUT - KANUKO

KOA - KOA

KOAH - KOAHA

KOALY - KOALI

KOBE - KOPE

KOBUS - KOPUKO

KOBY - KOPI

KODEE - KOKE

KODIAK - KOKIAKA

KODIE - KOKIE

KODY - KOKI

KOETA - KOEKA

KOHEN - KOHENI

KOHL - KOHULU

KOHSHEEN - KOHUKENI

KOI - KOI

KOKLEY - KOKULEI

KOLAWOLE - KOLAWOLE

KOLBY - KOLUPI

KOLDEN - KOLENI

KOLE - KOLE

KOLETON - KOLEKONU

KOLIN - KOLINE

KOLLIN - KOLINE

KOLT - KOLUKU

KOLTON - KOLUKONU

KOMAL - KOMALA

KOMARII - KOMALI

KONA - KONA

KONDA - KONUKA

KONG - KONU

KONI - KONI

KONLAN - KONULANA

KONNER - KONELI

KONOU - KONOU

KONRAD - KONULAKA

KONSTANTINE - KONUKANAKINE

KONTRIVA - KONULIWA

KOOBAN - KOPANA

KOPEN - KOPENI

KORAKOT - KOLAKOKU

KORALEE - KOLALE

KORANA - KOLANA

KORBIN - KOLUPINE

KORBY - KOLUPI

KORDELL - KOLUKELI

KOREEN - KOLENI

KOREENA - KOLENA

KOREN - KOLENI

KORENE - KOLENE

KOREY - KOLEI

KOREYAH - KOLEIAHA

KORI - KOLI

KORIN - KOLINE

KORISSA - KOLIKA

KORLEE - KOLE

KORMASA - KOLUMAKA

KORRIE - KOLIE

KORRINE - KOLINE

KORTEZ - KOKEKI

KORTNEE - KOKUNE

KORTNEY - KOKUNEI

KORTNIE - KOKUNIE

KORY - KOLI

KORYNN - KOLINE

KOSKE - KOKUKE

KOSSIVI - KOKIWI

KOSTA - KOKA

KOSTAS - KOKAKA

KOUEN - KOUENI

KOU-JUNG - KOU-IUNO

KOURTNEY - KOUKONEI

KOURTNI - KOUKONI

KOUSTUBH - KOUKUPOHO

KOVETTE - KOWEKE

KOY - KOI

KOYO - KOIO
KRAMER - KALAMELI
KREED - KALEKI
KREGAN - KALEKANA
KRENDLE - KALENIKILE
KRENESHIA - KALENEKIA
KRENSHAW - KALENIKAWA
KRESHAWNA - KALEKAWANA
KRICKET - KALIKEKEKI
KRINA - KALINA
KRIS - KALIKE
KRISANN - KALIKANA
KRISETTE - KALIKEKE
KRISH - KALIKE
KRISHA - KALIKA
KRISHANNA - KALIKANA
KRISHAUN - KALIKAUNO
KRISHMA - KALIKEMA
KRISHNA - KALIKENA
KRISHNAN - KALIKENANA
KRISLYN - KALIKELINE
KRISSEL - KALIKELI
KRISSINDA - KALIKINEKA
KRISS-KRINA - KALIKE-EKELINA
KRISSY - KALIKI
KRISTA - KILIKIKA
KRISTABEL - KALIKAPELI
KRISTAL - KALIKALA
KRISTANA - KALIKANA
KRISTEL - KALIKELI

KRISTELYS - KALIKELIKE
KRISTEN - KILIKINA
KRISTHEL - KALEKELI
KRISTI - KILIKI
KRISTIAN - KALIKIANA
KRISTIANA - KALIKIANA
KRISTANNE - KALIKANE
KRISTIE - KALIKIE
KRISTILYN - KALIKILINE
KRISTIN - KILIKINA
KRISTINA - KILIKINA
KRISTINE - KILIKINA
KRISTOFER - KALIKOPELI
KRISTOFFER - KALIKOPELI
KRISTOL - KALIKOLU
KRISTOPHER - KILIKOPELA
KRISTY - KILIKI
KRISTYN - KALIKINE
KRISTYNA - KALIKINA
KITABU - KIKAPU
KRITI - KALIKI
KRIZIA - KALIKIA
KRIZ-LYN - KALIKE-ELINE
KROY - KALOI
KRUM - KALUMO
KRUNALI - KALUNALI
KRUTHI - KALUKI
KRUZ - KALUKO
KRYN - KALINE
KRYSTA - KALIKA

KRYSTAFER - KALIKAPELI

KRYSTA - KALIKA

KRYSTAL - KALIKALA

KRYSTEE - KALIKE

KRYSTELLE - KALIKELE

KRYSTEN - KALIKENE

KRYSTIE - KALIKIE

KRYSTIN - KALIKINE

KRYSTLE - KALIKELE

KRZYSZTOF - KALAKIKEKEKOPU

KSENYA - KAKENIA

K'TREISHA - KA'ALEIKA

KUANG - KUANA

KUNDAVI - KUNOKAWI

KULANI - KULANI

KULDEEP - KULEPI

KULJEET - KULIEKI

KULVEER - KULOWELI

KUM -KUMO

KUMASI - KUMAKI

KUMIKO - KUMIKO

KUN - KUNO

KUNAL - KUNALA

KUNESHIA - KUNEKIA

KUNGA - KUNA

KUNTA - KUNOKA

KUNTHOS - KUNOKOKU

KUNWAR - KUNOWALA

KURIAN - KULIANA

KURSTY - KULOKI

KURSTYNE - KULOKINE

KURT - KELEKA

KURTIS - KUKIKE

KURTWOOD - KUKOWOKU

KUSUM - KUKUMO

KUUNG-WEI - KUNO-OWEI

KUV - KUWO

KWABENA - KAWAPENA

KWAI - KAWAI

KWAME - KAWAME

KWAN - KAWANA

KWEEHOWE - KAWEHOWE

KY -KI

KYA - KIA

KYAH - KIAHA

KYAN - KIANA

KYANNA - KIANA

KYARA - KIALA

KYARAH - KIALAHA

KYE - KIE

KYET - KIEKI

KYHAMALICH - KIHAMALIKE

KYI - KII

KYITA - KIIKA

KYLA - KILA

KYLAN - KILANA

KYLE - KAILA

KYLEE - KILE

KYLEEN - KILENI

KYLEIGH - KILEIKEHE

KYLEIGHT - KILEIKEHEKE
KYLEN - KILENI
KYLER - KILELI
KYLESHA - KILEKA
KYLEY - KILEI
KYLIA - KILIA
KYLIE - KILIE
KYLLIAN - KILIANA
KYLON - KILONU
KYLONNA - KILONA
KYLYNN - KILINE
KYM – KIME
KYMBERLY - KIMEPELI
KYMESHIA - KIMEKIA
KYMONIE - KIMONIE
KYNAN - KINANA
KYNDALL - KINEKALA
KYNDALLYN - KINEKALINE
KYNDRA - KINEKELA
KYNSLIE - KINEKELIE
KYON - KIONU
KYONEE - KIONE
KYRA - KILA
KYRAN - KILANA
KYREN - KILENI
KYRENE - KILENE
KYRIAN - KILIANA

L

FIRST NAMES

LA'A - LA'A

LAARNI - LALANI

LABAN - LAPANA

LABARBARA - LAPALAPALA

LABDHI - LAPAKAHI

LABRAYA - LAPALAIA

LACALL - LAKALA

LACARA - LAKALA

LACE - LAKE

LACENA - LAKENA

LACEY - LAKEI

LACHANNA - LAKANA

LACHASA - LAKAKA

LACHELLE - LAKELE

LACHERYL - LAKELILE

LACHLAN - LAKALANA

LACHRISA - LAKALIKA

LACI - LAKI

LACIE - LAKIE

LACINDER - LAKINEKELI

LACINDRA - LAKINEKELA

LACOLLE - LAKOLE

LACOSTA - LAKOKA

LACOSTIA - LAKOKIA

LACOUNTISS - LAKOUNOKIKE

LACRETIA - LAKALEKIA

LACY - LAKI

LADAISHA - LAKAIKA

LADANIEL - LAKANIELI

LADARIUS - LAKALIUKO

LADAWN - LAKAWANA

LADAWNA - LAKAWANA

LADD - LAKA

LADDIE - LAKIE

LADELLE - LAKELE

LADENE - LAKENE

LADESSIA - LAKEKIA

LADETRA - LEKELA

LADETTE - LAKEKE

LADOICE - LAKOIKE

LADONNA - LAKONA

LADONYA - LAKONIA

LADORIS - LAKOLIKE

LADORPHEUS - LAKOLUPEUKO

LADRIAN - LAKALIANA

LAEL - LAELI

LAERCIO - LAELIKIO

LAETITIA - LAEKIKIA

LAFAYE - LAPAIE

LAFONZO - LAPONUKO

LAGIMAINA - LAKIMAINA

LAGRATTA - LAKALAKA

LAGRETTA - LAKALEKA

LAHOMA - LAHOMA

LAI - LAI

LAI'ANNA - LAI'ANA

LAIGEN - LAIKENI

LAIKYN - LAIKINE

LAILA- LAILA

LAILAN - LAILANA

LAIMA - LAIMA

LAINA - LAINA

LAINE - LAINE

LAINEY - LAINEI

LAINIE - LAINIE

LAION - LAIONU

LAIRD - LAILEKE

LAISA - LAIKA

LAISSEN -LAIKENI

LAITH - LAIKE

LAJHE - LAIHE

LAKARL - LAKALA

LAKE - LAKE

LAKEESHA - LAKEKA

LAKEETHIA - LAKEKIA

LAKEN - LAKENI

LAKENIA - LAKENIA

LAKESHA - LAKEKA

LAKETRA - LAKELA

LAKIAH - LAKIAHA

LAKINYA - LAKINIA

LAKISHA - LAKIKA

LAKITA - LAKIKA

LAKKYN - LAKINE

LAKOTA - LAKOKA

LAKRESHA - LEKALEKA

LAKSHMI - LAKAKAMI

LALAH - LALAHA

LALAINE - LALAINE

LALANYA - LALANIA

LALINDA - LALINEKA

LALING - LALINE

LALITHA - LALIKA

LALU - LALU

LALY - LALI

LAMAE - LAMAE

LAMAR - LAMALA

LAMBERT - LAMAPEKI

LAMBIE - LAMAPIE

LAMEEK - LAMEKI

LAMESHA - LAMEKA

LAMIAD - LAMIAKA

LAMIKA - LAMIKA

LAMINE - LAMINE

LAMOYNE - LAMOINE

LAMPUNG - LAMAPUNO

LAMONT - LAMONUKU

LAN - LANA

LANA - LANA

LANAE - LANAE

LANAIJA - LANAIIA

LANANCY - LANANAKI

LANARIA - LANALIA

LANAYE - LANAIE

LANAY'E - LANAI'E

LANAYIA - LANAIIA

LANAYTTE - LANAIKE

LANCE - LANAKE

LANCY - LANAKI

LAND - LANAKA

LANDEE - LANAKE

LANDEN - LANAKENI

LANDER - LANAKELI

LANDIS - LANAKIKE

LANDON - LANAKONU

LANDRY - LANAKALI

LANDYN - LANAKINE

LANE - LAINA

LANEAH - LANEAHA

LANEDRA - LANEKILA

LANEI - LANEI

LANELL - LANELI

LANESA - LANEKA

LANETTE - LANEKE

LANEY - LANEI

LANG - LANA

LANGSTON - LANAKONU

LANI - LANI

LANIAY - LANIAI

LANICE - LANIKE

LANIE - LANIE

LANIEY - LANIEI

LANIQUE - LANIKE

LANISE - LANIKE

LANISHA - LANIKA

LANISIA - LANIKIA

LANISSA - LANIKA

LANITA - LANIKA

LANNA - LANA

LANNESA - LANEKA

LANNEY - LANEI

LANYA - LANIA

LAOTI - LAOKI

LAPACEK - LAPAKEKI

LAPERRYREA - LAPELILEA

LAPRENZA - LAPALENIKA

LAPRIA - LAPALIA

LAQUAN - LAKANA

LAQUANA - LAKUKANA

LAQUANDA - LAKUKANAKA

LAQUANTA - LAKANAKA

LAQUENCIA - LAKENIKIA

LAQUENTIS - LAKENIKIKE

LAQUESHA - LAKEKA

LAQUETTA - LAKEKA

LAQUISHA - LAKIKA

LAQUITA - LAKIKA

LARA - LALA

LARAE - LALAE

LARAH - LALAHA

LARCHAE - LALAKAE

LARAINE - LALAINE

LARAMIE - LALAMIE

LARANDA - LALANAKA

LARAYNE - LALAINE

LAREEN - LALENI

LAREINA - LALEINA

LARENE - LALENE

LARESSA - LALEKA

LARETTA - LALEKA

LAREVA - LALEWA

LAREVIA - LALEWIA

LARHONDA - LALAHONUKA

LARIE - LALIE

LARIJO - LALIIO

LARINA - LALINA

LARINDA - LILINEKA

LARIONNE - LALIONE

LARISA - LALIKA

LARISSA - LALIKA

LARIZZA - LALIKA

LARK - LAKA

LARKIN - LAKINE

LARNELL - LALANELI

LARNESE - LALANEKE

LARNETTA - LALANEKA

LAROMAN - LALOMANA

LARONDA - LALONUKA

LAROSHA - LALOKA

LARRA - LALA

LARRELL - LALELI

LARRY - LALI

LARS - LALAKA

LARSEN - LALAKENI

LARUE - LALUE

LASAIAH - LAKAIAHA

LASAUNDRIA - LAKAUNOKOLIA

LASCELLES - LAKAKELEKI

LASHAAD - LAKAKA

LASHANDA - LAKANAKA

LASHAUN - LAKAUNO

LA SHAUNDRA - LA KAUNOKOLA

LASHAWN - LAKAWANA

LASHAWNDA - LAKAWANAKA

LASHAY - LAKAI

LASHAYA - LAKAIA

LASHE' - LAKE'I

LASHEA - LAKEA

LASHEILIA - LAKEILIA

LASHEKA - LAKEKA

LASHELL - LAKELI

LASHERRIE - LAKELIE

LASHI - LAKI

LASHIYAH - LAKIIAHA

LASHLEY - LAKALEI

LASHMY - LAKAMI

LASHON - LAKONU

LASHONDA - LOKONUKA

LASHUN - LUKUNO

LASONDRA - LAKONUKULA

LASSANA - LAKANA

LASSE - LAKE

LASSITY - LAKIKI

LASTLY - LAKALI

LASZLO - LAKAKALO

LATA - LAKA

LATABEN - LAKAPENI

LATAMBER - LAKAMAPELI

LATANYA - LAKANIA

LATASHA - LAKAKA

LATAVIA - LAKAWIA
LATAWNA - LAKAWANA
LATESHA - LAKEKA
LATHAN - LAKANA
LATHYN - LAKINE
LATI - LAKI
LATIFAH - LAKIPAHA
LATIMER - LAKIMELI
LATISHA - LAKIKA
LATONYA - LAKONIA
LATORIE - LAKOLIE
LATOSHA - LAKOKA
LATOYA - LAKOIA
LATOYIA - LAKOIIA
LATRAIL - LALAILE
LATRAYION - LALAI'IONU
LATREECIA - LALEKIA
LATRELLE - LALELE
LATRENA - LALENA
LATRENDA - LALENIKA
LATRESE - LALEKE
LATRESSA - LALEKA
LATRISHA - LALIKA
LAUDEN - LAUKENI
LAUDI - LAUKI
LAUGHREN - LAUKOHOLENI
LAUGHTON - LAUKOHOKONU
LAUNA - LAUNA
LAUNI - LAUNI
LAURA - LALA

LAURAINE - LAULAINE
LAURE - LAULE
LAUREAN - LAULEANA
LAUREANO - LAULEANO
LAUREN - LALENA
LAUREEN - LAULENA
LAURENNE - LAULENE
LAURETTA - LAULEKA
LAURETTE - LAULEKE
LAUREL - LALELA
LAURELL - LALELA
LAUREN - LAULENA
LAURENA - LAULENA
LAURENE - LAULENE
LAURENCE - LAULENIKE
LAUREN JO - LAULENI IO
LAURENT - LAULENIKI
LAURETA - LAULEKA
LAURIE - LALI
LAURIE-ANNE - LAULIE-ANE
LAURINDA - LAULINEKA
LAURISSA - LAULIKA
LAURITA - LAULIKA
LAURYN - LAULINE
LAUTICE - LAUKIKE
LAUVER - LAUWELI
LAVADA - LAWAKA
LAVAN - LAWANA
LAVANNA - LAWANA
LAVAR - LAWALA

LAVELLE - LAWELE

LAVENE - LAWENE

LAVENIA - LAWENIA

LAVERL - LAWELI

LAVERN - LAWELINI

LAVERNA - LAWELINA

LAVERNE - LAWELINE

LAVETTA -LAWEKA

LAVID - LAWIKE

LAVINA -LAWINA

LAVON - LAWONU

LAVONA - LAWONA

LAVONDA - LAWONUKA

LA'VONDAY - LA'AWONUKAI

LAVONNE - LAWONE

LAVORIS - LAWOLIKE

LAWANA - LAWANA

LAWANDA - LAWANAKA

LAWANNI - LAWANI

LAWNY - LAWANI

LAWREN - LAWALENI

LAWRENCE – LAULENEKE

LAWRIN - LAWALINE

LAWSON - LAWAKONU

LAWTON - LAWAKONU

LAYCEE - LAIKE

LAYLA - LAILA

LAYNE – LAINA

LAYNETTE - LAINEKE

LAYTAN - LAIKANA

LAYTON - LAIKONU

LAYONIE - LAIONIE

LAZARO -LAKALO

LAZARUS - LAKALUKO

L'DORESSA - LA'AKOLEKA

LEA - LEA

LEAH – LEA

LEAHANN - LEAHANA

LEALA – LEALA

LEAMON - LEAMONU

LEANA - LEANA

LEANDA - LEANAKA

LEANDER - LEANAKELI

LEANDRA - LEANAKALA

LEANDRO - LEANAKALO

LEANESS - LEANEKI

LEANIAH - LEANIAHA

LEANN - LEANA

LEANNA - LEANA

LEANNE - LEANE

LEANOR - LEANOLU

LEAR - LEALA

LEASHAY - LEAKAI

LEASETT - LEAKEKI

LEATRICE - LIAKIKI

LECILIN - LEKILINE

LECLAIR - LEKILAILE

LEDA - LEKA

LEDESMA - LEKEKIMA

LEDINE - LEKINE

LEDOR - LEKOLU
LEE - LI
LEEANE - LEANE
LEE-ANN - LE-ANA
LEEANN - LIANA
LEEDA - LEKA
LEE ENG - LI ENI
LEEISA - LEIKA
LEELA - LELA
LEENA - LENA
LEEOR - LEOLU
LEERANEZ - LELANEKI
LEESA - LEKA
LEESHA - LEKA
LEETIE - LEKIE
LEFTY - LEPIKI
LEGACY - LEKAKI
LEGARE - LEKALE
LEHA - LEHA
LEHIGH - LEHIKEHE
LEI - LEI
LEIA - LEIA
LEIANN - LEIANA
LEIDY - LEIKI
LEIF - LEIPE
LEIFJE - LEIPIE
LEIGH - LEI
LEIGHA - LEIKEHA
LEIGHANN - LEIKEHANA
LEIGHERA - LEIKEHELA

LEIGHTON - LEIKEHEKONU
LEIKI - LEIKI
LEILA - LEILA
LEILANI - LEILANI
LEILIA - LEILIA
LEILINA - LEILINA
LEIR - LEILE
LEISA - LEIKA
LEISHA - LEIKA
LEISHAWN - LEIKAWANA
LEITH - LEIKE
LEITICIA - LEKIKIA
LEIZA - LEIKA
LEIZELL - LEIKELI
LEKESHIA - LEKEKIA
LEKEYA - LEKEIA
LEKITA - LEKIKA
LELA - LELA
LELAND - LELANA
LELET - LELEKI
LELIA - LELIA
LELLA - LELA
LELLIE - LELIE
LEMERLE - LEMELE
LEMMEL - LEMELI
LEMON - LEMONU
LE'MON - LE'IMONU
LEMUEL - LEMUELI
LEN - LENA
LENA - LINA

LENAY - LENAI
LENDORA - LENIKOLA
LENE - LENE
LENESSA - LENEKA
LENG CHOO - LENI KO
LENISE - LENIKE
LENKA - LENIKA
LENN - LENI
LENNIE - LENIE
LENNON - LENONU
LENNY - LENI
LENORA - LENOLA
LENORE - LENOLE
LENOXX - LENOKU
LENSON - LENIKONU
LENYELLE - LENIELE
LENYSSE - LENIKE
LEO - LIO
LEOBARDO - LEOPALAKO
LEOLA - LEOLA
LEOMAR - LEOMALA
LEON - LEONA
LEONA - LEONA
LEONARD – LEONAKA
LEONARDO - LEONALAKO
LEONE - LEONE
LEONETTE - LEONEKE
LEONID - LEONIKE
LEONIDA - LEONIKA
LEONIDES - LEONIKEKI

LEONIE - LEONIE
LEONILA - LEONILA
LEONOR - LEONOLU
LEONORA - LEONOLA
LEONTYNE - LEONUKINE
LEOPARD - LEOPALAKA
LEORA - LENOLA
LEOSANTI - LEOKANAKI
LEOTA - LEOKA
LEOTIST - LEOKIKE
LEOVINO - LEOWINO
LEQUETTA - LEKEKA
LEQUISHA - LEKEIKA
LEQUNE - LEKUNE
LERAH - LELAHA
LEREN - LELENI
LERENE - LELENE
LERMA - LELIMA
LERIN - LELINE
LERLINE - LELINE
LEROSS - LELOKU
LEROY - LELOI
LERTON - LEKONU
LERTRINA - LELINA
LES - LEKI
LESA - LEKA
LESHA - LEKA
LESHAUN - LEKAUNO
LESHELL - LEKELI
LESIA - LEKIA

LESIELI - LEKIELI

LESLEE - LEKILE

LESLEIGH - LEKILEIKEHE

LESLEY - LEKILEI

LESLEYANN - LEKILEIANA

LESLIE - LEKILI

LESSIE - LEKIE

LESTAT - LEKAKA

LESTER - LEKELA

LESTINA - LEKINA

LESTOLA - LEKOLA

LETA - LEKA

LETAH - LEKAHA

LELET - LELEKI

LETERRA - LEKELA

LETHA - LEKA

LETHU - LEKU

LETICIA - LEKIKIA

LETISHA - LEKIKA

LETITIA - LEKIKIA

LETRESA - LELEKA

LETTIE - LEKIE

LETTY - LEKI

LETYCIA - LEKIKIA

LEUM - LEUMO

LEURLINE - LEULINE

LEV - LEWI

LEVETTE - LEWEKE

LEVI - LIWAI

LEVINA - LEWINA

LEVISHA - LEWIKA

LEVITA - LEWIKA

LEVITICUS - LEWIKIKUKO

LEVON - LEWONU

LEWELLEN - LEWELENI

LEVIA - LEWIA

LEW - LEWI

LEWY - LEWI

LEWIS - LUI

LEX - LEKI

LEXA - LEKA

LEXANI - LEKANI

LEXI - LEKI

LEXIA - LEKIA

LEXIE - LEKIE

LEXINE - LEKINE

LEXIS - LEKIKE

LEXUS - LEKUKO

LEXXIE - LEKIE

LEXXUS - LEKUKO

LEXY - LEKI

LEYLA - LEILA

LEYTON - LEIKONU

LEZANDRA - LEKANAKALA

L'HOUCINE - LA'AHOUKINE

LIA - LIA

LIAM - LIAMA

LIAN - LIANA

LIANA - LIANA

LIANDREW - LIANAKALEWI

LIANE - LIANE
LIANI - LIANI
LIANN - LIANA
LIANNA - LIANA
LIB - LIPE
LIBAN - LIPANA
LIBBIE - LIPI
LIBBREY - LIPELEI
LIBBY - LIPI
LIBERTY - LIPEKI
LIBRA - LIPELA
LICHELLE - LIKELE
LIDA - LIKA
LIDDY - LIKI
LIDIA - LIKIA
LIEF - LIEPI
LIEKE - LIEKE
LIELEN - LIELENI
LIEONAL - LIEONALA
LIEPA - LIEPA
LIESJE - LIEKIE
LIESL - LIEKILI
LIETTE - LIEKE
LIFE - LIPE
LIFNA - LIPENA
LIGAYA - LIKAIA
LIGIA - LIKIA
LIHONG - LIHONU
LIINA - LINA
LIISA - LIKA

LIISI - LIKI
LILA - LILA
LILENE - LILENE
LILET - LILEKI
LILIA - LILIA
LILIANA - LILIANA
LILIANE - LILIANE
LILIBETH - LILIPEKI
LILITH - LILIKI
LILLA - LILA
LILLIA - LILIA
LILLIAM - LILIAMA
LILLIAN - LILIANA
LILLIE - LILIE
LILLY - LILIA
LILLYAN - LILIANA
LILLYANNE - LILIANE
LILO - LILO
LILY - LILIA
LILY-ROSE - LILI-ELOKE
LIM - LIME
LIMA - LIMA
LIMIAH - KUNUAGA
LIMOR - LIMOLU
LIN - LINE
LINA - LINA
LINCEY - LINEKEI
LINCHIE - LINEKIE
LINCOLN - LINEKOLUNU
LINDA - LINAKA

LINDE - LINEKE
LINDLEY - LINEKELEI
LINDSAY - LINAKE
LINDSEY - LINEKEKEI
LINDY - LINEKI
LINDYN - LINEKINE
LINET - LINEKI
LINETTE - LINEKE
LINH - LINEHE
LINK - LINEKE
LINKER - LINEKELI
LINLEY - LINELEI
LINNEA - LINEA
LINNEALL - LINEALA
LINNIE - LINIE
LINO - LINO
LINORA - LINOLA
LINSEY - LINEKEI
LINT - LINEKE
LINUS - LINO
LINWARD - LINEWALAKA
LINZIE - KINEKIE
LINZY - LINEKI
LIONEL - LAIONELA
LIONIRES - LIONILEKI
LIONITA - LIONIKA
LIPE - LIPE
LIS - LIKE
LISA - LIKA
LISABETH - LIKAPEKI

LISAGEAN - LIKAKEANA
LISANNE - LIKANE
LISE - LIKE
LISELLE - LIKELE
LISHA - LIKA
LISKA - LIKEKA
LISMORE - LIKEMOLE
LISSA - LIKA
LISSETTE - LIKEKE
LISSY - LIKI
LITA - LIKA
LITHA - LIKA
LITIA - LIKIA
LITITTIA - LIKIKIA
LITO - LIKO
LITSA - LIKA
LITTY - LIKI
LITZA - LIKEKA
LIV - LIWE
LIVANA - LIWANA
LIVIA - LIWIA
LIVIANNA - LIWIANA
LIYADSI - LIIAKAKI
LIYAH - LIIAHA
LIYANA - LIIANA
LIZ - LIKE
LIZA - LIKA
LIZANNE - LIKANE
LIZBETH - LIKEPEKI
LIZEL - LIKELI

LIZETTE - LIKEKE

LIZZIE - LIKIE

LIZZY - LIKI

LJEAN - LIEANA

LLEROME - LELOME

LLEWELLYNNE - LEWELINE

LLEWYN - LEWINE

LLIJ - LII

LLISA - LIKA

LLOYD - LOEKA

LLWELLYN - LAWELINE

LOANE - LOANE

LOANN - LOANA

LOC - LOKU

LODEMA - LOKEMA

LOEL - LOELI

LOERA - LOELA

LOESJE - LOEKIE

LOGAN - LOKANA

LOGANNE - LOKANE

LOHRY - LOHULI

LOIDA - LOIKA

LOIS - LOIKA

LOISE - LOIKE

LOKESH - LOKEKI

LOLA - LOLA

LOLANDRA - LOLANAKALA

LOLI - LOLI

LOLIDA - LOLIKA

LOLINA - LOLINA

LOLITA - LOLIKA

LOLLY - LOLI

LOLO - LOLO

LOMESIA - LOMEKIA

LOMETA - LOMEKA

LON - LONA

LONA - LONA

LONDON - LONUKONU

LONE - LONE

LONG-HAI - LONU-UHAI

LONNA - LONA

LONNEKE - LONEKE

LONNELL - LONELI

LONNETTE - LONEKE

LONNIE - LONIE

LONNY - LONI

LONZELL - LONUKELI

LOOD - LOKU

LOQUACIOUS - LOKAKIOUKO

LOQUETTA - LOKEKA

LORA - LOLA

LORAINE - LOLAINE

LORALEE - LOLALE

LORALIE - LOLALIE

LORAMIL - LOLAMILE

LORANN - LOLANA

LORAYNE - LOLAINE

LORE - LOLE

LOREA - LOLEA

LOREAL - LOLEALA

LORECE - LOLEKE

LOREDANA - LOLEKANA

LOREE - LOLE

LOREEN - LOLENI

LORELEE- LOLELE

LORELEI - LOLELEI

LORELLE - LOLELE

LOREN - LOLENA

LORENA - LOLENA

LORENDA - LOLENIKA

LORENE - LOLENE

LORENZA - LOLENIKA

LORENZE - LOLENIKE

LORENZO - LOLENEKO

LORESA - LOLEKA

LORETTA - LOLEKA

LORETTE - LOLEKE

LORI - LOLI

LORIA - LOLIA

LORIANN - LOLIANA

LORI-ANN - LOLI-ANA

LORIE - LOLIE

LORIEL - LOLIELI

LORILAC - LOLILAKA

LORIN, LORINA – LOLINA

LORINDA - LOLINEKA

LORING - LOLINE

LORIS - LOLIKE

LORISE - LOLIKE

LORISSA - LOLIKA

LORNA - LOLENA

LORNE - LOLUNE

LORRAINE - LOLEINA

LORRIE - LOLI

LORRINE - LOLINE

LORRY - LOLI

LORUHAMA - LOLUHAMA

LORYN - LOLINE

LOSANA - LOKANA

LOSEL - LOKELI

LOSHI - LOKI

LOSTON - LOKONU

LOTEIRA - LOKEILA

LOTOMAU - LOKOMAU

LOTTA - LOKA

LOTTIE - LOKIE

LOTUS - LOKUKO

LOU - LOU

LOUANN -LOUANA

LOUANNE - LOUANE

LOUCRETIA - LOUKOLEKIA

LOUDAN - LOUKANA

LOUELLA - LUELA

LOUENDA - LOUENIKA

LOUGHRAN - LOUKOHOLANA

LOUIE - LOKE

LOUIEBEL - LOUIEPELI

LOUIS - LUI

LOUISA - LOUIKA

LOUISE - LUIKA

LOULA - LOULA
LOULIE JO - LOULIE IO
LOURY - LOULI
LOURDES - LOULOKEKI
LOURINE - LOULINE
LOUVENIA - LOUWENIA
LOVEDY - LOWEKI
LOWAYNE - LOWAINE
LOWEEN - LOWENI
LOWELL - LOWELA
LOWRIE - LOWULIE
LOVEL - LOWELI
LOVELLENE – LOWELENE
LOVELYN - LOWELINI
LOVETTA - LOWEKA
LOVETTE - LOWEKE
LOVEY - LOWEI
LOVING - LOWINE
LOVONIA - LOWONIA
LOWAILEI - LOWAILEI
LOWAN - LOWANA
LOY - LOI
LOYAA - LOIA
LOYAL - LOIALA
LSIAN - LAKIANA
LUA - LUA
LUANA - LUANA
LUANN - LUANA
LUANNE - LUANE
LUBA - LUPA

LUBEANA - LUPEANA
LUC - LUKO
LUCA - LUKA
LUCAS - LUKAKA
LUCENA - LUKENA
LUCETTE - LUKEKE
LUCHO - LUKO
LUCIA - LUKIA
LUCIANA - LUKIANA
LUCIANO - LUKIANO
LUCIE - LUKIE
LUCIEN - LUKIENI
LUCILLA - LUKILA
LUCILLE - LUKILA
LUCINDA - LUKINA
LUCINE - KUKINE
LUCING - LUKINE
LUCIUS - LUKIO
LUCKY - LUKOKI
LUCO - LUKO
LUCRETIA - LOKOLEKIA
LUCY - LUKE
LUCYBEL - LUKIPELI
LUCYNTHIA - LUKINEKIA
LUDMILA - LUKOMILA
LUDOVICO - LUKOWIKO
LUDWIK - LUKOWIKE
LUDY - LUKI
LUE - LUE
LUELLA - LUELA

LUFI - LUPI

LUGENE - LUKENE

LUIANNE - LUIANE

LUIGI - LUIKI

LUIS - LUIKE

LUISA - LUIKA

LUISE - LUIKE

LUISITO - LUIKIKO

LUIZA - LUIKA

LUJUANA - LUIUANA

LUKA - LUKA

LUKE – LUKA

LULA - LULA

LULETTE - LULEKE

LULU - LULU

LULWA - LULOWA

LUMI - LUMI

LUMING - LUMINE

LUNA - LUNA

LUND - LUNOKO

LUNELLE - LUNELE

LUNING - LUNINE

LUONG - LUONU

LUPE - LUPE

LUPHILIA - LUPILIA

LUPITA - LUPIKA

LURA - LULA

LURDES - LULOKEKI

LURIA - LULIA

LURIE - LULIE

LURLEEN - LULENI

LUTHER - LUKELI

LUTHIEN - LUKIENI

LUTHURE - LUKELA

LUTICIA - LUKIKIA

LUTZ - LUKOKO

LUVERNE - LUWELINE

LUWANA - LUWANA

LUWEN - LUWENI

LUZ - LUKO

LU-ZAHN - LU-OKAHANA

LUX - LUKO

LUZILLE - LUKILE

LUZITA - LUKIKA

LYA - LIA

LYANGIE - LIANIE

LYBA - LIPA

LYCI - LIKI

LYDA - LIKA

LYDELL - LIKELI

LYDIA - LUKIA

LYGIA - LIKIA

LYLA - LILA

LYLE - LAILE

LYLENE - LILENE

LYLY - LILI

LYMAN - LIMANA

LYN - LINE

LYNA - LINA

LYNDA - LINEKA

LYNDAL - LINEKALI   LYSSA - LIKA
LYNDALL - LINEKALI   LYON - LIONU
LYNDEL - LINEKELI   LYTISHA - LIKIKA
LYNDON - LINEKONA   LYUDMILA - LIUKOMILA
LYNDRA - LINEKELA   LYVIA - LIWIA
LYNDSE - LINEKEKE
LYNDSEY -LINEKEKEI
LYNECIA - LINEKIA
LYNESE - LINEKE
LYNESSA - LINEKA
LYNETTE - LINEKE
LYNLY - LINELI
LYNN - LINA
LYNNA - LINA
LYNNAE - LINAE
LYNNAN - LINANA
LYNNANNE - LINANE
LYNNDE - LINEKE
LYNNE - LINE
LYNNEL - LINELI
LYNNELE - LINELE
LYNNETTE - LAWELI
LYNNWOOD - LINEWOKU
LYNSEY - LINEKEI
LYNTREAL - LINELEALA
LYNZIE - LINEKIE
LYNZI - LINEKI
LYRA - LILA
LYRIC - LILIKE
LYSANDRA - LIKANAKALA

M

FIRST NAMES

MAAIKE - MAIKE

MAALIYA - MALIIA

MAARJA - MALIA

MAARTEN - MAKENI

MABEL - MAPELI

MABETH - MAPEKI

MABLE - MEIPALA

MAC - MAKA

MACAIL - MAKAILE

MACARTHUR - MAKAKULO

MACAULEY - MAKAULEI

MACE - MAKE

MACEE - MAKE

MACENZIE - MAKENIKIE

MACGUIRE - MAKAKUILE

MACHAELLAH - MAKAELAHA

MACHEL - MAKELI

MACHELL - MAKELI

MACHELLE - MAKELE

MACHO - MAKO

MACI - MAKI

MACIA - MAKIA

MACIE - MAKIE

MACIEL - MAKIELI

MACK - MAKA

MACKENNA - MAKAKENA

MACKENNAH - MAKAKENAHA

MACKENZIE - MAKAKENKIE

MACKIE - MAKAKIE

MACKINLEY - MAKAKINELEI

MACKLIN - MAKAKALINE

MACOLE - MAKOLE

MACON - MAKONU

MACQUEL - MAKAKELI

MACRINA - MAKALINA

MACSYN - MAKAKINE

MACY - MAKI

MADAISHA - MAKAIKA

MADALEINE - MAKALEINE

MADALENA - MAKALENA

MADALYN - MAKALINE

MADALYNN - MAKALINE

MADASON - MAKAKONU

MADCHEN - MAKAKENI

MADDEN - MAKENI

MADDEX - MAKEKI

MADDIE - MAKIE

MADDISON - MAKIKONU

MADDIX - MAKIKE

MADDOCK - MAKOKUKU

MADDOX - MAKOKU

MADDY - MAKI

MADELAYNE - MAKELAINE

MADELEINE - MAKELEINE

MADELENE - MAKELENE

MADELINE - MAKELINA

MADELYN - MAKELINE

MADGE - MAKAKE

MADHAVI - MAKAHAWI

MADHURI - MAKAHULI

MADIA - MAKIA

MADIHA - MAKIHA

MADHU - MAKAHU

MADIE - MAKIE

MADIGAN - MAKIKANA

MADILYN - MAKILINE

MADISON - MAKIKONU

MADISYN - MAKIKINE

MADLI - MAKALI

MADONNA - MAKONA

MADRICA - MAKALIKA

MADY - MAKI

MADYSON - MAKIKONU

MAE - MAE

MAEANA - MAEANA

MAEDZ - MAEKIKI

MAEFRIZE - MAEPILIKE

MAEGAN - MAEKANA

MAELEE - MAELE

MAELON - MAELONU

MAERENE - MAELENE

MAESYN - MAEKINE

MAEVE - MAEWE

MAGALA - MAKALA

MAGALI - MAKALI

MAGALITA - MAKALIKA

MAGAN - MAKANA

MAGDA - MAKAKA

MAGDALENA - MAKALENA

MAGDALIA - MAKAKALIA

MAGDY - MAKAKI

MAGELYS - MAKELIKE

MAGEN - MAKENI

MAGGIE - MAKIE

MAGIC - MAKIKE

MAGNHILD - MAKANAHILE

MAGNOLIA - MAKANOLIA

MAGID - MAKIKE

MAGNUS - MAKANUKO

MAGUIRE - MAKUILE

MAHA - MAHA

MAHAD - MAHAKA

MAHAGONY - MAHAKONI

MAHAL - MAHALA

MAHALA - MAHALA

MAHALI - MAHALI

MAHAYLA - MAHAILA

MAHEALANI - MAHEALANI

MAHENDRA - MAHENIKILA

MAHER - MAHELI

MAHIMA - MAHIMA

MAHINDER - MAHINEKELI

MAHLIA - MAHALIA

MAHLIK - MAHALIKE

MAHLON - MAHALONA

MAHREN - MAHALENI

MAHUMD - MAHUMOKO

MAI - MAI

MAIA - MAIA

MAIDA - MAIKA

MAIGRET - MAIKELEKI

MAIHAN - MAIHANA

MAIJU - MAIIU

MAIKAYA - MAIKAIA

MAIKEN - MAIKENI

MAIKER - MAIKELI

MAIKOU - MAIKOU

MAILE - MAILE

MAILEE - MAILE

MAINE - MAINE

MAIRE - MAILE

MAIREAD - MAILEAKA

MAIRELI - MAILELI

MAISE - MAIKE

MAISHA - MAIKA

MAISIE - MAIKIE

MAISSA - MAIKA

MAISY - MAIKI

MAISYN - MAIKINE

MAITE - MAIKE

MAITLYN - MAIKELINE

MAITRAYA - MAILAIA

MAIVEN - MAIWENI

MAIYA - MAIIA

MAIYEE - MAIIE

MAJ - MAI

MAJA - MAIA

MAJED - MAIEKI

MAJEEDAH - MAIEKAHA

MAJESCA - MAIEKIKA

MAJESTA - MAIEKA

MAJKEN - MIKENI

MAJOR - MAIOLU

MAJORIE - MAIOLIE

MAJURE - MAIULE

MAKALAH - MAKALAHA

MAKALI - MAKALI

MAKALL - MAKALA

MAKARLIE - MAKALIE

MAKARRA - MAKALA

MAKAYA - MAKAIA

MAKAYELA - MAKAIELA

MAKAYLA - MAKAILA

MAKAYLEIGH - MAKAILEIKEHE

MAKAYLEN - MAKAILENI

MAKEDA - MAKEKA

MAKEEBA - MAKEPA

MAKELLA - MAKELA

MAKENA - MAKENA

MAKENNA - MAKENA

MAKENZIE - MAKENIKIE

MAKI - MAKI

MAKIESE - MAKIEKE

MAKIMA - MAKIMA

MAKINON - MIKINONU

MAKIYA - MAKIIA

MAKOTO - MAKOKO

MAL - MALA

MALA - MALA

MALACHA - MALAKA

MALACHI - MALAKI

MALAIKA - MALAIKA

MALAINA - MALAINA

MALAKA - MALAKA

MALAKAI - MALAKAI

MALAKIYA - MALAKI'IA

MALAN - MALANA

MALANI - MALANI

MA'LAURA - MA'ALAULA

MALAYA - MALAIA

MALAYATHONG - MALAIAKONU

MALAYNA - MALAINA

MALAYSIA - MALAIKIA

MALCOLM - MALAKOMA

MALEAH - MALEAHA

MALEENA - MALENA

MALEK - MALEKI

MALENA - MALENA

MALENA - MALENA

MALERIE - MALELIE

MALGORZATA - MALAKOLUKAKA

MALIA - MALIA

MALIE - MALIE

MALIK - MALIKE

MALIKA - MALIKA

MALINA - MALINA

MALINDA - MALINEKA

MALINI - MALINI

MALISA - MALIKA

MALISIA - MALIKIA

MALISSA - MALIKA

MALIYA - MALIIA

MALIYAH - MALIIAHA

MALKA - MALAKA

MALLAK - MALAKA

MALLARI - MALALI

MALLIE - MALIE

MALLIKA - MALIKA

MALLORI - MALOLI

MALLORIE - MALOLIE

MALLORY - MALELIA

MALORIE - MALOLIE

MALTEE - MALAKE

MALVINA - MALAWINA

MALYN - MALINE

MALYNA - MALINA

MALYNDA - MALINEKA

MALYSSA - MALIKA

MALYTHA - MALIKA

MAMIE – MAME

MAMTA - MAMAKA

MAN - MANA

MANA - MANA

MANAHIL - MANAHILE

MANASA - MANAKA

MANASI - MANAKI

MANDA - MANAKA

MANDADI - MANAKAKI

MANDALE - MANAKALE

MANDANA - MANAKANA

MANDI - MANAKI

MANDIE - MANAKIE

MANDIP - MANAKIPE

MANDY - HENOHENO

MANDYE - MANAKIE

MANELLA - MANELA

MANELITO - MANELIKO

MANG - MANA

MANGIE - MANIE

MANGO - MANO

MANI - MANI

MANISH - MANIKE

MANISHA - MANIKA

MANFRED - MANAPALEKI

MANJARI - MANIALI

MANJI - MANII

MANJIT - MANIIKE

MANMING - MANAMINE

MANNA - MANA

MANNIE - MANIE

MANNING - MANINE

MANNY - MANI

MANOLO - MANOLO

MANON - MANONU

MANOU - MANU

MANSUR - MANAKULO

MAN-SZE - MANA-AKAKE

MANTEESHA - MANAKEKA

MANU - MANU

MANUEL – MANUELA

MANUELA - MANUELA

MANUKA - MANUKA

MANVEER - MANAWELI

MANVILLE - MANAWILE

MANVIR - MANAWILE

MANYA - MANIA

MAQUEL - MAKELI

MARA - MALA

MARAEA - MALAEA

MARAH - MALAHA

MARALENE - MALALENE

MARANDA - MALANAKA

MARANEE - MALANE

MARAYE - MALAIE

MARBELYS - MALAPELIKE

MARC - MALAKA

MARCAYLA - MALAKAILA

MARCEL - MALAKELI

MARCELINA - MALAKELINA

MARCELINHO - MALAKELINEHO

MARCELL - MALAKELI

MARCELLA - MAKELA

MARCELLE - MALAKELE

MARCELLINA - MALAKELINA

MARCELLUS - MALAKELUKO

MARCELO - MALAKELO

MARCENA - MALAKENA

MARCENE - MALAKENE

MARCH - MALAKA

MARCHANT - MALAKANAKA

MARCHE - MALAKE

MARCHELLE - MALIKALA

MARCI - MALAKI

MARCIA - MALAKIA

MARCIAL - MALAKIALA

MARCIANA - MALAKIANA

MARCIE - MALAKIA

MARCIN - MALAKINE

MÁRCIO - MAÁALAKIO

MARCO - MALAKO

MARCOS - MALAKOKU

MARCUS - MALAKUKO

MARCY - MALAKI

MARDEE - MALAKE

MARDEEN - MALAKENI

MARDELL - MALAKELI

MARDELLA - MALAKELA

MARDELLE - MALAKELE

MARDI - MALAKI

MAREE - MALE

MAREK - MALEKI

MARELLA - MALELA

MARELLE - MALELE

MAREN - MALENI

MARENA - MALENA

MAREON - MALEONU

MARESA - MALEKA

MARESSA - MALEKA

MARET - MALEKI

MARETA - MALEKA

MARG - MAKA

MARGARET - MAKALEKA

MARGARETE - MAKALEKE

MARGARITA - MAKALIKA

MARGARITE - MAKALIKE

MARGAUX - MAKAUKO

MARGE - MAKE

MARGEE - MAKE

MARGENE - MAKENE

MARGERY - MAKELI

MARGIE - MALAKI

MARGIT - MAKIKE

MARGO - MAKO

MARGOT - MAKOKA

MARGRET - MAKALEKI

MARGRETHE - MAKALEKE

MARGUERITE - MAKALIKA

MARI - MALI

MARIA - MALIA

MARIADIANA - MALIAKIANA

MARIAH - MALIAHA

MARIAM - MALIAMA

MARIAN - MALIANA

MARIANA - MALIANA

MARIANITA - MALIANIKA

MARIANNA - MALIANA

MARIANNE - MELEANA

MARIANO - MALIANO

MARIANTHI - MALIANAKI

MARIASCHELLE - MALIAKAKELE

MARIBEL - MALIPELI

MARIBELE - MALIPELE

MARIBETH - MALIPEKI

MARICAR - MALIKALA

MARICARMEN - MALIKALAMENI

MARICELA - MALIKELA

MARICELES - MALIKELEKI

MARICIA - MALIKIA

MARICOR - MALIKOLU

MARIDSA - MALIKEKA

MARIE - MALIA

MARIEA - MALIEA

MARIEL - MALIELI

MARIELA - MALIELA

MARIELENA - MALIELENA

MARIELLA - MALIELA

MARIELLE - MALIELE

MARIENA - MALIENA

MARIETINA - MALIEKINA

MARIETJIE - MALIEKIIE

MARIETTA - MALIEKA

MARIXA - MALIKA

MARJ - MALI

MARIDEN - MALIKENI

MARIJO - MALIIO

MARIKA - MALIKA

MARIKO - MALIKO

MARILEE - MALILE

MARILENA - MALILENA

MARILIIS - MALILIKE

MERILIN - MELILINE

MARILOLY - MALILOLI

MARILOU - MALILOU

MARILYN - MELELINA

MARIMAR - MALIMALA

MARIN - MALINE

MARINA - MALINA

MARINCHI - MALINEKI

MARINDA - MALINEKA

MARINELLA - MALINELA

MARINELLE - MALINELE

MARINO - MALINO

MARIO - MALIA

MARIOLA - MALIOLA

MARION - MALIONA

MARIPAZ - MALIPAKA

MARIS - MALIKE

MARISA - MALIKA

MARISE - MALIKE

MARISHA - MALIKA

MARISKA - MALIKEKA

MARISSA - MALIKA

MARISOL - MALIKOLU

MARIETTE - MALIEKE

MARINE - MALINE

MARINEL - MALINELI

MARINETTE - MALINEKE

MARISELA - MALIKELA

MARISSA - MALIKA

MARISA - MALIKA

MARISELA - MALIKELA

MARISOL - MALIKOLU

MARISSA - MALIKA

MARIT - MALIKE

MARITA - MALIKA

MARITESS – MALIKEKI

MYSTINA - MIKINA

MYUNG JIN - MIUNO IINE

MARITJIE - MALIKIIE

MARITZA - MALIKEKA

MARIUS - MALIUKO

MARIVEL - MALIWELI

MARIVI - MALIWI

MARIVIC - MALIWIKE

MARIYA - MALIIA

MARIYAM - MALIIAMA

MARIZ - MALIKE

MARIZA - MALIKA

MARIZEL - MALIKELI

MARIZEN - MALIKENI

MARIZITA - MALIKIKA

MARJANI - MAKIANI

MARJORIE - MAKOLI

MARJOURIE - MALIOULIE

MARK - MALEKO

MARKAY - MAKAI

MARKAYLA - MAKAILA

MARKEDA - MAKEKA

MARKEETH - MAKEKI

MARKEIS - MAKEIKE

MARKEL - MAKELI

MARKETHA - MAKEKA

MARKETTA - MAKEKA

MARKEVYA - MAKEWIA

MARKIE - MAKIE

MARKITA - MAKIKA

MARKO - MAKO

MARKUS - MAKUKO

MARLA - MALA

MARLALEE - MALALE

MARLANA - MALANA

MARLANE - MALANE

MARLEDYS - MALEKIKE

MARLEE - MALE

MARLEIGH - MALEIKEHE

MARLEIGHA - MALEIKEHA

MARLENA - MALENA

MARLENE - MALENA

MARLES - MALEKI

MARLEY - MALEI

MARLIE - MALIE

MARLIN - MALINE

MARLINI - MALINI

MARLIS - MALIKE

MARLISE - MALIKE

MARLISSE - MALIKE

MARLIZ - MALIKE

MARLL - MALA

MARLON – MALONA

MARSALETE - MALAKELAKE

MARLOUS - MALO'UKO

MARSALIS - MALAKALIKE

MARLOW - MALOWU

MARSELLA - MALAKELA

MARLYN - MALINE

MARSHA - MALEKA

MARLYS - MALIKE

MARSHALEEN - MALAKALENI

MARNA - MALANA

MARSHALL - MALEKALA

MARNE - MALANE

MARSHAY - MALAKAI

MARNEL - MALANELI

MAR SHEI - MALA KEI

MARNERY - MALANELI

MARSHEILA - MALAKEILA

MARNETTA - MALANEKA

MARSHIDA - MALAKIKA

MARNI - MALANI

MARSIA - MALAKIA

MARNIE - MALANIE

MARSTON - MALAKONU

MARNY -MALANI

MART - MAKA

MARONDA - MALONUKA

MARTA - MAKA

MARQUALYA - MALAKALIA

MARTHA - MALEKA

MARQUAN - MALAKANA

MARTI - MAKI

MARQUELL - MALAKELI

MARTICIA - MAKIKIA

MARQUERITE - MAKALIKA

MARTIE - MAKIE

MARQUES - MALAKEKI

MARTIKA - MAKIKA

MARQUIC - MALAKAIKE

MARTIN - MALAKINA

MARQUIE - MALAKIE

MARTINA - MALAKINA

MARQUISE - MALAKIKE

MARTINE - MAKINE

MARQUISHA - MALAKIKA

MARTINEZ - MAKINEKI

MARQUITA - MALAKIKA

MARTINI - MAKINI

MARQUIZE - MALAKUIKE

MARTISHA - MAKIKA

MARRINNA - MALINA

MARTIZA - MAKIKA

MARRIS - MALIKE

MARTRAIL - MALAILE

MARRISA - MALIKA

MARTRISHA - MALIKA

MARRISSA - MALIKA

MARTY - MALEKI

MARV - MALAWA

MARVA - MALAWA

MARVANNA - MALAWANA

MARVEL - MALAWELI

MARVELL - MALAWELI

MARVELLA - MALAWELA

MARVI - MALAWI

MARVIN - MALAWINA

MARVIS - MALAWIKE

MARVIVE - MALAWIWE

MARVONTE - MALAWONUKE

MARWYN - MALAWINE

MARX - MALAKA

MARXA - MALAKA

MARY - MALIA

MARYA - MALIA

MARYAH - MALIAHA

MARYAL - MALIALA

MARYALICE - MALIALIKE

MARYAM - MALIAMA

MARYANN - MELEANA

MARYANNE - MELEANA

MARYBETH - MALIPEKI

MARYBROCK - MALIPELOKUKU

MARYBROOK - MALIPELOKU

MARYCARM - MALIKALAMA

MARYELIZABETH - MALIELIKAPEK

MARY ELLE - MALIA ELE

MARYELLEN - MALIELENI

MARYETTA - MALIEKA

MARYFRANCES - MALIPELANAKEKI

MARYAH - MALIAHA

MARYHERBERT - MALIHELIPEKI

MARYJANE - MALIIANE

MARYJEAN - MALIIEANA

MARYJO- MALI'IO

MARY-JOAN - MALI-IOANA

MARYKATE - MALIKAKE

MARYKATHRYN - MALIKALINE

MARYKAY - MALIKAI

MARYKAYE - MALIKAIE

MARYKE - MALIKE

MARYLA - MALILA

MARY LEA - MALI LEA

MARYLEE - MALILE

MARYLINE - MALILINE

MARYLLIS - MALILIKE

MARYLOU - MELELU

MARYLYN - MALILINE

MARYLYNN - MALILINE

MARYNA - MALINA

MARYNINE - MALINENI

MARYROSE - MALILOKE

MARYSE - MALIKE

MARY SUE - MALIA KU

MARYSUE - MALIKUE

MARYVETTE - MALIWEKE

MARZ - MALAKA

MARZANA - MALAKANA

MARZENA - MALAKENA

MARZETTA - MALAKEKA

MARZIEH - MALAKIEHI

MASAKO - MAKAKO

MASANI - MAKANI

MASASU - MAKAKU

MASATO - MAKAKO

MASKIT - MAKAKIKE

MASON - MAKONU

MASOUD - MAKOUKO

MASSEY - MAKEI

MASSIMO - MAKIMO

MASUMI - MAKUMI

MATAI - MAKAI

MATALEE - MAKALE

MATAYA - MAKAIA

MATEAH - MAKEAHA

MATEO - MAKEO

MATET - MAKEKI

MATEUS - MAKEUKO

MATHEA - MAKEA

|MATHESON - MAKEKONU

MATHEW - MAKEWI

MATHIAS - MAKIAKA

MATHIEU - MAKIEU

MATHIJS - MAKIIKE

MATHILDE - MAKILE

MATHLEEN - MAKALENI

MATHYS - MAKIKE

MATIAS - MAKIAKA

MATIGAN - MAKIKANA

MATILDA - MAKILA

MATIS - MAKIKA

MATIUS - MAKIUKO

MATS - MAKA

MATT - MAKAIO

MATTEA - MAKEA

MATTEO - MAKEO

MATTHAYA - MAKAIA

MATTHEW - MAKAIO

MATTHIAS - MAKIAKA

MATTI - MAKI

MATTIE - MAKIE

MATTY - MAKI

MAUDE - MAUKE

MAULIK - MAULIKE

MAULIBEL - MAULIPELI

MAULINE - MAULINE

MAUNAYIA - MAUNAIIA

MAURA - MAULA

MAUREEN - MAULENA

MAURICE - MAULIKE

MAURICIO - MAULIKIO

MAURIE - MAULIE

MAURINE - MAULINE

MAURO - MAULO

MAUTINOA - MAUKINOA

MAVEL - MAWELI

MAVERICK - MAWELIKEKE

MAVIS - MEWIKE

MAX – MAKI

MAXI-LEE - MAKI ELE

MAXIM - MAKIME

MAXIMUS - MAKIMO

MAXINE - MAKINA

MAXON - MAKONU

MAXSON - MAKAKONU

MAXWELL - MAKAWELI

MAY - MEI

MAYA - MAIA

MAYBELLE - MEIPELA

MAYBELLINE - MAIPELINE

MAYBORN - MAIPOLUNU

MAYCEE - MAIKE

MAYDELLE - MAIKELE

MAYE - MAIE

MAYEBELLE - MAIEPELE

MAYELIN - MAIELINE

MAYGAN - MAIKANA

MAYLEA - MAILEA

MAYLEE - MAILE

MAYLENI - MAILENI

MAYLIE - MAILIE

MAYNARD - MEINALA

MAYOWA - MAIOWA

MAYRA - MAILA

MAYREE - MAILE

MAYRENE - MAILENE

MAYRIN - MAILINE

MAYSON - MAIKONU

MAYTEE - MAIKE

MAYUMI - MAIUMI

MAYURI - MAIULI

MAYURPANKHI - MAIULOPANAKAHI

MAZEL - MAKELI

MAZEN - MAKENI

MAZIE - MAKIE

MAZY - MAKI

MAZZI - MAKI

MCARIA - MAKALIA

MCCABE - MAKAPE

MCCALL - MAKALA

MCCASLIN - MAKAKALINE

MCCAULEY - MAKAULEI

MCCLELLAN - MAKALELANA

MCCRAE - MAKALAE

MCCREARY - MAKALEALI

MCCAULEY - MAKAULEI

MCGEE - MAKAKE

MCINNIS - MAKINIKE

MCKAE - MAKAKAE

MCKALYNNE - MAKAKALINE

MCKAY - MAKAKAI

MCKAYLA - MAKAKAILA

MCKAYLEE - MAKAKAILE

MCKAYLEY - MAKAKAILEI

MCKEE - MAKAKE

MCKENLEE - MAKAKENILE

MCKENNA - MAKAKENA

MCKENZEE - MAKAKENIKE

MCKENZI - MAKAKENIKI

MCKENZIE - MAKAKENIKIE

MCKINLEY - MAKAKINELEI

MCKINSLEY - MAKAKINEKELEI

MCLEAN - MAKALEANA

MCMURRY - MAKAMULI

MCNALLY - MAKANALI

MEAC - MEAKA

MEADE - MEAKE

MEADOW - MEAKOWU

MEAGAN - MEAKANA

MEAGHAN - MEAKAHANA

MEARA - MEALA

MEASHEARA - MEAKEALA

MEAZA - MEAKA

MECCA - MEKA

MEDEA - MEKEA

MEDHA - MEKIHA

MEDHAVI - MEKIHAWI

MEDINA - MEKINA

MEDORA - MEKOLA

MEDY - MEKI

MEE - ME

MEECHIE - MEKIE

MEEJIN - MEIINE

MEENA - MENA

MEERA - MELA

MEESHA - MEKA

MEETA - MEKA

MEETESH - MEKEKI

MEEYA - MEIA

MEG - MEKI

MEGALA - MEKALA

MEGAN - MEKANA

MEGGAN - MEKANA

MEGGEN - MEKENI

MEGGIE - MEKIE

MEGHAN - MEKANA

MEGHA - MEKIHA

MEAGHN - MEAKAHANA

MEGHNA - MEKIHINA

MEGIN - MEKINE

MEGUMI - MEKUMI

MEHDI - MEHIKI

MEHENDI - MEHENIKI

MEHWISH - MEHIWIKE

MEHYAR - MEHIALA

MEI - MEI

MEIBH - MEIPEHE

MEIGEN - MEIKENI

MEIKE - MEIKE

MEILANI - MEILANI

MAILENE - MAILENE

MEILIN - MEILINE

MEIRA - MEILA

MEISHA - MEIKA

MEKAYLA - MEKAILA

ME'KELL - ME'IKELI

MEKENZIE - MEKENIKIE

MEKHAIL - MEKIHAILE

MEKHI - MEKIHI

MEKIA - MEKIA

MEKIEL - MEKIELI

MEKISHA - MEKIKA

MEKO - MEKO

MEKONNEN - MEKONENI

MEL - MELI

MELADEE - MELAKE

MELAINA - MELAINA

MELANEY - MELANEI

MELANIE - MELANI

MELAYA - MELAIA

MELBA - MELIPA

MELBOURNE - MELIPOULONE

MELDA - MELA

MELEA - MELEA

MELEAH - MELEAHA

MELEANA - MELEANA

MELECA - MELEKA

MELECIO - MELEKIO

MELIA - MELIA

MELINA - MELINA

MELIND - MELINEKE

MELINDA - MELINAKA

MELIS - MELIKE

MELISA - MELIKA

MELISHA - MELIKA

MELISSA - MELIKA

MELISSIA - MELIKIA

MELITA - MELIKA

MELLANIE - MELANIE

MELLE - MELE

MELLEN - MELENI

MELLETTE - MELEKE

MELLIE - MELIE

MELODIE - MELOKIE

MELODY - MELOKIA

MELONEY - MELONEI

MELONIE - MELONIE

MELVA - MELIWA

MELVELLINE - MELIWELINE

MELVI - MELIWI

MELVILLE - MELIWILE

MELVIN – MELEWINA

MELVILYN - MELIWILINE

MELVIRICK - MELIWILIKEKE

MELYCHER - MELIKELI

MELYNA - MELINA

MEMMY - MEMI

MEMPHIS - MEMIPIKE

MENA - MENA

MENCHIE - MENIKIE

MENG - MENI

MENGKONG - MENIKONU

MENZER - MENIKELI

MEOKA - MEOKA

MEONA - MEONA

MER - MELI

MERAB - MELAPA

MERANDA - MELANAKA

MERAYA - MELAIA

MERCEDES - MEKEKE

MERCELLE - MELIKELE

MERCHAND - MELIKANAKA

MERCURY - MELIKULI

MERCY - MELIKI

MEREDITH - MELEKIKE

MERI - MELI

MERIAH - MELIAHA

MERICIA - MELIKIA

MERIDA - MELIKA

MERIDETH - MELIKEKI

MERILEE - MELILE

MERIL LEE - MELILE LI

MERINA - MELINA

MERIRAE - MELILAE

MERISSA - MELIKA

MERIT - MELIKE

MERITA - MELIKA

MERKO - MEKO

MERLAYNA - MELAINA

MERLE - MELE

MERLENE – MELENE

MERLI - MELI

MERLIN - MELINE

MERLITA - MELIKA

MERLOT - MELOKU

MERLY - MELI

MERNA - MELINA

MEROLYN - MELOLINE

MERRAN - MELANA

MERRELL - MELELI

MERRIA - MELIA

MERRIAL - MELIALA

MERRICK - MELIKEKE

MERRILL - MELILE

MERRILLYN - MELILINE

MERRILY - MELILI

MERRITT - MELIKE

MERRY - MELI

MERRYN - MELINE

MERT - MEKI

MERTON - MEKONU

MERVAT - MELIWAKA

MERVIN - MELIWINE

MERYL - MELILE

MESEAN - MEKEANA

MERSENDA - MELIKENIKA

MESHA - MEKA

MESHEOLA - MEKEOLA

MESSINA - MEKINA

MESSLINA - MEKILINA

META - MEKA

METIT - MEKIKI

METRICE - MELIKE

METTE - MEKE

MEUY - MEUI

MEYAUNA - MEIAUNA

MEYDALYN - MEIKALINE

MEYERS - MEIELIKI

MEYGAN - MEIKANA

MHAJRIKA - MAHAILIKA

MHEALYSSAH - MAHEALIKAHA

MHYRES - MAHILEKI

MIA – MIA

MIAENN - MIAENI

MIAN - MIANA

MIANEH - MIANEHI

MIANNA - MIANA

MIARI - MIALI

MIAYA - MIAIA

MICAELA - MIKAELA

MICAH - MIKA

MICAIAH - MIKAIAHA

MICAILA - MIKAILA

MICAYLA - MIKAILA

MICHA - MIKA

MICHAE - MIKAE

MICHAEL - MIKALE

MICHAELA - MIKAELA

MICHAELIS - MIKAELIKE

MICHAELLE - MIKAELE

MICHAELYN - MIKAELINE

MICHAL - MIKALA

MICHALEEN - MIKALENI

MICHEL, MICHELL - MIKALE

MICHELA - MIKELA

MICHELE - MIKALA

MICHELINE - MIKALINA

MICHELLE – MIKALA

MICHEON - MIKEONU

MICHI - MIKI

MICHICKIA - MIKIKEKIA

MICHIKO - MIKIKO

MICHIO - MIKIO

MICHLLE - MIKELE

MICHOLETTE - MIKOLEKE

MICHQUEL - MIKEKAELI

MICK - MIKEKE

MICKE - MIKEKE

MICKELL - MIKEKELI

MICKELLE - MIKEKELE

MICKEY - MIKEKEI

MICKIE - MIKEKIE

MICKIELA - MIKEKIELA

MIDGE - MIKEKE

MIDIRISE - MIKILIKE

MIDORI - MIKOLI

MIE - MIE

MIEKE - MIEKE

MIEOSHA - MIEOKA

MIESHA - MIEKA

MIGLING - MIKELINE

MIGUEL - MIKUELA

MIGUELA - MIKUELA

MIHAI - MIHAI

MIHIR - MIHILE

MIHO - MIHO

MIJA - MIIA

MIJI - MIII

MIJOI - MIIOI

MIJOY - MIIOI

MIKA - MIKA

MIKAEL - MIKAELI

MIKAELA - MIKAELA

MIKALA - MIKALA

MIKASA - MIKAKA

MIKAYA - MIKAIA

MIKAYLA - MIKAILA

MIKAYLI - MIKAILI

MIKAYLIE - MIKAILIE

MIKE - MIKALA

MIKEL - MIKELI

MIKELLE - MIKELE

MIKENZIE - MIKENIKIE

MIKESHA - MIKEKA

MIKEY - MIKEI

MIKHAIL - MIKEHAILE

MIKHAYLA - MIKEHAILA

MIKI - MIKI

MIKIA - MIKIA

MIKIJO - MIKIIO

MIKKEL - MIKELI

MIKKI - MIKI

MIKKO - MIKO

MIKOLAJ - MIKOLAI

MILA - MILA

MILAGRO - MILAKALO

MILAGROS - MILAKALOKU

MILAN - MILANA

MILAR - MILALA

MILAYNA - MILAINA

MILCA - MILEKA

MILDRED - MILIKELEKA

MILEAH - MILEAHA

MILEDYS - MILEKIKE

MILENA - MILENA

MILERKA - MILEKA

MILES - MILEKA

MI'LEXUS - MI'ELEKUKO

MILEY - MILEI

MILFORD - MILEPOLUKU

MILISSA - MILIKA

MILLA - MILA

MILLARD - MILALAKA

MILLER - MILELI

MILLET - MILEKI

MILLICENT - MILIKENA

MILLIE - MILE

MILLS - MILEKE

MILO - MILO

MILTON - MILIKONA

MILUSKA - MILUKOKA

MIMI - MIMI

MIMS - MIMEKE

MIN - MINE

MINA - MINA

MINAL - MINALA

MINDE - MINEKE

MINDEE - MINEKE

MINDEN - MINEKENI

MINDY - MINEKI   MIRANDA - MILANAKA

MINE - MINE   MIRAYA - MALAIA

MINECIA - MINEKIA   MIRCEA - MILEKEA

MINERVA - MINELIWA   MIRELLA - MILELA

MINETTA - MINEKA   MIREYA - MILEIA

MING - MINE   MIRI - MILI

MINGA - MINA   MIRIAHA - MILIAHA

MING KIAT - MINE KIAKA   MIRIAM - MILIAMA

MINH - MINEHE   MIRKO - MIKO

MINHTHU - MINEHEKU   MIRL - MILE

MINHVIEN - MINEHEWIENI   MIRNA - MILENA

MINIFIE - MINIPIE   MIRO - MILO

MINIS - MINIKE   MIROS - MILOKU

MINJEE - MINIE   MIRSHA - MILEKA

MINJI - MINII   MIRTA - MIKA

MINKY - MINEKI   MIRYT - MILIKE

MINNA - MINA   MIRZA - MILEKA

MINNACHHI - MINAKI   MISA - MIKA

MINNELLI - MINELI   MISAHEL - MIKAHELI

MINNIE - MINE   MISATU - MIKAKU

MINOOR - MINOLU   MISCHA - MIKEKA

MINOR - MINOLU   MISHA - MIKA

MINTA - MINEKA   MISHANNDA - MIKANAKA

MIO - MIO   MISHKA - MIKEKA

MIQUITA - MIKIKA   MISSY - MIKI

MIRA - MILA   MISTI - MIKI

MIRABELLE - MILEPELE   MISTY - MIKI

MIRACLE - MILAKALE   MISTYMAE - MIKIMAE

MIRAIS - MILAIKE   MITALI - MIKALI

MIRAL - MILALA   MITCH - MIKEKE

MITCHELL – MIKELA

MOESHA - MOEKA

MITCHELLEE - MIKEKELE

MOHAMMED - MOHAMEKA

MITCHI - MIKEKI

MOHAN - MOHANA

MI-TONG - MI-EKONU

MOH-DEH - MOHU-UKEHI

MITSUKO - MIKUKO

MOHIT - MOHIKE

MITZI - MIKEKI

MOHSEN - MOHUKENI

MIYA - MIIA

MOIRA - MOILA

MIYAH - MIIAHA

MOISE - MOIKE

MIYAN - MIIANA

MOISHA - MOIKA

MI-YEE - MI-IE

MOJGAN - MOIKANA

MIYOKO - MIIOKO

MOLLEE - MOLE

M'KAILA - MA'AKAILA

MOLLEY - MOLEI

MMELIKA - MELIKA

MOLLIE- MOLIE

MLEE - MALE

MOLLY - MOLI

M'LEIGH - MA'ALEIKEHE

MOMOKO - MOMOKO

MLETA - MALEKA

MONA - MONA

M'LYNN - MA'ALINE

MONAE - MONAE

MO - MO

MONALISA - MONALIKA

MOACIR - MOAKILE

MONCADA - MONUKAKA

MOAMEN - MOAMENI

MONCHI - MONUKI

MOBI - MOPI

MONDI - MONUKI

MOBINA - MOPINA

MONDLA - MONUKULA

MOBIUS - MOPIUKO

MONDO - MONUKO

MOBY - MOPI

MONE - MONE

MODENA - MOKENA

MONETTE - MONEKE

MODESTA - MOKEKA

MONIAH - MONIAHA

MODESTO - MOKEKO

MONICA - MONIKA

MOE - MOE

MONIER - MONIELI

MOEED - MOEKI

MONIKA - MONIKA

MOEENA - MOENA

MONIKA JO - MONIKA IO

MONINA - MONINA

MONIQUE - MONIKE

MONIR - MONILE

MONISHA - MONIKA

MONJA - MONIA

MONKEY - MONUKEI

MONNA - MONA

MONNIE - MONIE

MONROE - MONULOE

MONTA - MONUKA

MONTANA - MONUKANA

MONTANNA - MONUKANA

MONTE - MONOKE

MONTEL - MONUKELI

MONTEZ - MONUKEKI

MONTGOMERY - MONUKUKOMELI

MONTIA - MONUKIA

MONTIEL - MONUKIELI

MONTINA - MONUKINA

MONTIQUA - MONUKIKA

MONTREAL - MONULEALA

MONTRELL - MONULELI

MONTSE - MONUKE

MONTSERRAT - MONUKELAKA

MONTY - MONOKE

MONVYL - MONUWILE

MONYQUA - MONIKA

MOOCHIE - MOKIE

MOOK - MOKU

MOOKIE - MOKIE

MOON - MONU

MOORE - MOLE

MOORRISON - MOLIKONU

MOOSE - MOKE

MORAG - MOLAKA

MORAIMA - MOLAIMA

MORANNA - MOLANA

MORAYO - MOLAIO

MORDECAI - MOLUKEKAI

MOREEN - MOLENI

MORENA - MOLENA

MORGAN - MOKANA

MORGANA - MOKANA

MORGANNE - MOKANE

MORGANSTAR - MOKANAKALA

MORGEN - MOKENI

MORI - MOLI

MORIAH - MOLIAHA

MORITA - MOLIKA

MORLEY - MOLEI

MORNÉ - MOLUNUÉU

MORRIS - MOLEKA

MORT - MOKU

MORTAKAI - MOKAKAI

MORTEN - MOKENI

MORTON - MOKONU

MORYN - MOLINE

MOSAAB - MOKAPA

MOSEA - MOKEA

MOSELYN - MOKELINE

MOSES - MOKE

MOSHE - MOKE

MOSTYN - MOKINE

MOTORIA - MOKOLIA

MOUNA - MOUNA

MOXLEY - MOKULEI

MOYA - MOIA

MOZA - MOKA

MOZAFFAR - MOKAPALA

MOZELLE - MOKELE

MSHINDA - MAKINEKA

MUFFY - MUPI

MUKESH - MUKEKI

MUKUND - MUKUNOKO

MUNAF - MANAPA

MUNEET - MUNEKI

MUNGA - MUNA

MUNGER - MUNELI

MUNIR - MUNILE

MUN KONG - MUNO KONU

MURAD - MULAKA

MURALI - MULALI

MURANILLI - MULANILI

MURIEL - MIULIELA

MURILO - MULILO

MURLINE - MULINE

MORONGOA - MOLONOA

MURPHY - MULOPI

MURRAY - MULAI

MURRY - MULI

MURSEL - MULOKELI

MURU - MULU

MURYAL - MULIALA

MUSA - MUKA

MUSETTE - MUKEKE

MUSTAFA - MUKAPA

MUTHANNA - MUKANA

MUTLEY - MUKOLEI

MY - MI

MYA - MIA

MYANA - MIANA

MYCHAELA - MIKAELA

MYCHAL - MIKALA

MYEISHA - MIEIKA

MYERS - MIELIKI

MYHALA - MIHALA

MY HONG - MI HONU

MYIANA - MIIANA

MYISHA - MI'IKA

MYJOI - MIIOI

MYKA - MIKA

MYKAELAH - MIKAELAHA

MYKAL - MIKALA

MYKAYLA - MIKAILA

MYKELTI - MIKELIKI

MYKIA - MIKIA

MYLA - MILA

MYLANG - MILANA

MYLEA - MILEA

MYLEE - MILE

MYLEEN - MILENI

MYLENE - MILENE

MYLES - MILEKI

MYLI - MILI

MYLINH - MILINEHE

MYLISSA - MILIKA

MYNDA - MINEKA

MYONG - MIONU

MYRA - MALIA

MYRANDA - MILANAKA

MYRL, MYRLE - MILE

MYRNA - MILENA

MYNIESH - MINIEKI

MYNOR - MINOLU

MYOUSHI - MIOUKI

MYRIAH - MILIAHA

MYRIAM - MILIAMA

MYRON - MAILONA

MYRRHANDA - MILEHANAKA

MYRTHA - MIKA

MYRTICE - MIKIKE

MYRTIEANNE - MIKIEANE

MYRTLE - MAKALA

MYSTI - MIKI

N

FIRST NAMES

NAADIRA - NAKILA

NAAJAH - NAIAHA

NAAMA - NAMA

NABERRIE - NAPELIE

NABIHA - NAPIHA

NABILA - NAPILA

NABILAH - NAPILAHA

NACHEBIA - NAKEPIA

NACHO - NAKO

NACOLE - NAKOLE

NADA - NAKA

NADALYN - NAKALINE

NADDER - NAKELI

NADEEMA - NAKEMA

NADEEN - NAKENI

NADELINE - NAKELINE

NADER - NAKELI

NADERAH - NAKELAHA

NADERIA - NAKELIA

NADIA - NAKIA

NADIAH - NAKIAHA

NADIDAH - NAKIKAHA

NADIF - NAKIPE

NADIM - NAKIME

NADINE - NAKINE

NADIR - NAKILE

NADIRAH - NAKILAHA

NADJA - NAKIA

NADYA - NAKIA

NAEEM - NAEMI

NAFISA - NAPIKA

NAHAL - NAHALA

NAHED - NAHEKI

NAHIRA - NAHILA

NAH' SHON - NAHA'A KONU

NAHUM - NAHUMO

NAI - NAI

NAIHJA - NAIHIA

NAILAH - NAILAHA

NAIMA - NAIMA

NAIRA - NAILA

NAISHUR - NAIKULO

NAIYA - NAIIA

NAJAH - NAIAHA

NAJARE - NAIALE

NAJD - NAIKE

NAJE' - NAIE'I

NAJEEB - NAIEPI

NAJEEMDEEN - NAIEMIKENI

NAJIA - NAIIA

NAJMA - NAIMA

NAJMI - NAIMI

NAKAYIA - NAKAIIA

NAKELLE - NAKELE

NAKIA - NAKIA

NAKISHA - NAKIKIA

NAKITA - NAKIKA

NAKIYAH - NAKIIAHA

NAKYA - NAKIA

NALE - NALE

NALENE - NALENE
NALINI - NALINI
NALOAH - NALOAHA
NALYA - NALIA
NAMID - NAMIKE
NAMITA - NAMIKA
NAMRADHA - NAMALAKAHA
NAMRATA - NAMALAKA
NAN - NANA
NANA - NANA
NANCEY - NANAKEI
NANCI - NANEKI
NANCY - NANEKI
NAND - NANAKA
NANDITA - NANAKIKA
NANDO - NANAKO
NANETTE - NANEKI
NANI - NANI
NANIDA - NANIKA
NANJI - NANII
NANNIE - NANIE
NANO - NANO
NAOKO - NAOKO
NAOMI - NAOMI
NAPOLEON - NAPOLEONU
NAQUELLE - NAKELE
NARAE - NALAE
NARAIN - NALAINE
NARCISCO - NALAKIKEKO
NARDA - NALAKA

NARDEGE - NALAKEKE
NARDOS - NALAKOKU
NARELLE - NALELE
NARGES - NAKEKI
NARJIT - NALIIKE
NARLENE - NALENE
NARI - NALI
NARIE - NALIE
NARIMON - NALIMONU
NARINE - NALINE
NARISSA - NALIKA
NASEEM - NAKEMI
NASH - NAKA
NASHAWN - NAKAWANA
NASHIRA - NAKILA
NASHIYA - NAKIIA
NASHON - NAKONU
NASIA - NAKIA
NASREEN - NAKALENI
NASRIN - NAKALINE
NASRULLAH - NAKALULAHA
NASSER - NAKELI
NASSIF - NAKIPE
NATAKA - NAKAKA
NATALEE - NAKALE
NATALIA - NAKALIA
NATALIE - NAKELI
NATALINA - NAKALINA
NATALYA - NAKALIA
NATARSHA - NAKALAKA

NATASCHA - NAKAKAKA
NATASHA - NAKAKA
NATASHYA - NAKAKIA
NATE - NAKE
NATERCIA - NAKELIKIA
NATESHA - NAKEKA
NATHALIE - NAKALIE
NATHALY - NAKALI
NATHAN - NAKANA
NATHANIA - NAKANIA
NATHANIEL - NAKANAELA
NATHASCHA - NAKAKAKA
NATHELYN - NAKELINE
NATHMANIEL - NAKAMANIELI
NATIANNA - NAKIANA
NATIEKA - NAKIEKA
NATIKA - NAKIKA
NATINOH - NAKINOHU
NATISHA - NAKIKA
NATIVIDAD - NAKIWIKAKA
NATIYA - NAKIIA
NATORIA - NAKOLIA
NATOYA - NAKOIA
NATRISHA - NALIKA
NATSUMI - NAKUMI
NAUNIE - NAUNIE
NAUREEN - NAULENI
NAUZIA - NAUKIA
NAVA - NAWA
NAVARRA - NAWALA

NAVARROW - NAWALOWU
NAVI - NAWI
NAVIN - NAWINE
NAVNEETH - NAWANEKI
NAVON - NAWONU
NAVYA - NAWIA
NAWKWEGEEJIG - NAWAKAWEKEIIKE
NAYA - NAIA
NAYANA - NAIANA
NAYDENE - NAIKENE
NAYELI - NAIELI
NAYIA - NAIIA
NAYIB - NAIIPE
NAYLANI - NAILANI
NAYOUNG - NAIOUNO
NAYSHA - NAIKA
NAZ - NAKA
NAZARAINA - NAKALAINA
NAZARUDDIN - NAKALUKINE
NAZEL - NAKELI
NAZIG - NAKIKE
NAZIMA - NAKIMA
NAZNIN - NAKANINE
N'DANTE - NA'AKANAKE
NEAH - NEAHA
NEAL - NIALA
NEALY - NEALI
NEANNA - NEANA
NEAOMA - NEAOMA
NECHAMA - NEKAMA

NECIAH - NEKIAHA

NECLAIR - NEKILAILE

NECIA - NEKIA

NED - NEKI

NEDDA - NEKA

NEDRA - NEKILA

NEDY - NEKI

NEEKA - NEKAI

NEELA - NELA

NEELAM - NELAMA

NEELY - NELI

NEEMER - NEMELI

NEENA - NENA

NEERAJ - NELAI

NEESHA - NEKA

NEETA - NEKA

NEEVE - NEWE

NEFRA - NEPILA

NEFTI - NEPIKI

NEGIN - NEKINE

NEGRON - NEKILONU

NEHA - NEHA

NEHEMIAH - NEHEMIA

NEHMAT - NEHIMAKA

NEIDA - NEIKA

NEIKHIA - NEIKEHIA

NEIL - NEILE

NEILIA - NEILIA

NEILSON - NEILEKONU

NEISIE - NEIKIE

NEJEEBA - NEIEPA

NEKA - NEKA

NEKAILA - NAKAILA

NEKIA - NEKIA

NELBERT - NELIPEKI

NELDA - NELA

NELEIGH - NELEIKEHE

NELIDA - NELIKA

NELKY - NELIKI

NELLIE - NELE

NELMA - NELEMA

NENA - NENA

NELENE - NELENE

NELIA - NELIA

NELL - NELI

NELLAINE - NELAINE

NELMARIE - NELIMALIE

NELS - NELIKI

NELSON - NELEKONA

NEMAIA - NEMAIA

NEMESIA - NEMEKIA

NEMIKO - NEMIKO

NEMRODITZ - NEMILOKIKEKE

NENA - NENA

NENITA - NENIKA

NEONA - NEONA

NEPHI - NEPI

NEPTUNE - NEPIKUNE

NEQUISHIA - NEKIIKIA

NEREIDA - NELEIKA

NEREL - NELELI

NERIAH - NELIAHA

NERISSA - NELIKA

NERLIN - NELINE

NERMINA - NELIMINA

NEROSHA - NELOKA

NERY - NELI

NERYMAR - NELIMALA

NESAN - NEKANA

NESS - NEKI

NESSIE - NEKIE

NESTA - NEKA

NESTONEL - NEKONELI

NESTOR - NEKOLU

NETA - NEKA

NETANA - NEKANA

NETHANIAL - NEKANIALA

NETTIE - NEKI

NEUSA - NEUKA

NEVA - NEWA

NEVADA - NEWAKA

NEVAEH - NEWAEHI

NEVDEEP - NEWIKEPI

NEVE - NEWE

NEVENKA - NEWENIKA

NEVIKA - NEWIKA

NEVIN - NEWINE

NEVINDER - NEWINEKELI

NEVIO - NEWIO

NEVLYN - NEWILINE

NEWANA - NEWANA

NEWELL - NEWELE

NEWERTON - NEWEKONU

NEWT - NEWIKI

NEWTON - NEWIKONU

NEYLA - NEILA

NEYSA - NEIKA

NEZAR - NEKALA

NEZARINE - NEKALINE

NGA - NA

NGAIRE - NAILE

NGHIA - NAHIA

NGOC - NOKU

NGURE - NULE

NGUYET - NUIEKI

NHANDECI - NAHANAKEKI

NHANEYA - NAHANEIA

NHU -NAHU

NIA - NIA

NIAMBI - NIAMAPI

NIAMH - NIAMAHA

NIARA - NIALA

NIAS - NIAKA

NIASHA - NIAKA

NIBY - NIPI

NICANOR - NIKANOLU

NICER - NIKELI

NICHELLE - NIKELE

NICHOLA - NIKOLA

NICHOLAS - NIKOLO

NICHOLAUS - NIKOLAUKO

NICHOLE - NIKOLE

NICHOLO - NIKOLO

NICK - NIKO

NICKEY - NIKEKEI

NICKI - NIKEKI

NICKIESHA - NIKEKIEKA

NICKLA - NIKEKELA

NICKOLE - NIKEKOLE

NICKY - NIKEKI

NICO - NIKO

NICOLA - NIKOLA

NICOLAI - NIKOLAI

NICOLAS - NIKOLAKA

NICOLE - NIKOLE

NICOLENA - NIKOLENA

NICOLETTE - NIKOLEKE

NICOLINA - NIKOLINA

NICOLO - NIKOLO

NIDA - NIKA

NIDIAM - NIKIAMA

NIECE - NIEKE

NIECY - NIEKI

NIEK - NIEKI

NIEKIHA - NIEKIHA

NIEL - NIELI

NIERVES - NIELIWEKI

NIEVA - NIEWA

NIEVE - NIEWE

NIEVES - NIEWEKI

NIGEL - NIKELI

NIHAL - NIHALA

NIHMAL - NIHEMALA

NIJINA - NIIINA

NIK - NIKE

NIKAELLA - NIKAELA

NIKESH - NIKEKI

NIKHILL - NIKEHILE

NIKI - NIKI

NIKIA - NIKIA

NIKIMA - NIKIMA

NIKISHA - NIKIKA

NIKITA - NIKIKA

NIKIYA - NIKIIA

NIKKA - NIKA

NIKKELLE - NIKELE

NIKKI - NIKI

NIKKOLE - NIKOLE

NIKO - NIKO

NIKOLAS - NIKOLAKA

NIKOLAUS - NIKOLAUKO

NIKOLAY - NIKOLAI

NIKOLE - NIKOLE

NIKOLETTA - NIKOLEKA

NIKOLETTE - NIKOLEKE

NIKOLI - NIKOLI

NILA - NILA

NILAN - NILANA

NILAND - NILANAKA

NILAY - NILAI

NILDA - NILA

NILEENA - NILENA

NILES - NILEKI

NILO - NILO

NILS - NILEKE

NILSA - NILEKA

NIMA - NIMA

NIMAL - NIMALA

NIMI - NIMI

NIMMI - NIMI

NIMON - NIMONU

NIMRIT - NIMELIKE

NIMSI - NIMEKI

NINA – NINA

NINET - NINEKE

NINETTE - NINEKE

NINFA - NINEPA

NING - NINE

NINI - NINI

NINIVAH - NINIWAHA

NINON - NINONU

NINSHENG - NINEKENI

NIOVIS - NIOWIKE

NIPA - NIPA

NIQUEL - NIKELE

NIQUI - NIKI

NIQUILENE - NIKILENE

NIRALI - NILALI

NIRAV - NILAWA

NIRUSHA - NILUKA

NIRVANA - NILEWANA

NISE - NIKE

NISHA - NIKA

NISHAN - NIKANA

NISHONDA - NIKONUKA

NISIN - NIKINE

NISSA - NIKA

NISSANA - NIKANA

NIT - NIKE

NITA - NIKA

NITTAYA - NIKAIA

NITU - NIKU

NITYA - NIKIA

NITZA - NIKEKA

NIVA - NIWA

NIVEDITA - NIWEKIKA

NIVIA - NIWIA

NIVIAH - NIWIAHA

NIXIE - NIKIE

NIXIETTA - NIKIEKA

NIXON - NIKONU

NIYA - NIIA

NIZAR - NIKALA

NJANSI - NIANAKI

NJERI - NIELI

N'KEBAH - NA'AKEPAHA

N'KEYAH - NA'AKEIAHA

NNAMDI - NAMAKI

NNEKA - NEKA

NNIROE - NILOE

NOAH - NOA

NOAL - NOALA

NOAM - NOAMA

NOBLE - NOPULE

NOBUKO - NOPUKO

NOCA - NOKA

NOE - NOE

NOEL - NOELA

NOELEEN - NOLENI

NOELENE - NOELENE

NOELIA - NOELIA

NOELLE - NOELE

NOELLINE - NOELINE

NOEMI - NOEMI

NOEVA - NOEWA

NOEY - NOEI

NOHELY - NOHELI

NOKE - NOKE

NOL - NOLU

NOLA - NOLA

NOLAN - NOLANA

NOLEAN - NOLEANA

NOLEND - NOLENIKI

NOM - NOMU

NOMITA - NOMIKA

NONA - NONA

NONI - NONI

NONIQUE - NONIKE

NONNIE - NONIE

NOON - NONU

NOONTAN - NONUKANA

NOOR - NOLU

NOOTAN - NOKANA

NORA - NOLA

NORAH - NOLAHA

NORAINI - NOLAINI

NORASHIKIN - NOLAKIKINE

NORBERT - NOLEPELEKO

NORBERTO - NOLUPEKO

NOREEN - NOLINA

NORELY - NOLELI

NORENE - NOLENE

NORIKO - NOLIKO

NORINE - NOLINE

NORITA - NOLIKA

NORKA - NOKA

NORLISHA - NOLIKA

NORLYN - NOLINE

NORM - NOLUMU

NORMA - NOMA

NORMAN - NOLEMANA

NORMANDIE - NOLUMANAKIE

NORREN - NOLENI

NORRIE - NOLIE

NORRIS - NOLEKA

NORRISA - NOLIKA

NORTHER - NOKELI

NORTON - NOKONU

NORVAL - NOLUWALA

NOSHEEN - NOKENI

NOU - NOU

NOUDJAL - NOUKIALA

NOVA - NOWA

NOVELLA - NOWELA

NOVLET - NOWULEKI

NOVLETTE - NOWULEKE

NOVIA - NOWIA

NOYAL - NOIALA

NRUPA - NALUPA

N'RYAH - NA'ALIAHA

NTSHOKO - NAKOKO

NUALA - NUALA

NUB - NUPO

NUMIA - NUMIA

NUNO - NUNO

NUOR - NUOLU

NUR - NULO

NURISSA - NULIKA

NURVIN - NULOWINE

NUTAN - NUKANA

NUZULA - NUKULA

NVEKA - NAWEKA

NWAMAKA - NAWAMAKA

NYAH - NIAHA

NYANNE - NIANE

NYASHA - NIAKA

NY'ASIA - NI'AKIA

NYCKOLAS - NIKEKOLAKA

NYDIA - NIKIA

NYECE - NIEKE

NYISHA - NIIKA

NYKO - NIKO

NYKOLE - NIKOLE

NYLA - NILA

NY'LEE - NI'ELE

NYLES - NILEKI

NYM - NIME

NYMPHA - NIMEPA

NYOKA - NIOKA

NYREE - NILE

NYSSA - NIKA

N'ZINGA - NA'AKINA

NZINGA - NAKINA

O

FIRST NAMES

OANH - OANAHA

OAKLEY - OAKALEI

OAKLY - OAKALI

OBAMA - OPAMA

OBDULIA - OPUKULIA

OBERLEIN - OPELEINE

OBI - OPI

OBINNA - OPINA

O'BRIAN - O'UPULIANA

O'BRIEN - O'UPULIENI

OCEAN - OKEANA

OCEANA - OKEANA

OCIE - OKIE

OCKE - OKUKE

OCTAVIA - OKAWIA

OCTAVIAN - OKAWIANA

OCTAVIO - OKAWIO

OCTAVIUS - OKAWIUKO

ODALIS - OKALIKE

ODALYS - OKALIKE

ODA MAE - OKA MAE

ODELIA - OKELIA

ODELL - OUKELI

ODEN - OKENI

ODESSA - OKEKA

ODETTE - OKEKE

ODIKA - OKIKA

ODILE - OKILE

ODIN - OKINE

OFELIA - OPELIA

OFIR - OPILE

OHENEBA - OHENEPA

OICHEE - OIKE

OIVIND - OIWINEKE

O'KEEFE - O'UKEPE

OKKE - OKE

OKSANA - OKUKANA

OLA - OLA

OLAITAN - OLAIKANA

OLAF - OLAPA

OLAFEMI - OLAPEMI

OLANDO - OLANAKO

OLAV - OLAWA

OLE - OLE

OLEG - OLEKI

OLGA - OLEKA

OGDEN - OKUKENI

OLGIE - OLUKIE

OLGUI - OLUKUI

OLENE - OLENE

OLETA - OLEKA

OLIHN - OLIHENE

OLIMPIA - OLIMEPIA

OLIN - OLINE

OLIVE - OLIWA

OLIVEA - OLIWEA

OLIVER – OLIWA

OLIVIA - OLIWIA

OLIVYA - OLIWIA

OLLA - OLA

OLLE - OLE

OLLIE - OLIE

OLLIFFE - OLIPE

OLLY - OLI

OLSEN - OLUKENI

OLU- OLU

OLUSEUN - OLUKEUNO

OLUYEMISI - OLUIEMIKI

OLYA - OLIA

OLYMPIA - OLIMIPIA

OMA - OMA

OMALA - OMALA

OMAR -OMALA

OMARA - OMALA

OMARAX - OMALAKA

OMARI - OMALI

OMAYRA - OMAILA

OMEDA - OMEKA

OMEGA - OMEKA

OMEISHCIA - OMEIKEKIA

OMER - OMELI

OMITA - OMIKA

ONA - ONA

ONALEE - ONALE

ONARGA - ONAKA

ONDINE - ONUKINE

ONDRA - ONUKULA

ONDRIA - ONUKULIA

ONECIMA - ONEKIMA

ONEIDA - ONEIKA

O'NEIL - O'UNEILE

ONESHA - ONEKA

ONESTY - ONEKI

ONG - ONU

ONIEKA - ONIEKA

ONIERA - ONIELA

ONIKA - ONIKA

ONIS - ONIKE

ONNIE - ONIE

ONUTE - ONUKE

OOLA - OLA

OONA - ONA

OONALEYNA - ONALEINA

OPAL - OPALA

OPALLINA - OPALINA

OPHELIA – OPELIA

OPRA - OPULA

OPREA - OPULEA

ORA - OLA

ORALIA - OLALIA

ORAPHIM - OLAPIME

ORBERT - OLUPEKI

ORDRA - OLUKULA

ORELIA - OLELIA

OREN - OLENI

ORETHA - OLEKA

ORESTES - OLEKEKI

ORETTA - OLEKA

ORI - OLI

ORIA - OLIA

ORIN – OLINA
ORION - OLIONU
ORISHA - OLIKA
ORIT - OLIKE
ORLA - OLA
ORLAUNDA - OLAUNOKA
ORLANDI - OLANAKI
ORLANDO - OLANAKO
ORLANTHIA - OLANAKIA
ORLENA - OLENA
ORLENE - OLENE
ORLIN - ORLINE
ORLINDA - OLINEKA
ORLIS - OLIKE
ORLY - OLI
ORNELLE - OLUNELE
ORNETTA - OLUNEKA
ORPAH - OLEPA
ORPHA - OLEPA
ORRIS - OLIKA
ORSON - OLUKONU
ORVALEE - OLUWALE
ORVAL - OLUWALA
ORVELINE - OLUWELINE
ORVIE - OLUWIE
ORVILLE- OLUWILE
OSAGYEFO - OKAKIEPO
OSAME - OKAME
OSBALDO - OKUPALO
OSCAR - OKA

OSHAELA - OKAELA
O'SHAY - O'UKAI
O'SHEA - O'UKEA
OSHEA - OKEA
O'SHEN - O'UKENI
OSHEN - OKENI
OSIE - OKIE
OSMAN - OKUMANA
OSMOND - OKUMONUKU
OSTARA - OKALA
OSTYN - OKINE
OSWALD - OKEWOLEKA
OTELIA - OKELIA
OTHA - OKA
OTILIO - OKILIO
OTIS - OKIKE
OTTO- OKA
OVADA - OWAKA
OVERLEAN - OWELEANA
OVIDIO - OWIKIO
OWEN - OWENA
OXY - OKI
OYA - OIA
OZEN - OKENI
OZLUM - OKULUMO
OZZIE - OKIE
OZZY - OKI

P

FIRST NAMES

PA - PA
PABLO - PAPALO
PACE - PAKE
PACEY - PAKEI
PACITA - PAKIKA
PACO - PAKO
PADEN - PAKENI
PADI - PAKI
PADMAVATHY - PAKAMAWAKI
PADMÉ - PAKAMAÉA
PAEA - PAEA
PAENG - PAENI
PAESE - PAEKE
PAGE - PAKE
PAIGE - PEIKE
PAISLEY - PAIKELEI
PAITEN - PAIKENI
PAKEE - PAKE
PALAK - PALAKA
PALLAS - PALAKA
PALMA - PALAMA
PALMER - PALAMELI
PALMIRA - PALAMILA
PALOMA - PALOMA
PAM - PAMA
PAMELA - PAMILA
PAMITA - PAMIKA
PANAGIOTI - PANAKIOKI
PANDORA - PANAKOLA
PANG - PANA

PANG IB - PANA IPE
PANKAJ - PANAKAI
PANSY - PANEKI
PANTELIS - PANAKELIKE
PAO - PAO
PAOLA - PAOLA
PAOLO - PAOLO
PAOULINE - PAOULINE
PAOULYNE - PAOULINE
PAPA - PAPA
PAPO - PAPO
PAR - PALA
PARA - PALA
PARAG - PALAKA
PARALEE - PALALE
PARASKEVI - PALAKAKEWI
PARDIS - PALAKIKE
PARESH - PALEKI
PARIMAL - PALIMALA
PARIS - PALIKE
PARISA - PALIKA
PARKE - PAKE
PARKER - PAKELI
PARKS - PAKAKA
PARLEY - PALEI
PARMINDER - PALAMINEKELI
PARRI - PALI
PARRISH - PALIKE
PARTH - PAKA
PARUL - PALULO

PARVATHY - PALAWAKI
PARVENDER - PALAWENIKELI
PARY - PALI
PASCAL - PAKAKALA
PASCOAL - PAKAKOALA
PASCUALA - PAKAKUALA
PASHA - PAKA
PASHEN - PAKENI
PASHOE - PAKOE
PASQUALE - PAKAKALE
PASTEL - PAKELI
PASTOR - PAKOLU
PASTORA - PAKOLA
PAT - PAKA
PATE - PAKE
PATIA - PAKIA
PATIENCE - AHONUI
PATIRA - PAKILA
PATON - PAKONU
PATRA - PALA
PATREE - PALE
PATREENA – PALENA
PATRICA - PALIKA
PATRICE - PALIKE
PATRICIA - PAKELEKIA
PATRICIO - PALIKIO
PATRICK - PAKELIKA
PATRIK - PALIKE
PATRISHA - PALIKA
PATROUSKI - PALOUKOKI

PATSY - PAKI
PATTERSON - PAKELIKONU
PATTI - PAKI
PATTY - PAKI
PAUL - PAULO
PAULA - PAULA
PAULETTE - POLOKE
PAULINA - PAULINA
PAULINE - POLINA
PAULIUS - PAULIUKO
PAULO - PAULO
PAULON - PAULONU
PAVALI - PAWALI
PAVEL - PAWELI
PAVLO - PAWALO
PAVLOS - PAWALOKU
PAXTON - PAKAKONU
PAYAL - PAIALA
PAYAM - PAIAMA
PAYGE - PAIKE
PAYNE - PAINE
PAYTON -PAIKONU
PAZ - PAKA
PEACE - PEAKE
PEACH - PEAKA
PEACHES - PEAKEKI
PEALER - PEALELI
PEANUT - PEANUKO
PEARL - MOMI
PEARLA - PEALA

PEARLINE - PEALINE

PEARLY - PEALI

PEARSON - PEALAKONU

PEATHON - PEAKONU

PEBBLES - PEPILEKI

PEDRO - PEKELO

PEER-MARIE - PELI-IMALIE

PEET - PEKI

PEG - PEKI

PEGGIE - PEKIE

PEGGY - PEKI

PEI GHEE - PEI KAHE

PEIGHTON - PEIKEHEKONU

PEKELO - PEKELO

PEK HOON - PEKI HONU

PELLAGIA - PELAKIA

PEMPI - PEMIPI

PENELOPE - PENELOPE

PENNY - PENI

PENSON - PENIKONU

PENTHEA - PENIKEA

PEONY - PEONI

PEPE - PEPE

PEPI - PEPI

PEPPER - PEPELI

PEPSI - PEPIKI

PER - PELI

PERCY - PELEKI

PERFECTO - PELIPEKO

PERI - PELI

PERILLA - PELILA

PERKIN - PEKINE

PERLA - PELA

PERNELL - PELINELI

PERNILLA - PELINILA

PERRI - PELI

PERRIN - PELINE

PERRINE - PELINE

PERRIS - PELIKE

PERRY - PELEKI

PERSEPHONE - PELIKEPONE

PERSIA - PELIKIA

PERSIS - PELIKIKE

PARVIN - PALAWINE

PETA - PEKA

PETE - PEKE

PETELLE - PEKELE

PETER - PIKA

PETERSON - PEKELIKONU

PATHMAKUMAR - PAKAMAKUMALA

PETRA - PELA

PETTER - PEKELI

PETTIS - PEKIKE

PETULA - PEKULA

PEYTEN - PEIKENI

PEYTON - PEIKONU

PFEIFFER - PAPEIPELI

PHAIDRA - PAIKELA

PHALISHA - PALIKA

PHANH - PANAHA

235.

PHARABY - PALAPI
PHAYVANH - PAIWANAHA
PHEAV - PEAWA
PHEBE - PEPE
PHEDIANA - PEKIANA
PHEDRA - PEKILA
PHELLY - PELI
PHENIX - PENIKE
PHIL - PILI
PHILAMER - PILAMELI
PHILANA - PILANA
PHILANH - PILANAHA
PHILBRICK - PILEPELIKEKE
PHILICIA - PILIKIA
PHILINE - PILINE
PHILIP - PILIPO
PHILIPPA - PILIPA
PHILIPPE - PILIPE
PHILL - PILE
PHILLIP - PILIPO
PHILIPOSE - PILIPOKE
PHILLIPPE - PILIPE
PHILLIPS - PILIPEKE
PHILOMINA - PILOMINA
PHIM - PIME
PHINNAEUS - PINAEUKO
PHI PHI - PI PI
PHOEBE - PO'IPE
PHOENIX - POENIKE
PHOUA - POUA

PHUC - PUKO
PHUONG - PUONU
PHYL - PILE
PHYLICIA - PILIKIA
PHYLLIDA - PILIKA
PHYLLIS - PILIKI
PIA - PIA
PIAMAN - PIAMANA
PICASSO - PIKAKO
PICHI - PIKI
PIERCE - PIELIKE
PIERRE - PIELE
PIERRICK - PIELIKEKE
PIERS - PELIKI
PIERSON - PIELIKONU
PIET - PIEKI
PIETRA - PIELA
PIETRO - PIELO
PILAR - PILALA
PILECE - PILEKE
PILUCA - PILUKA
PINA - PINA
PINING - PININE
PING - PINE
PINKY - PINEKI
PIO-PYO - PIO-UPIO
PIPA - PIPA
PIPAY - PIPAI
PIPER - PIPELI
PISEY - PIKEI

PIYUSH - PIIUKO
PLACIDO - PALAKIKO
PLEAS - PALEAKA
PLEXICO - PALEKIKO
PLEZ - PALEKI
PLINY - PALINI
PLUMMER - PALUMELI
POANA - POANA
POE - POE
POGISA - POKIKA
POH YIN - POHU IINE
POI - POI
POLET - POLEKI
POLIANA - POLIANA
POLYA - POLIA
PO-LIN - PO-ULINE
POLINA - POLINA
POLLY - POLE
POLLYANNA - POLIANA
PONA - PONA
PONCECA - PONUKEKA
PONDA - PONUKA
PONDER - PONUKELI
PONG - PONU
PONSI - PONUKI
POOJA - POIA
POONAM - PONAMA
POORNIMA - POLUNIMA
POOVESHINI - POWEKINI
POPCORN - POPUKOLUNU

POPPY - POPI
PORCHA - POLUKA
PORFIDIA - POLUPIKIA
PORTER - POKELI
PORTIA - POLIKIA
PORTZ - POKUKU
PORYA - POLIA
POTTER - POKELI
POVL - POWULU
PRABHAKAR - PALAPAHAKALA
PRABHJOT - PALAPAHIOKU
PRACHI - PALAKI
PRAFUL - PALAPULO
PRAISE - PALAIKE
PRAKASH - PALAKAKA
PRAMILA - PALAMILA
PRANAV - PALANAWA
PRAPTI - PALAPAKI
PRASAD - PALAKAKA
PRASANNA - PALAKANA
PRASHANT - PALAKANAKA
PRASHANTI - PALAKANAKI
PRATHYUSHA - PALAKIUKA
PRATIKSHA - PALAKIKEKA
PRATIMA - PALAKIMA
PRAVALLIKA - PALAWALIKA
PRAVEEN - PALAWENI
PRAXEDES - PALAKEKEKI
PREBAH - PALEPAHA
PRECIOUS - PALEKIOUKO

PREDERICK - PALEKELIKEKE

PREECE - PALEKE

PREET - PALEKI

PREETH - PALEKI

PREETHA - PALEKA

PREETI - PALEKI

PREETIKA - PALEKIKA

PREM - PALEMI

PREMLATHA - PALEMILAKA

PREN - PALENI

PRENESS - PALENEKI

PRENNA - PALENA

PRENTISS - PALENIKIKE

PRESCIOUS - PALEKIKIOUKO

PRESHA - PALEKA

PRESLEE - PALEKILE

PRESLEY - PALEKILEI

PRESSLIE - PALEKILIE

PRESTINE - PALEKINE

PRESTON - PELEKONA

PREVAL - PALEWALA

PRICE - PALIKE

PRISCILLA - PELEKILA

PRIMROSE – PALIMELOKE

PRINCE - PALINEKE

PRINCESS - PALINEKEKI

PRINTOUS - PALINEKOUKO

PRISKA - PALIKEKA

PRISSY - PALIKI

PRISTINE - PALIKINE

PRITHVRI - PALIKEWELI

PRITPAL - PALIKEPALA

PRIYA - PALIIA

PRIYANKA - PALIIANAKA

PROMISE - PALOMIKE

PROMMYSE - PALOMIKE

PROSE - PALOKE

PROVIDENCE - PALOWIKENIKE

PROVIDENCIA - PALOWIKENIKIA

PRISCILLA - PELIKILA

PRISMA- PALIKIMA

PRIYA - PALIIA

PROMISE - PALOMIKE

PRU - PALU

PRUDENCE - PELUKINA

PRUDENCIA - PALUKENIKIA

PRYAM - PALIAMA

PTOLEMY - PAKOLEMI

PUI - PUI

PUIYAN - PUIIANA

PUFF - PUPO

PUNIT - PUNIKE

PURITA - PULIKA

PURING - PULINE

PURSHOTAM - PULIKOKAMA

PURVI - PULOWI

PUSHPA - PUKOPA

PUTZIE - PUKOKIE

PYONG - PIONU

PYTHAGORAS - PIKAKOLAKA

Q

FIRST NAMES

QABIL - KAPILE

QAYLYN - KAILINE

QA'TICIA - KA'AKIKIA

QIANA - KIANA

QIN - KINE

QINA - KINA

QINYL - KINILE

QINZHU - KINEKEHU

QUADE - KAKE

QUAID - KAIKE

QUAKE - KAKE

QUALEEM - KALEMI

QUALLS - KALAKA

QUAN - KUKANA

QUANA - KUKANA

QUANG - KA'ANA

QUANIESHA - KANIEKA

QUANTAVIOUS - KANAKAWIOUKO

QUANTAY - KANAKAI

QUANTERIUS - KANAKELIUKO

QUANTIA - KANAKIA

QUANTRICIA - KANALIKIA

QUARDESHA - KALAKEKA

QUASHAYA - KAKAIA

QA'SHEEN - KA'AKENI

QUAY - KAE

QUAYSON - KAEKONU

QUE - KE

QUEENESTER - KENEKELI

QUEENIE – KU'ENE

QUEHNITAH - KEHINIKAHA

QUEINT - KEINEKE

QUENTIN - KENEKINA

QUERUBE - KELUPE

QUERUBIN - KELUPINE

QUETZALI - KEKIKALI

QUIANNA - KIANA

QUILLA JUNE - KILA IUNE

QUIMBY - KIMEPI

QUINA - KENA

QUINCE - KINEKE

QUINCY - KINEKI

QUINDETTA - KINEKEKA

QUINETTA - KINEKA

QUINLAN - KAINELANA

QUINN - KINA

QUINNY - KINI

QUINTELLA - KINEKELA

QUINTEN - KINEKENI

QUINTESSENCE - KINEKEKENIKE

QUINTEZ - KINEKEKI

QUINTIN - KINEKINE

QUINTO -KINEKO

QUINTON - KINEKINA

QUINYRA - KINILA

QUIRA - KILA

QUISHAWN - KIKAWANA

QUIXOTE - KIKOKE

QURUM - KULUMO

QU' SHENA - KU'O KENA

QUTATSHEIA - KUKAKEIA
QUVANTE - KUWANAKE
QUYEN- KIENI
QUYENANH - KIENANAHA
QWAN - KAWANA
QYLA - KILA
QUYNH - KINEHE
QYYANTAHH - KIANAKAHA

R

FIRST NAMES

RAADHA - LAKAHA

RAANIN - LANINE

RA'ANN - LA'ANA

RAASHAND - LAKANAKA

RABA - LAPA

RABIA - LAPIA

RABIATUL - LAPIAKULO

RABORN - LAPOLUNU

RACE - LAKE

RACHANA - LAKANA

RACHAEL - LAKAELI

RACHAL - LAKALA

RACHEAL - LAKEALA

RACHEL - LEIKELI

RACHELIN - LAKELINE

RACHELL - LEIKELI

RACHELLE - LAKELE

RACHEYAL - LAKEIALA

RACHID - LAKIKE

RACHNA - LAKANA

RACHON - LAKONU

RACHYL - LAKILE

RACQUELL - LAKAKELI

RADA - LAKA

RADEEN - LAKENI

RADHAKRISHNA - LAKAHAKALIKENA

RADHIKA - LAKAHIKA

RADISLAV - LAKIKELAWA

RADKA - LAKAKA

RADMILLA - LAKAMILA

RADON - LAKONU

RADONNA - LAKONA

RAE - LAE

RAEANNA - LAEANA

RAED - LAEKI

RAE' DAWN - LAE'I KAWANA

RAEGAN - LAEKANA

RAELENE - LAELENE

RAELLEAH - LAELEAHA

RAELYN - LAELINE

RAENA - LAENA

RAESEAN - LAWKEANA

RAEVEN - LAEWENI

RAEYLE - LAEILE

RAFAEL - LAPAELI

RAFAL - LAPALA

RAFE - LAPE

RAFFEHA - LAPEHA

RAFFERTY - LAPEKI

RAFIA - LAPIA

RAFIK - LAPIKE

RAGAN - LAKANA

RAGHAV - LAKAHAWA

RAGHU - LAKAHU

RAGNHILD - LAKANAHILE

RAHAMAT - LAHAMAKA

RAHAYU - LAHAIU

RAHEEM - LAHEMI

RAHIM - LAHIME

RAHIMAH - LAHIMAHA

RAHMA - LAHAMA

RAHMAD - LAHAMAKA

RAHSAAN - LAHAKANA

RAHUL - LAHULO

RAIANNE - LAIANE

RAICHELLE - LAIKELE

RAIDA - LAIKA

RAIF - LAIPE

RAIK - LAIKE

RAIN - LAINE

RAINA - LAINA

RAINE - LAINE

RAINELLE - LAINELE

RAINER - LAINELI

RAINHARDT - LAINEHALAKAKA

RAINY - LAINI

RA'ISAH - LA'IKAHA

RAISS - LAIKE

RAIZA - LAIKA

RAJ - LAI

RAJA - LAIA

RAJAGURU - LAIAKULU

RAJAN - LAIANA

RAJAT - LAIAKA

RAJEEVE - LAIEWE

RAJESH - LAIEKI

RAJI - LAII

RAJIV - LAIIWE

RAJNA - LAINA

RAJNI - LAINI

RAJRANI - LAILANI

RAJVIR - LAIWILE

RAKAYLA - LAKAILA

RAKELLE - LAKELE

RAKESH - LAKEKI

RAKHIM - LAKAHIME

RAKIA - LAKIA

RAKISHA - LAKIKA

RAKSHA - LAKAKA

RAKSHAW - LAKAKAWA

RAKSHU - LAKAKU

RALEIGH - LALEIKEHE

RALEN - LALENI

RALITSA - LALIKA

RALFRED - LALAPALEKI

RALONDIA - LALONUKIA

RALPH - LALEPA

RALSTON - LALAKONU

RAM - LAMA

RAMA - LAMA

RAMAEL - LAMAELI

RAMAKOTAIAH - LAMAKOKAIAHA

RAMAKOTI - LAMAKOKI

RAMAYA - LAMAIA

RAMBO - LAMAPO

RAMECCA - LAMEKA

RAMEEZ - LAMEKI

RAMESH - LAMEKI

RAMESUS - LAMEKUKO

RAMIL - LAMILE

RAMINDER - LAMINEKELI   RANGARAJAN - LANALAIANA
RAMIRO - LAMILO   RANGER - LANELI
RAMOJUS - LAMOIUKO   RANGIE - LANIE
RAMON – LAMONA   RANIA - LANIA
RAMONA - LAMONA   RANIER - LANIELI
RAMONDA - LAMONUKA   RANIERY - LANIELI
RAMONE - LAMONE   RANIT - LANIKE
RAMSES - LAMAKEKI   RANITTA - LANIKA
RAMSEY - LAMAKI   RANJAN - LANIANA
RAMUS - LAMUKO   RANKIN - LANAKINE
RAMY - LAMI   RANNIE - LANIE
RANA - LANA   RANNIKA - LANIKA
RANAE - LANAE   RANSEL - LANAKELI
RANAH - LANAHA   RANSOM - LANAKOMU
RANCE - LANAKE   RANYL - LANILE
RAND - LANAKA   RAO - LAO
RANDA - LANAKA   RAOUL - LAOULO
RANDAL - LANAKALA   RAPH - LAPA
RANDALE - LANAKALE   RAPHAEL – LAPA'ELA
RANDALL - LANAKALA   RAPHE - LAPE
RANDELL - LANAKELI   RAPUNZAL - LAPUNOKALA
RANDEN - LANAKENI   RAQUEL - LAKALI
RANDI - LANAKI   RASA - LAKA
RANDLE - LANAKALE   RASEENEE - LAKENE
RANDOLPH - LANAKOLUPU   RASHAAD - LAKAKA
RANDOLYN - LANAKOLINE   RASHAAL - LAKALA
RANDY – LANAKI   RASHAD - LAKAKA
RANEE - LANE   RASHADA - LAKAKA
RANESA - LANEKA   RASHANA - LAKANA
RANGA - LANA   RA'SHANN - LA'AKANA

RASHAUN - LAKAUNO

RASHAUNI - LAKAUNI

RASHEED - LAKEKI

RASHEEN - LAKENI

RASHELLE - LAKELE

RASHIA - LAKIA

RASHID - LAKIKE

RASHIDA - LAKIKA

RASHIKA - LAKIKA

RASHITHA - LAKIKA

RASHMI - LAKAMI

RASHMIKA - LAKAMIKA

RASIDI - LAKIKI

RASMUS - LAKAMUKO

RASSIDA - LAKIKA

RASTON - LAKONU

RATAN - LAKANA

RATANA - LAKANA

RATHEANY - LAKEANI

RATNA - LAKANA

RATSAMY - LAKAMI

RAUBIN - LAUPINE

RAUDHAH - LAUKOHAHA

RAUL - LAULA

RAUNAY - LAUNAI

RAVEENA - LAWENA

RAVEN - LAWENI

RAVENNA - LAWENA

RAVI - LAWI

RAVID - LAWIKE

RAVIN - LAWINE

RAWD - LAWAKA

RAWLE - LAWALE

RAWLEY - LAWALEI

RAY - LEI

RAYA - LAIA

RAYAH - LAIAHA

RAYAN - LAIANA

RAYANADA - LAIANAKA

RAYANNE - LAIANE

RAYCE - LAIKE

RAYCHELLE - LAIKELE

RAYE - LAIE

RAYECHELLE - LAIEKELE

RAYFORD - LAIPOLUKU

RAYLEE - LAILE

RAYLEEN - LAILENI

RAYLEN - LAILENI

RAYLENE - LAILENE

RAYLI - LAILI

RAYLIAH - LAILIAHA

RAYLYNN - LAILINE

RAYLYNNE - LAILINE

RAYMA - LAIMA

RAYME - LAIME

RAYMON - LAIMONU

RAYMONA - LAIMONA

RAYMOND - LEIMANA

RAYMUND- LAIMUNOKO

RAYNA - LAINA

RAYNAR - LAINALA

RAYNE - LAINE

RAYNELL - LAINELI

RAYNETTE - LAINEKE

RAYNIKA - LAINIKA

RAYNOLD - LAINOLU

RAYTEVIA - LAIKEWIA

RAYVEN - LAIWENI

RAZAK - LAKAKA

RAZALI - LAKALI

RAZEL - LAKELI

RAZIYA - LAKIIA

REA - LEA

REAGAN - LEAKANA

REAGHAN - LEAKAHANA

REAKY - LEAKI

REAL - LEALA

REANELL - LEANELI

REANN - LEANA

REANNA - LEANA

REARICK - LEALIKEKE

REAS - LEAKA

REBA - LEPA

REBECA - LEPEKA

REBECCA - LEPEKA

REBEKAH - LEPEKAHA

REBEL - LOPELI

RECHEA - LEKEA

RECY - LEKI

RED - LEKI

REDA - LEKA

REDDY - LEKI

REDIJAH - LEKIIAHA

REDITH - LEKIKE

REDMOND - LEKIMONUKU

REDONDA - LOKONUKA

REDZWAN - LEKIKIWANA

REE - LE

REECE - LEKE

REED - LEKI

REEGIN - LEKINI

REEK'QUAN - LEKI'IKANA

REEM - LEMI

REENA - LENA

REESE - LEKE

REESHA - LEKA

REESHAWNA - LEKAWANA

REEVES - LEWEKI

REEYA - LEIA

REEZA - LEKA

REEZAH - LEKAHA

REEZAMARIE - LEKAMALIE

REFUGIO - LEPUKIO

REGALINE - LEKALINE

REGAN - LEKANA

REGEAN - LEKEANA

REGGAYE - LEKAIE

REGGIE - LEKIE

REGINA - LEKINA

REGINAE - LEKINAE

REGINALD - LEKINALA

REGINE - LEKINE

REGINO - LEKINO

REGIS - LEKIKE

RÉGIS - LAÉAKIKE

REGOR - LEKOLU

REID - LEIKE

REIGAN - LEIKANA

REIKO - LEIKO

REILEY - LEILEI

REILLY - LEILI

REIME - LEIME

REINA - LEINA

REINABETH - LEINAPEKI

REINHARDT - LEINEHALAKAKA

REINHOLD - LEINEHOLU

REINO - LEINO

REISHA - LEIKA

REISS - LEIKE

REITA - LEIKA

REJEAN - LEIEANA

REKAH - LEKAHA

REKHA - LEKIHA

RELEINA - LELEINA

RELINA - LELINA

RELLA - LELA

RELLE - LELE

RELLY - LELI

REM - LEMI

REMEDIOS - LEMEKIOKU

REMEL - LEMELI

REMI - LEMI

REMICK - LEMIKEKE

REMINGTON - LEMINEKONU

REMJO - LEMIO

REMY - LEMI

REMZO - LEMIKO

REN - LENI

RENA - LOWENA, LINA

RENAE - LENAE

RENALDA - LENALA

RENALDO - LENALO

RENALITA - LENALIKA

RENARTA - LENAKA

RENATA - LENAKA

RENATE - LENAKE

RENATO - LENAKO

RENAY - LENAI

RENCHIE - LENIKIE

RENDA - LENIKA

RENDELL - LENIKELI

RENDEN - LENIKENI

RENDY - LENIKI

RENE – LINEI

RENEA - LENEA

RENEAKA - LENEAKA

RENEE – LINEI

RENELLE - LENELE

RENELYN - LENELINE

RENESSA - LENEKA

RENETTE - LENEKE

RENEY - LENEI

RENHAN - LENIHANA

RENI - LENI

RENIAH - LENIAHA

RENISH - LENIKE

RENITA - LENIKA

RENJITHA - LENIIKA

RENNARD - LENALAKA

RENNER - LENELI

RENNETTA - LENEKA

RENNIE - LENIE

RENNY - LENI

RENO - LENO

RENS - LENIKI

RENSI - LENIKI

RENUKA - LENUKA

RENZ - LENIKI

RENZY - LENIKI

REQUASHA - LEKAKA

RESA - LEKA

RESERVED - LEKELIWEKI

RESHAD - LEKAKA

RESHAM - LEKAMA

RESHAY - LEKAI

RESHMA - LEKIMA

RESHMI - LEKIMI

RESHONDA - LEKONUKA

RESMI - LEKIMI

RESS - LEKI

RESTI - LEKI

RETA - LEKA

RETHA - LEKA

REUBEN - LEUPENA

REUVEN - LEUWENI

REVA - LEWA

REVAL - LEWALA

REVATI - LEWAKI

REVENA - LEWENA

REVESHINI - LEWEKINI

REVIA - LEWIA

REVONDA - LEWONUKA

REX - LEKE

REXANN - LEKANA

REXANNA - LEKANA

REXFORD - LEKIPOLUKU

REXINE - LEKINE

REXINOR - LEKINOLU

REXY - LEKI

REY - LEI

REYES - LEIEKI

REYLINA - LEILINA

REYMES - LEIMEKI

REYMUNDO - LEIMUNOKO

REYNA - LEINA

REYNALDO - LEINALO

REYNANTE - LEINANAKE

REYNARD - LEINALAKA

REYNOLDS - LEINOLUKU

REZNY - LEKINI

RHAINNE - LAHAINE

RHANDA - LAHANAKA

RHAPSODY - LAHAPAKOKI

RHAQUEL - LAHAKELI

RHASHANI - LAHAKANI

RHEA - LEHEA

RHEANNE - LAHEANE

RHEANNON - LAHEANONU

RHEN - LEHENI

RHENA - LAHENA

RHESSA - LAHEKA

RHETT - LAHEKI

RHETTE - LAHEKE

RHEZ - LAHEKI

RHIANNA - LAHIANA

RHIANNON - LAHIANONU

RHINA - LAHINA

RHODA - LONAKA

RHODORA - LAHOKOLA

RHOJAI - LAHOIAI

RHOLANDA - LAHOLANAKA

RHONA - LAHONA

RHONDA - LONAKA

RHONNI - LAHONI

RHYANN - LAHIANA

RHYANNON - LAHIANONU

RHYEN - LAHIENI

RHYNER - LAHINELI

RHYS - LAHIKE

RHYTHM - LAHIKEME

RHYU - LAHIU

RHYZEL - LAHIKELI

RIA - LIA

RIAAD - LIAKA

RIAAN - LIANA

RIAN - LIANA

RIANA - LIANA

RIANNA - LIANA

RIANNE - LIANE

RIASHAUNA - LIAKAUNA

RIC - LIKE

RICAH - LIKAHA

RICANN - LIKANA

RICARDO - LIKALAKO

RICCA - LIKA

RICCI - LIKI

RICH - LIKE

RICHANDA - LIKANAKA

RICHANNE - LIKANE

RICHARD - LIKEKE

RICHELE - LIKELE

RICHELLA - LIKELA

RICHELLE - LIKELE

RICHETTA - LIKEKA

RICHIA - LIKIA

RICHIE - LIKIE

RICHIK - LIKIKE

RICHY - LIKI

RICK - LIKA

RICKY - LIKI

RICO - LIKO

RIDGE - LIKEKE

RIDGELY - LIKEKELI

RIDLEY - LIKELEI

RIEDELL - LIEKELI

RIEVON - LIEWONU

RIGEL - LIKELI

RIGGIN - LIKINE

RIGGS - LIKEKE

RIGOBERTO - LIKOPEKO

RIGZEN - LIKEKENI

RIIKKA - LIKA

RIKA - LIKA

RIKAKO - LIKAKO

RIKHYAH - LIKEHIAHA

RIKKE - LIKE

RIKKI - LIKI

RILEA - LILEA

RILEE - LILE

RILEY - LILEI

RIM - LIME

RIMA - LIMA

RIMANTAS - LIMANAKAKA

RIMAS - LIMAKA

RINA - LINA

RINDA - LINEKA

RINGO - LINO

RINKOO - LINEKO

RIO - LIO

RIOGHNACH - LIOKUHANAKA

RIORDAN - LIOLUKANA

RIP - LIPE

RIPLEY - LIPELEI

RISA - LIKA

RISCHAN - LIKEKANA

RISE - LIKE

RISHA - LIKA

RISHI - LIKI

RISHOO - LIKO

RISTO - LIKO

RITA - LIKA

RITAM - LIKAMA

RITCHIE - LIKEKIE

RITHIKA - LIKIKA

RITHVIK - LIKEWIKE

RIVA - LIWA

RIVER - LIWELI

RIVELINO - LIWELINO

RIVON - LIWONU

RIYA - LIIA

RIZWANA - LIKEWANA

RIZZA - LIKA

ROANN - LOANA

ROANNE - LOANE

ROARKE - LOAKE

ROB - LOPU

ROBANN - LOPANA

ROBBIE - LOPIE

ROBBY - LOPI

ROBEL - LOPELI

ROBEN - LOPENI

ROBERT - LOPAKA

ROBERTA - LOPEKA

ROBERTO - LOPEKO

ROBI - LOPI

ROBIN - LOPINE

ROBINETTE - LOPINEKE

ROBS - LOPUKU

ROBY - LOPI

ROBYN - LOPINE

ROCCHINA - LOKINA

ROCCO - LOKO

ROCENA - LOKENA

ROCH - LOKU

ROCHEL - LOKELI

ROCHELLE – LOKELE

ROCIO - LOKIO

ROCK - LOKUKU

ROCKFORD - LOKUKUPOLUKU

ROCKNE - LIKINE

ROCKY - LOLUKI

ROD - LOKA

RODAN - LOKANA

RODANIEL - LOKANIELI

RODDA - LOKA

RODDIE - LOKIE

RODDY - LOKI

RODEL - LOKELI

RODERICK - LOKELIKA

RODGER - LOKUKELI

RODIN - LOKINE

RODINA - LOKINA

RODLYN - LOKULINE

RODLYNN - LOKULINE

RODNEY - LOKENE

RODOLFO - LOKOLUPO

RODRIGO - LUKULIKO

ROE -LOE

ROEDER - LOEKELI

ROEINA - LOEINA

ROEL - LOELI

ROELOF - LOELOPU

ROENA - LOENA

ROGA - LOKA

ROGAN - LOKANA

ROGEL - LOKELI

ROGELENE - LOKELENE

ROGELIO - LOKELIO

ROGER - LOKELA

ROHAN - LOHANA

ROHANI - LOHANI

ROHIL - LOHILE

ROHIT - LOHIKE

ROHITASWAR - LOHIKAKAWALA

ROHN - LOHUNU

ROHSHELL - LOHUKELI

ROISIN - LOIKINE

ROJEAN - LOIEANA

ROLA - LOLA

ROLANA - LOLANA

ROLAND - LOLANA   RONAN - LONANA
ROLANDO - LOLANAKO   RONANDO - LONANAKO
ROLENE - LOLENE   RONDA - LONUKA
ROLF – LOLAPA   RONDAL - LONUKALA
ROLIN - LOLINA   RONDELL - LONUKELI
ROLINDA - LOLINEKA   RONDY - LONUKI
ROLLANDE - LOLANAKE   RONELL - LONELI
ROLLIE - LOLIE   RONELLA - LONELA
ROLLIN - LOLINE   RONENE - LONENE
ROMA - LOMA   RONESHIA - LONEKIA
ROMAN - LOMANA   RONETTE - LONEKE
ROMANA - LOMANA   RONI - LONI
ROMANE - LOMANE   RONIKA - LONIKA
ROMANO - LOMANO   RONIN - LONINE
ROMARIO - LOMALIO   RONISHA - LONIKA
ROMAYA - LOMAIA   RONITA - LONIKA
ROMEO - LOMEO   RONJA - LONIA
ROMERO - LOMELO   RONKE - LONUKE
ROMI - LOMI   RONKYLE - LONUKILE
ROMICHE - LOMIKE   RONNA - LONA
ROMINA - LOMINA   RONNALEE - LONALE
ROMMEL - LOMELI   RONNELL - LONELI
ROMULO - LOMULO   RONNESSA - LONEKA
ROMY - LOMI   RONNI - LONI
RON - LONA   RONNIE - LONIE
RONA - LONA   RONOEL - LONOELI
RONALD - LONALA   RONSON - LONUKONU
RONALDINE - LONALINE   RONYA - LONIA
RONALDO - LONALO   RONYAN - LONIANA
RONALYNN - LONALINE   ROOKS - LOKUKU

ROOPA - LOPA

ROOPAL - LOPALA

ROOPWANTI - LOPUWANAKI

ROOSEVELT - LOKEWELIKI

ROPE - LOPE

ROPER - LOPELI

RORY - LOLI

ROS - LOKU

ROSA - LOKA

ROSAEL - LOKAELI

ROSAKI - LOKAKI

ROSALBA - LOKALAPA

ROSALEE - LOKALE

ROSALI - LOKALI

ROSALIA - LOKALIA

ROSALIE - LOKALIE

ROSALINA - LOKALINA

ROSALIND - LOKALINEKE

ROSALINDA - LOKALINEKA

ROSALITA - LOKALIKA

ROSALYN - LOKALINE

ROSAMOND - LOKAMONUKU

ROSAN - LOKANA

ROSANDA - LOKANAKA

ROSANNA - LOKANA

ROSANGELA - LOKANELA

ROSARIA - LOKALIA

ROSARINHA - LOKALINEHA

ROSARIO - LOKALIO

ROSAURA - LOKAULA

ROSBELI - LOKUPELI

ROSCOE - LOKUKOE

ROSE - LOKE

ROSEANNE - LOKEANA

ROSEBELINDA - LOKEPELINEKA

ROSELIA - LOKELIA

ROSELINE - LOKELINE

ROSELLA - LOKELA

ROSELYN - LOKELINE

ROSEMARIE - LOKEMALIE

ROSEMARY - LOKEMELE

ROSEN - LOKENI

ROSENDO - LOKENIKO

ROSENID - LOKENIKE

ROSETTA - LOKEKA

ROSEZELLIA - LOKEKELIA

ROSHAUNDA - LOKAUNOKA

ROSHELLE - LOKELE

ROSHNI - LOKUNI

ROSIE - LOKIE

ROSILE - LOKILE

ROSINA - LOKINA

ROSITA - LOKIKA

ROSLYN - LOKULINE

ROSS - LOKE

ROSSANI - LAKANI

ROSSANO - LOKANO

ROSSI - LOKI

ROSTISLAV - LOKIKELAWA

ROTALIA - LOKALIA

ROTEM - LOKEMI

ROUEL - LOUELI

ROWAN - LOWANA

ROWDY - LOWUKI

ROWELL - LOWELI

ROWENA - LOWENA

ROWIN - LOWINE

ROXANA - LOKANA

ROXANE - LOKANE

ROXANN - LOKANA

ROXANNE - LOKANA

ROXY - LOKI

ROY - LOI

ROYA - LOIA

ROYAL - LOIALA

ROYALTY - LOIALAKI

ROYANN - LOIANA

ROYCE - LOIKE

ROYDEN - LOIKENA

ROYDON - LOIKONU

ROYLENE - LOILENE

ROYSTON - LOIKONU

ROZA - LOKA

ROZANN - LOKANA

ROZANNE - LOKANE

ROZARIAN - LOKALIANA

ROZELLE - LOKELE

ROZILYN - LOKILINE

RUAIRI - LUAILI

RUBA - LUPA

RUBAL - LUPALA

RUBEN - LUPENA

RUBERTA - LUPEKA

RUBEUS - LUPEUKO

RUBINA - LUPINA

RUBY - LUPE

RUBYE - LUPIE

RUBYMER - LUPIMELI

RUCHIK - LUKIKE

RUCHIKA - LUKIKA

RUDI - LUKI

RUDOLFO - LUKOLOPO

RUDOLPH – LUKOLOPA

RUDY - LUKI

RUDYLINDA - LUKILINEKA

RUEDIGER - LUEKIKELI

RUEGER - LUEKELI

RUELLA - LUELA

RUENELLE - LUENELE

RUFF -LUPO

RUFINA - LUPINA

RUFO - LUPO

RUFUS - LUPE

RUGER - LUKELI

RUI - LUI

RUKHSANA - LUKOHOKANA

RUKMINI - LUKOMINI

RULA - LULA

RULON - LULONU

RUMINA - LUMINA

RUMOR - LUMOLU
RUNE - LUNE
RUNETTE - LUNEKE
RUNK - LUNOKO
RUPA - LUPA
RUPAL - LUPALA
RUPAUL - LUPAULO
RUPEE - LUPE
RUPERT - LUPEKO
RUPIN - LUPINE
RUPINDER - LUPINEKELI
RUSH - LUKO
RUSHDEEYEE - LUKOKEIE
RUSLAN - LUKOLANA
RUSS - LUKE
RUSSELL - LUKELA
RUSSIE - LUKIE
RUSSLEY - LUKOLEI
RUSTICA - LUKIKA
RUSTIN - LUKINE
RUSTON - LUKONU
RUSTY - LUKI
RUSZA - LUKOKA
RUTGER - LUKOKELI
RUTH - LUKA
RUTHANN - LUKANA
RUTHELLA - LUKELA
RUTHIE - LUKIE
RUY - LUI
RUY-DAN - LUI-EKANA

RUZELLE - LUKELE
RUZMIR - LUKOMILE
RYAH - LIAHA
RYAN - LIANA
RYANN - LIANA
RYANNE - LIANE
RYCHEE' - LIKE'I
RYCHELLE - LIKELE
RYCKE - LIKEKE
RYDEN - LIKENI
RYDER - LIKELI
RYEA - LIEA
RYEN - LIENI
RYHAD - LIHAKA
RYKER - LIKELI
RYKKEYYIA - LIKEIIA
RYLAN - LILANA
RYLAND - LILANAKA
RYLEE - LILE
RYLEIGH - LILEIKEHE
RYLER - LILELI
RYLEY - LILEI
RYLIE - LILIE
RYLIN - LILINE
RYMIA - LIMIA
RYNE - LINE
RYNESHA - LINEKA
RYNO - LINO
RYO - LIO
RYOKO - LIOKO

RYQUEL - LIKELI
RYSON - LIKONU
RYU - LIU

S

FIRST NAMES

SAACHI - KAKI

SADIKA - KAKIKA

SAADIAH - KAKIAHA

SADIYAH - KAKIIAHA

SAARAH - KALAHA

SADURI - KAKULI

SABARAH - KAPALAHA

SAEDA - KAEKA

SABELLA - KAPELA

SAEED - KAEKI

SABERA - KAPELA

SAEROMY - KAELOMI

SABET - KAPEKI

SAEVLEN - KAEWILENI

SABIKA - KAPIKA

SAFA - KAPA

SABINA - KAPINA

SAFET - KAPEKI

SABINE - KAPINE

SAFYA - KAPIA

SABLE - KAPALE

SAGAN - KAKANA

SABON - KAPONU

SAGE - KAKE

SABRA - KAPALA

SAGEL - KAKELI

SABREENA - KAPALENA

SAGESSE - KAKEKE

SABRENNA - KAPALENA

SAGHAR - KAKAHALA

SABRI - KAPALI

SAGITA - KAKIKA

SABRIE - KAPALIE

SAGRA - KAKALA

SABRINA - KAPALINA

SAGRARIO - KAKALALIO

SABRYNN - KAPALINE

SAHAR - KAHALA

SABRYNNA - KAPALINA

SAHARA - KAHALA

SABYN - KAPINI

SAHDIA - KAHAKIA

SACARIO - KAKALIO

SAHIL - KAHILE

SACHA - KAKA

SAHRA - KAHALA

SACHIKO - KAKIKO

SAHRIE - KAHALIE

SACHIN - KAKINE

SAI - KAI

SACHSEN - KAKAKENI

SAID - KAIKE

SADAF - KAKAPA

SAIDA - KAIKA

SADE - KAKE

SAIDY - KAIKI

SADEE - KAKE

SAIFOLAU - KAIPOLAU

SADIE - KAKIE

SAIGE - KAIKE

SAIJO - KAIIO

SALOME - KALOME

SAIKARUNA - KAIKALUNA

SALOMON - KALOMONU

SAILOR - KAILOLU

SALONI - KALONI

SAINT - KAINEKE

SALVADOR - KALAWAKOLU

SAINT JOHN - KAINEKE IOHUNU

SALVATORRE - KALAWAKOLE

SAI-ON - KAI-ONU

SALWA - KALAWA

SAJAN - KAIANA

SALYNA - KALINA

SAJITHA - KA'IKA

SAM – KAMA

SAJNA - KAINA

SAMANTHA -KAMANAKA

SAKARA - KAKALA

SAMANTHA-JO - KAMANAKA-IO

SAKEENAH - KAKENAHA

SAMARA - KAMALA

SAKIRA - KAKILA

SAMARE' - KAMALE'I

SAKISHA - KAKIKA

SAMARIA - KAMALIA

SAKTHI - KAKAKI

SAMARNSGRI - KAMALANAKAKALI

SAKURA - KAKULA

SAMEER - KAMELI

SAL - KALA

SAMEYAH - KAMEIAHA

SALA - KALA

SAMI - KAMI

SALEA - KALEA

SAMIA - KAMIA

SALEENA - KALENA

SAMIJO - KAMIIO

SALEM - KALEMI

SAMIR - KAMILE

SALENA - KALENA

SAMIRA - KAMILA

SALETH - KALEKI

SAMIT - KAMIKE

SHALI - KALI

SAMIYAH - KAMIIAHA

SALINA - KALINA

SAMMEEJO - KAMEIO

SALINY - KALINI

SAMMIE - KAMIE

SALLIE - KALIE

SAMMIE-ANGEL - KAMIE-ANELI

SALLIEANNA - KALIEANA

SAMMY - KAMI

SALLY - KALE

SAMONE - KAMONE

SALMA - KALAMA

SAMSON - KAMEKONA

SALMAN - KALAMANA

SAMUAL - KAMUALA

SAMUDRO - KAMUKOLO

SAMUEL - KAMUELA

SAMYA - KAMIA

SANA - KANA

SANADA - KANAKA

SANAZ - KANAKA

SANCHIA - KANAKIA

SANDA - KANAKA

SANDHYA - KANAKAHIA

SANDEE - KANAKE

SANDEEP - KANAKEPI

SANDERSON - KANAKELIKONU

SANDHYA - KANAKAHIA

SANDI - KANAKI

SANDIE - KANI

SANDON - KANAKONU

SANDOR - KANAKOLU

SANDRA - KANELA

SANDRINE - KANAKALINE

SANDRO - KANAKALO

SANDY - KANI

SANEESHA - KANEKA

SANG - KANA

SANGEETA - KANEKA

SANIYA - KANIIA

SANJAY - KANIAI

SANJAYA - KANIAIA

SANJEEV - KANIEWI

SANJIT - KANIIKE

SANJITA - KANIIKA

SANJU - KANIU

SANSRI - KANAKALI

SANTA - KANAKA

SANTANA - KANAKANA

SANTAYVIA - KANAKAIWIA

SANTI - KANAKI

SANTIAGO - KANAKIAKO

SANTINA - KANAKINA

SANTINO - KANAKINO

SANTO - KANAKO

SANTOS – KANAKOKU

SAOIRSE - KAOILEKE

SAPHRONIA - KAPALONIA

SAPRINA - KAPALINA

SAPPHA - KAPA

SAPPHIRA - KAPILA

SAPPHIRE - KAPILE

SAQQARA - KAKALA

SARA - KALA

SARAFINA - KALAPINA

SARANN - KALANA

SARAH - KALA

SARAI - KALAI

SARAHITY - KALAHIKI

SARALIA - KALALIA

SARANTY - KALANAKI

SARAY - KALAI

SARAYA - KALAIA

SAREE - KALE

SAREENA - KALENA

SAREL - KALELI
SARELLE - KALELE
SARETTE - KALEKE
SARGE - KAKE
SARGON - KAKONU
SARHA - KALAHA
SARI - KALI
SARIKA - KALIKA
SARIMAH - KALIMAHA
SARIN - KALINE
SARINA - KALINA
SARIS - KALIKE
SARKA - KAKA
SAROM - KALOMU
SARIAH - KALIAHA
SARIANNA - KALIANA
SARINN - KALINE
SARITA - KALIKA
SARIYA - KALIIA
SARFRAZ - KALAPALAKA
SARTHAK - KAKAKA
SARYNNA - KALINA
SASCHELLE - KAKAKELE
SASHA – KAKA
SASI - KAKI
SASIDHAR - KAKIKEHALA
SASKIA - KAKAKIA
SASNA - KAKANA
SASS - KAKA
SATCHEL - KAKAKELI

SATHARA - KAKALA
SATHY - KAKI
SATIN - KAKINE
SATIRA - KAKILA
SATISH - KAKIKE
SATORIE - KAKOLIE
SATOSHI - KAKOKI
SATTERTHWAITEBE - KAKEKIWAIKEPE
SATVIR - KAKAWILE
SATYA - KAKIA
SATYEN - KAKIENI
SAUGA - KAUKA
SAUL - KAULO
SAU-LIN - KAU-OLINE
SAULIUS - KAULIUKO
SAULNETTE - KAULONEKE
SAUNDERS - KAUNOKELIKI
SAUNDRA - KAUNOKOLA
SAVANA - KAWANA
SAVANNA - KAWANA
SAVANNAH - KAWANAHA
SAVEENA - KAWENA
SAVEN - KAWENI
SAVINO - KAWINO
SAVION - KAWIONU
SAVITABEN - KAWIKAPENI
SAVONNA - KAWONA
SAVVY - KAWI
SAVY - KAWI
SAWAKO - KAWAKO

SAWANTA - KAWANAKA
SAWNEY - KAWANEI
SAWYER - KAWIELI
SAXON - KAKONU
SAXTON - KAKAKONU
SAYA - KAIA
SAYAN - KAIANA
SAYDEE - KAIKE
SAYDIE - KAIKIE
SAYFORD - KAIPOLUKU
SAYLOR - KAILOLU
SAYNIA - KAINIA
SAYONARA - KAIONALA
SCEFRENNA - KAKEPILENA
SCHAE - KAKAE
SCHAEFER - KAKAEPELI
SCHALAH - KAKALAHA
SCHENLEY - KAKENILEI
SCHIEFER - KAKIEPELI
SCHNIGHDER - KAKANIKEHEKELI
SCARFF - KAKALAPA
SCARLETT - KAKALEKI
SCETLANA - KAKEKILANA
SCHARLEAN - KAKALEANA
SCHEHERAZADE - KAKEHELAKAKE
SCHEKELA - KAKEKELA
SCHENELLE - KAKENELE
SCHMITTY - KAKAMIKI
SCHUYLER - KAKUILELI
SCHYLER - KAKILELI

SCHYRELL - KAKILELI
SCHZARVETTE - KAKAKALAWEKE
SCIERA - KAKIELA
SCIP - KAKIPE
SCOOTER - KAKOKELI
SCOTIA - KAKOKIA
SCOTLAND - KAKOKULANAKA
SCOTLYN - KAKOKULINE
SCOTT – KOKA
SCOTTY - KAKOKI
SCOTTIE - KAKOKIE
SCOUT - KAKOUKO
SCOUTER - KAKOUKELI
SEADETA - KEAKEKA
SEAMUS – KEAMUKA
SEAN – KANA
SEANA - KEANA
SEANTELL - KEANAKELI
SEARA - KEALA
SEARCI - KEALAKI
SEASON - KEAKONU
SEB - KEPI
SEBASTIAN – KEPAKIANO
SEBASTIANA - KEPAKIANA
SEBNEM - KEPINEMI
SEBRINA - KEPILINA
SECOYA - KEKOIA
SEDA - KEKA
SEDEF - KEKEPI
SEDLEY - KEKILEI

SEDONA - KEKONA	SELINDA - KELINEKA
SEEHUM - KEHUMO	SELISA – KELIKA
SEE LAI - KE LAI	SELMA - KELIMA
SEEMA - KEMA	SELWYN - KELIWINE
SEENA - KENA	SELVA - KELIWA
SEF - KEPI	SELVAA - KELIWA
SEFIK - KEPIKE	SELVENI - KELIWENI
SEGUNDINA - KEKUNOKINA	SELVI - KELIWI
SEHAR - KEHALA	SELVIJE - KELIWIIE
SEHER - KEHELI	SELVINI - KELIWINI
SEIJI - KEIII	SELYA - KELIA
SEIKO - KEIKO	SEMAJ - KEMAI
SEIROSA - KEILOKA	SEMRA - KEMILA
SEITA - KEIKA	SENAIDA - KENAIKA
SEKU - KEKU	SENAYET - KENAIEKI
SEKUJUANNA - KEKUIUANA	SENECA - KENEKA
SELA - KELA	SENEN - KENENI
SELAH - KELAHA	SENERITA - KENELIKA
SELAMAT - KELAMAKA	SENITA - KENIKA
SELBY - KELIPI	SENNY - KENI
SELENA - KELENA	SENORA - KENOLA
SELENCI - KELENIKI	SENTILA - KENIKILA
SELENCIA - KELENIKIA	SEONA - KEONA
SELENE - KELENE	SEPH - KEPI
SELENY - KELENI	SEPHRA - KEPILA
SELETA - KELEKA	SEQUOIA - KEKOIA
SELETHA - KELEKA	SERA - KELA
SELIME - KELIME	SERAN - KELANA
SELIN - KELINE	SERE - KELE
SELINA - KELINA	SERENA - KELENA

SERENIDY - KELENIKI

SERENITY - KELENIKI

SEREY - KELEI

SERGE - KEKE

SERGEI - KEKEI

SERGEANT - KEKEANAKA

SERGIL - KEKILE

SERGIO - KEKIO

SERGIUS – KELEKIO

SERGUY - KEKUI

SERI - KELI

SERITA - KELIKA

SERRA - KELA

SERRANO - KELANO

SESSAHLEE - KEKAHALE

SESSALY - KEKALI

SETE - KEKE

SETH – KEKA

SETIANI - KEKIANI

SETORIA - KEKOLIA

SETRAK - KELAKA

SETTA - KEKA

SEUNGJOO - KEUNIO

SEVAK - KEWAKA

SEVA - KEWA

SEVALA - KEWALA

SEVANISTA - KEWANIKA

SEVERINO - KEWELINO

SEVERITA - KEWELIKA

SEVIL - KEWILE

SEVIN - KEWINE

SEVINE - KEWINE

SEWARD - KEWALAKA

SEYMOUR - KEIMOULO

SHA - KA

SHAAN - KANA

SHAAYAN - KAIANA

SHA'CARI - KA'AKALI

SHAD - KAKA

SHADANA - KAKANA

SHADE - KAKE

SHADERIA - KAKELIA

SHADIE - KAKIE

SHADOE - KAKOE

SHADREN - KAKALENI

SHADY - KAKI

SHAE - KAE

SHAELAN - KAELANA

SHAELIN - KAELINE

SHAELYN - KAELINE

SHAE-LYNN - KAE-ILINE

SHAELZIMAH - KAELIKIMAHA

SHAFALLI - KAPALI

SHAFINA - KAPINA

SHAFIQA - KAPIKA

SHAGUFTA - KAKUPA

SHAHAR - KAHALA

SHAHEEMAH - KAHEMAHA

SHAHEEN - KAHENI

SHAHIN - KAHINE

SHAHIR - KAHILE
SHAHITA - KAHIKA
SHAHLA - KAHALA
SHAHRZAD - KAHALAKAKA
SHAI - KAI
SHAIDA - KAIKA
SHAILA - KAILA
SHAILEE - KAILE
SHAILEND - KAILENIKI
SHAILO - KAILO
SHAILOS - KAILOKU
SHAINA - KAINA
SHAIRE - KAILE
SHAJITH - KAIIKE
SHAK - KAKA
SHAKAELA - KAKAELA
SHA'KEE - KA'AKE
SHAKEELA - KAKELA
SHAKEIA - KAKEIA
SHAKEY - KAKEI
SHAKIA - KAKIA
SHAKIL - KAKILE
SHAKILAH - KAKILAHA
SHAKIRA - KAKILA
SHALA - KALA
SHALAN - KALANA
SHALANE - KALANE
SHALANNE - KALANE
SHALAYNA - KALAINA
SHALBHA - KALAPAHA

SHALEA - KALEA
SHALEEN - KALENI
SHALEIA - KALEIA
SHALEQUA - KALEKA
SHALER - KALELI
SHALET - KALEKI
SHALETHA - KALEKA
SHALEY - KALEI
SHALIEYA - KALIEIA
SHALIKA - KALIKA
SHALIMAR - KALIMALA
SHALIN - KALINE
SHALINDA - KALINEKA
SHALINI - KALINI
SHALIONDEL - KALIONUKELI
SHALISSA - KALIKA
SHALLAN - KALANA
SHALON - KALONU
SHALONDRA - KOLONUKULA
SHALVA - KALAWA
SHAM - KAMA
SHAMAIYA - KAMAIIA
SHAMAR - KAMALA
SHAMARA - KAMALA
SHAMAREE - KAMALE
SHAMAYNE - KAMAINE
SHAMBRAY - KAMAPALAI
SHAMUBIN - KAMUPINE
SHAMUS - KAMUKO
SHAMEKA - KAMEKA

SHAMETRA - KAMELA
SHAMI -KAMI
SHAMIELA - KAMIELA
SHAMIKA - KAMIKA
SHAMIKIA - KAMIKIA
SHAMIN - KAMINE
SHAMONA - KAMONA
SHAMONICA - KAMONIKA
SHAMONTIEL - KAMONUKIELI
SHAMRA - KAMALA
SHAMSA - KAMAKA
SHAMYAH - KAMIAHA
SHAN - KANA
SHANA - KANA
SHANAE - KANAE
SHANAEL - KANAELI
SHANAH - KANAHA
SHAND - KANAKA
SHANDA - KANAKA
SHANDERLON - KANAKELONU
SHANDHIYA - KANAKAHIIA
SHANDI - KANAKI
SHANDLEY - KANAKALEI
SHANDON – KANOKONA
SHANDRA - KANAKALA
SHANDRIANNA - KANAKALIANA
SHANE - KANE
SHANEA - KANEA
SHANEE - KANE
SHANEEN - KANENI

SHANEEQ'A - KANEKI'A
SHANEKA - KANEKA
SHANEKIA - KANEKIA
SHANELL - KANELI
SHANENE - KANENE
SHANEQUA - KANEKUA
SHANEQUAH - KANEKAHA
SHANESA - KANEKA
SHANETTE - KANEKE
SHANEVA - KANEWA
SHANG - KANA
SHANI - KANI
SHANIA - KANIA
SHANICE - KANIKE
SHANIE - KANIE
SHANIECE - KANIEKE
SHANIQUA - KANIKA
SHANIQUE - KANEKAKE
SHANISA - KANIKA
SHANIAH - KANIAHA
SHANITA - KANIKA
SHANKEZIA - KANAKEKIA
SHANLEE - KANALE
SHANLEIGH - KANALEIKEHE
SHANNA - KANA
SHANNELI - KANELI
SHANNELL - KANELI
SHANNEN - KANENI
SHANN HOO - KANA HO
SHANNON - KANONU

SHANOAH - KANOAHA

SHANON - KANONU

SHAN-SHAN - KANA-AKAHANA

SHANSHAN - KANAKAHANA

SHANTAE - KANAKAE

SHANTANIQUE - KANAKANIKUE

SHANTAVIA - KANAKAWIA

SHANTEE' - KANEKE'I

SHANTEL - KANAKELI

SHANTELL - KANAKELI

SHANTELLE - KANAKELE

SHANTERRIA - KANAKELIA

SHANTI - KANAKI

SHANTIE - KANAKIE

SHANYA - KANIA

SHANZA - KANAKA

SHARMILLA - KALAMILA

SHAO YU - KAO IU

SHAOLIN - KAOLINE

SHAPRISE - KAPALIKE

SHAQOYA - KAKOIA

SHAQUANDA - KAKANAKA

SHAQUANTIS - KAKANAKIKE

SHAQUETTA - KAKEKA

SHAQUIESHA - KAKIEKIHA

SHAQUILLA - KAKILA

SHAQUILLE - KAKEILE

SHAQUIRA - KAKILA

SHARA - KALA

SHARAD - KALAKA

SHARALEE - KALALE

SHARANE - KALANE

SHARAYA - KALAIA

SHARBEL - KALAPELI

SHARCORRIA - KALAKOLIA

SHARDE - KALAKE

SHAREEN - KALENI

SHAREL - KALELI

SHARLA - KALA

SHARMAINE - KALAMAINE

SHARREE - KALE

SHARRELL - KALELI

SHARETTA - KALEKA

SHARI - KALI

SHARICE - KALIKE

SHARIDAH - KALIKAHA

SHARIFA - KALIPA

SHARIKA - KALIKA

SHARI-LYNN - KALI-ELINE

SHARIFF - KALIPE

SHARILYN - KALILINE

SHARINA - KALINA

SHARION - KALIONU

SHARITA - KALIKA

SHARLA - KALA

SHARLENE - KALENE

SHARLETHA - KALEKA

SHARLYN - KALINE

SHARMA - KALAMA

SHARMAINE - KALAMAINE

SHARMAN - KALAMANA
SHARNÉ - KALANAÉA
SHARNICE - KALANIKE
SHARNITA - KALANIKA
SHAROD - KALOKU
SHARON – KALONA
SHARONDA - KALONUKA
SHARONLYN - KALONULINE
SHARONYKA - KALONIKA
SHARR - KALA
SHARRAH - KALAHA
SHARRIE - KALIE
SHARRIET - KALIEKI
SHARRON - KALONU
SHARTEEL - KAKELI
SHARVARI - KAKELI
SHARYL - KELELA
SHARYN - KALINE
SHARYNE - KALINE
SHASI - KAKI
SHASTA - KAKA
SHASTHRA - KAKALA
SHATIAH - KAKIAHA
SHATIKA - KAKIKA
SHATIMA - KAKIMA
SHATOI'IA - KAKOI'IA
SHATOYA - KAKOIA
SHATZE - KAKAKE
SHAUGHNESSY - KAUKOHONEKI
SHAUHIN - KAUHINE

SHAUN - KAUNO
SHAUNA - KAUNA
SHAUNAE - KAUNAE
SHAUNAK - KAUNAKA
SHAUNDA - KAUNOKA
SHAUNDRA - KAUNOKOLA
SHAUNDREA - KAUNOKOLEA
SHAUNICE - KAUNIKE
SHAUNNA - KAUNA
SHAUNT - KAUNOKO
SHAUNTE - KAUNOKE
SHAUNTEL - KAUNOKELI
SHAUNTELLE - KAUNOKELE
SHAUREE - KAWALE
SHAVALIER - KAWALIELI
SHAVANDA - KAWANAKA
SHAVARGUS - KAWAKUKO
SHAVODKA - KAWOKUKA
SHAVON - KAWONU
SHAW - KAWA
SHAWGONNIAH - KAWAKONIAHA
SHAWN - KAWANA
SHAWNA - KAWANA
SHAWNAE - KAWANAE
SHAWNDA - KAWANAKA
SHAWNDARA - KAWANAKALA
SHAWNEE - KAWANE
SHAWNELLE - KAWANELE
SHAWNETTE - KAWANEKE
SHAWNEY - KAWANEI

SHAWNNA - KAWANA

SHAWNTAY - KAWANAKAI

SHAWNTE - KAWANAKE

SHAWNTREL - KAWANALELI

SHAWNY - KAWANI

SHAY - KAI

SHAYAN - KAIANA

SHAYDA - KAIKA

SHAYDEE - KAIKE

SHAYELLE - KAIELE

SHAYLA - KAILA

SHAYLAH - KAILAHA

SHAYLEE - KAILE

SHAYLEEN - KAILENI

SHAYLEN - KAILENI

SHAYLYN - KAILINE

SHAYLYNN - KAILINE

SHAYMUS - KAIMUKO

SHAYNA - KAINA

SHAYNE - KAINE

SHAZIA - KAKIA

SHEA - KEA

SHEALYN - KEALINE

SHEALYNN - KEALINE

SHEAN - KEANE

SHEANA - KEANA

SHEARON - KEALONU

SHEAVONE - KEAWONU

SHEDDRIKA - KEKILIKA

SHEDRICK - KEKILIKEKE

SHEEBA - KEPA

SHEELA - KELA

SHEEN - KENI

SHEENA - KENA

SHEETAL - KEKALA

SHEFFIA - KEPIA

SHEHLA - KEHILA

SHEHRYAR - KEHILIALA

SHEILA - KILA

SHEILAH - KEILAHA

SHEILDA - KEILA

SHEKEIVA - KEKEIWA

SHEKERA - KEKELA

SHEKHAR - KEKIHALA

SHEKINAH - KEKINAHA

SHELAGH - KELAKAHA

SHELAUGH - KELAUKOHO

SHELBA - KELIPA

SHELBIE - KELIPIE

SHELBY - KELIPI

SHELDON - KELONU

SHELEAN - KELEANA

SHELELA - KELELA

SHELIA - KELIA

SHELL - KELI

SHELLA - KELA

SHELLEE - KELE

SHELLEI - KELEI

SHELLENA - KELENA

SHELLEY - KELEI

SHELLEYMAR - KELEIMALA
SHELLI - KELI
SHELLIE - KELIE
SHELLONE - KELONE
SHELLY - KELI
SHELTON - KELIKONU
SHELVA - KELIWA
SHEMAIAH - KEMAIAHA
SHEMAR - KEMALA
SHE'MARRI - KE'IMALI
SHEMEKA - KEMEKA
SHENAIAH - KENAIAHA
SHENAY - KENAI
SHENDELLE - KENIKELE
SCHENELLE - KAKENELE
SHENICA - KENIKA
SHENIDA - KENIKA
SHENIQUINAE - KENIKANAE
SHENNA - KENA
SHENNITTA - KENIKA
SHERA - KELA
SHERAHL - KELAHALA
SHERARD - KELALAKA
SHEREE - KELE
SHEREKA - KELEKA
SHEREL - KELELI
SHERELLE - KELELE
SHERENE - KELENE
SHERESE - KELEKE
SHERI - KELIKA

SHERIA - KELIA
SHERICE - KELIKE
SHERIDAN - KELIKANA
SHERIDEE - KELIKE
SHERIE - KELIE
SHERILYN - KELILINE
SHERISSA - KELIKA
SHERITA - KELIKA
SHERLITHIA - KELIKIA
SHERIVAH - KELIWAHA
SHERLE - KELE
SHERLOCK - KELOKUKU
SHERMA - KELIMA
SHERMAN – KELEMANA
SHERMOND - KELIMONUKU
SHEROLD - KELOLU
SHERON - KELONU
SHERONDA - KELONUKA
SHERRAD - KELAKA
SHERRI - KELI
SHERRICK - KELIKEKE
SHERRIE - KELIE
SHERRIL - KELILE
SHERRIN - KELINE
SHERRING - KELINE
SHERRON - KELONU
SHERRY - KELI
SHERWIN - KELIWINE
SHERYL – KELIA
SHERYLDENE - KELILENE

SHERYLL - KELILE
SHERYLYN - KELILINE
SHERYNE - KELINE
SHESHA - KEKIHA
SHEYENNE - KEIENE
SHIANA - KIANA
SHIANITA - KIANIKA
SHIANNE - KIANE
SHIGEKO - KIKEKO
SHIHO - KIHO
SHIJU - KIIU
SHIJUANA - KIIUANA
SHIKHA - KIKEHA
SHIKIN - KIKINE
SHILAR - KILALA
SHILL - KILE
SHILLEENA - KILENA
SHILO - KILO
SHILOH - KILOHU
SHILPA - KILEPA
SHILU - KILU
SHIMON - KIMONU
SHINA - KINA
SHINATA - KINAKA
SHINESHA - KINEKIHA
SHING-SHING - KINE-EKEHINE
SHINIKA - KINIKA
SHINIKIA - KINIKIA
SHINNELL - KINELI
SHINNETTE - KINEKE

SHIONA - KIONA
SHIRA - KILA
SHIRECE - KILEKE
SHIREEKA - KILEKA
SHIREEN - KILENI
SHIRELLE - KILELE
SHIRIN - KILINE
SHIRISHA - KILIKEHA
SHIRL - KILE
SHIRLANN - KILANA
SHIRLEEN - KILENI
SHIRLEY – KELI
SHIROI KUMO - KILOI KUMO
SHITAL - KIKALA
SHIVANGI - KIWANI
SHIVANI - KIWANI
SHIVAR - KIWALA
SHIVAUN - KIWAUNO
SHIVONNE - KIWONE
SH'KELA - KA'AKELA
SHLOMO - KALOMO
SHMUEL - KAMUELI
SHOBA - KOPA
SHOBNA - KOPUNA
SHOHREH - KOHULEHI
SHOKOUFEH - KOKOUPEHI
SHOLA - KOLA
SHOLOM - KOLOMU
SHOMARI - KOMALI
SHON - KONU

SHONA - KONA

SHONDA - KONUKA

SHONDRA - KONUKULA

SHONETTE - KONEKE

SHONN - KANA

SHONNA - KONA

SHONNIE - KONIE

SHONTE' - KONUKE'I

SHOSHANA - KOKUHANA

SHOSHO - KOKUHO

SHOUA - KOUA

SHOVA - KOWA

SHOVINE - KOWINE

SHQIPE - KAKIPE

SHREE - KALE

SHREENAH - KALENAHA

SHREYA - KALEIA

SHRINA - KALINA

SHRINIVAS - KALINIWAKA

SHRSYA - KALAKIA

SHRUTI - KALUKI

SHTERNA - KAKELINA

SHUANGLI - KUANALI

SHU-HSIEN - KU-OHOKIENI

SHU-XIA - KU KIA

SHUBHA - KUPOHA

SHUBHANGI - KUPOHANI

SHUBHANKAR - KUPOHANAKALA

SHUBHEN - KUPOHENI

SHUBY - KUPI

SHUKRI - KUKOLI

SHULTZ - KULOKOKO

SHUNDA - KUNOKA

SHUNNA - KUNA

SHUNTAE - KUNOKAE

SHUNTAY - KUNOKAI

SHUNTEE' - KUNOKE'I

SHUNTERIKA - KUNOKELIKA

SHUNTINE - KUNOKINE

SHUSKA - KUKOKA

SHUTE - KUKE

SHUWEN - KUWENI

SHUYING - KUIINE

SHYA - KIA

SHYAMALAN - KIAMALANA

SHYANE - KIANE

SHYANNE - KIANE

SHYEASHA - KIEAKAHA

SHYHEIM - KIHEIME

SHYLA - KILA

SHYLAND - KILANAKA

SHYLER - KILELI

SHYLON - KILONU

SHYNE - KINE

SHYRA - KILA

SHYROLON - KILOLONU

SHZELLE - KAKELE

SHIA - KIA

SI - KI

SIA - KIA

SIAH - KIAHA

SIAN - KIANA

SIANA - KIANA

SIANING - KIANINE

SIANNAH - KIANAHA

SIANNE - KIANE

SIARA - KIALA

SIATTA - KIAKA

SIAVOSH - KIAWOKU

SIBREN - KIPELENI

SIBY - KIPI

SIBYL – KIPILA

SICA - KIKA

SICCO - KIKO

SICELY - KIKELI

SID - KIKE

SIDDHARTHA - KIKEHAKA

SIDEOUS - SIDEOUS

SIDEYIN - KIKEIINE

SIDINA - KIKINA

SIDNEY – KIKANI

SIDONIA - KIKONIA

SIDRA - KIKELA

SIEGBERT - KIEKIPEKI

SIEGFRIED - KIEKIPILIEKI

SIENNA - KIENA

SIERAH - KIELAHA

SIERRA - KIELA

SIEW - KIEWI

SIEW CHENG - KIEWI KENI

SIEW CHUN - KIEWI KUNO

SIEW LUM - KIEWI LUMO

SIEW TAN - KIEWI KANA

SIEWYEAN - KIEWIEANA

SIFA - KIPA

SIG - KIKE

SIGBERTO - KIKEPEKO

SIGI - KIKI

SIGNA - KIKENA

SIGNE - KIKENE

SIGRID - KIKELIKE

SIINA - KINA

SILAS - KILA

SI'LESHIA - KI'ELEKIA

SILICIA - KILIKIA

SILINA - KILINA

SILIVA - KILIWA

SILKE - KILEKE

SILMARA - KILEMALA

SILVA - KILEWA

SILVANA - KILEWANA

SILVER - KILEWELI

SILVERIO - KILEWELIO

SILVIA - KILEWIA

SILVIANO - KILEWIANO

SILVIE - KILEWIE

SILVIO - KILEWIO

SIM - KIMI

SIMA - KIMA

SIMALUA - KIMALUA

SIMEON - KIMEONA

SIMER - KIMELI

SIMI - KIMI

SIMINA - KIMINA

SIMME - KIME

SIMON – KIMONA

SIMONA - KIMONA

SIMONE - KIMONE

SIMORA - KIMOLA

SIMOTE - KIMOKE

SIMRAN - KIMELANA

SIMS - KIMEKE

SIMSMEYUN - KIMEKEMEIUNO

SIMYOU - KIMIOU

SINA - KINA

SINAI - KANAI

SINAN - KINANA

SINATRA - KINALA

SINAYA - KINAIA

SINDY - KINEKI

SINE - KINE

SINEAD - KINEAKA

SINGIE - KINIE

SINJIN - KINIINE

SINJON - KINIONU

SINTA - KINEKA

SINTHUJAH - KINEKUIAHA

SIOBAHN - KIOPAHANA

SIOBBHAN - KIOPUHANA

SIOBHAN - KIOPUHANA

SIOMARA - KIOMALA

SION - KIONU

SI'ON - KI'ONU

SIONE - KIONE

SIQIAN - KIKIANA

SIQOURNEY - KIKOULONEI

SIRA - KILA

SIRI - KILI

SIRINA - KILINA

SIRIUS - KILIUKO

SIRIVAN - KILIWANA

SIRKKA - KILIKA

SIRVONTA - KILEWONUKA

SIS - KIKE

SISCO - KIKEKO

SISKA - KIKEKA

SISKO - KIKEKO

SISLEY - KIKELEI

SISSEL - KIKELI

SISSY - KIKI

SISTER - KIKELI

SITARA - KIKALA

SITH - KIKE

SITI - KIKI

SIU - KU

SIV - KIWE

SIVA - KIWA

SIYAVASH - KIIAWAKA

SKIP - KAKIPE

SLATON - KALAKONU

SLIM - KALIME
SLY - KAKI
SLYE - KAKIE
SKEET - KAKEKI
SKEETER - KAKEKELI
SKY - KAKI
SKYE - KAKIE
SKYELAR - KAKIELALA
SKYELYNN - KAKIELINE
SKYLA - KAKILA
SKYLAR - KAKILALA
SKY-LENE - KAKI-ELENE
SKYLER - KAKILELI
SKYLEY - KAKILEI
SKYLIER - KAKILIELI
SKYWALKER - KAKIWALAKELI
SLADE - KALAKE
SLADJANA - KALAKIANA
SLAG - KALAKA
SLATER - KALAKELI
SLAVA - KALAWA
SLAVOMIR - KALAWOMILE
SLAWEK - KALAWEKI
SLAYTON - KALAIKONU
SLIEMAN - KALIEMANA
SLOAN - KALOANA
SLONE - KALONE
SLY - KALI
SMAILA - KAMAILA
SMITA - KAMIKA

SMOKE - KAMOKE
SMOOTHEE - KAMOKE
SNEAD - KAMEAKA
SNEHA - KANEHA
SNEZANA - KANEKANA
SNJEZANA - KANIEKANA
SNOOPY - KANOPI
SNOW - KANOWU
SOANA - KOANA
SOBRENA - KOPULENA
SOCORRO - KOKOLO
SOCRATES - KOKALAKE
SODA - KOKA
SOEN - KOENI
SOFIA - KOPIA
SOFRONA - KOPULONA
SOHAIL - KOHAILE
SOHAM - KOHAMA
SOILA - KOILA
SOJIM - KOIIME
SOKHAM - KOKUHAMA
SOKTHEA - KOKUKEA
SOL - KOLU
SOLANA - KOLANA
SOLANGE - KOLANE
SOLARRA - KOLALA
SOLE - KOLE
SOLEIL - KOLEILE
SOLENA - KOLENA
SOLIMAR - KOLIMALA

SOLINE - KOLINE

SOLLY - KOLI

SOLOMON - KOLOMONA

SOLON - KOLONU

SOLVEI - KOLUWEI

SOMAIA - KOMAIA

SOMERLYN - KOMELINE

SOMERS - KOMELIKI

SOMESH - KOMEKI

SOMESHWAR - KOMEKIWALA

SOMINIQUE - KOMINIKE

SOMMER - KOMELI

SOMPORN - KOMUPOLUNU

SON - KONU

SONA - KONA

SONALI - KONALI

SONAMJEET - KONAMIEKI

SONDIE - KONUKIE

SONDRA - KONUKULA

SONEST - KONEKI

SONG - KONU

SONGCHAU - KONUKAU

SONGSIRI - KONUKILI

SONIA - KONIA

SONITA - KONIKA

SONJA - KONIA

SON MIN - KONU MINE

SONNA - KONA

SONNET - KONEKI

SONNIE - KONIE

SONNY - KONI

SONOKO - KONOKO

SONSENIORA` - KONUKENIOLA'A

SONSURAY - KONUKULAI

SONTINA - KONUKINA

SONYA - KONIA

SOOKIE - KOKIE

SOOSH - KOKU

SOPHAL - KOPALA

SOPHIA - KOPIA

SOPHIE - KOPI

SOPHINA - KOPINA

SOPHON - KOPONU

SOPNA - KOPUNA

SOR - KOLU

SORAIDA - KOLAIKA

SORAYA - KOLAIA

SORCHA - KOLUKA

SOREN - KOLENI

SORIEN - KOLIENI

SORIYA - KOLIIA

SOROCHI - KOLOKI

SOSEFINA - KOKEPINA

SOSIE - KOKIE

SOTERIA - KOKELIA

SOTERO - KOKELO

SOTHY - KOKI

SOTIRIA - KOKILIA

SOUA CHOUA - KOUA KOUA

SOUKIE - KOUKIE

SOULEYMA - KOULEIMA
SOUMINI - KOUMINI
SOURI - KOULI
SOUSAN - KOUKANA
SOVANDY - KOWANAKI
SOVANN - KOWANA
SOVANNA - KOWANA
SOVRIN - KOWULINE
SOWARI - KOWALI
SOWJANYA - KOWIANIA
SPACIE - KAPAKIE
SPANKY - KAPANAKI
SPARKLE - KAPAKALE
SPARKY - KAPAKI
SPARROW - KAPALOWU
SPEED-LEE - KAPEKI-ILE
SPENCE - KAPENIKE
SPENCER - KEPENEKELA
SPERA - KAPELA
SPICY - KAPIKI
SPIKE - KAPIKE
SPIRO - KAPILO
SPOR - KAPOLU
SPRING - KUPULAU
SPROUT - KAPALOUKO
SPYROS - KAPILOKU
SQUIGGY - KAKAIKI
SREKAR - KALEKALA
SREY - KALEI
SRIDEVI - KALIKEWI

SRINIDHI - KALINIKEHI
SRINU - KALINU
SRIRAJA - KALILAIA
SRIYA - KALIIA
SRUTHI - KALUKI
SRUTHY - KALUKI
STACEY - KAKEI
STACI - KAKI
STACIA - KAKIA
STACIE - KAKIE
STACLYN - KAKALINE
STACY - KAKI
STAFFORD - KAPOLUKU
STALEY - KALEI
STALIN - KALINE
STAN - KANA
STANA - KANA
STANFORD - KANAPOLA
STANISLAV - KANIKELAWA
STANLEY - KANALE
STATAN - KAKANA
STANTASIA - KANAKAKIA
STATEN - KAKENI
STANTON - KANAKONU
STANZIE - KANAKIE
STARCIA - KALAKIA
STAR KALA
STARA - KALA
STARLA - KALA
STARLET - KALEKI

STARLYNN - KALINE

STEPHANIE - KEKEPANIA

STARR - KALA

STEPHANJA - KEPANIA

STAS - KAKA

STEPHANNIE - KEKEPANIA

STASA - KAKA

STEPHANO - KEPANO

STASE - KAKE

STEPHANY - KEPANI

STASH - KAKA

STEPHEN – KEPANO

STASIA - KAKIA

STEPHENA - KEPENA

STASSI - KAKI

STEPHENIE - KEPENIE

STATON - KAKONU

STERGIO - KEKIO

STAV - KAWA

STERLING - KELINA

STAVA - KAWA

STESHA - KEKA

STAVROS - KAWALOKU

STETSON - KEKONU

STAYTON - KAIKONU

STEVE - KIWI

STEDE - KEKE

STEVEN - KIWINI

STEELE - KELE

STEVI - KEWI

STEF - KEPI

STEVIE - KEWIE

STEFAN - KEPANA

STEWART, STUART - KEWALAKA

STEFANI - KEPANI

STHEMBILE - KEMIPILE

STEFANIA - KEPANIA

STINA - KINA

STEFANIE - KEPANIE

STITCH - KIKEKE

STEFANU - KEPANU

STOCKTON - KOKUKUKONU

STEFFEN - KEPENI

STONE - KONE

STEFON - KEPONU

STONEY - KONEI

STEIFON - KEIPONU

STORM - KOLUMU

STELEE - KELE

STORMI - KOLUMI

STELL - KELI

STORMIE - KOLUMIE

STELLA - KELA

STORMY - KOLUMI

STEN - KENI

STORY - KOLI

STEPH - KEPI

STRATTON - KALAKONU

STEPHAN - KEPANA

STRAUSS - KALAUKO

STRAWN - KALAWANA

STU - KU

STUART - KUAKA

STUBBLES - KUPOLEKI

STUBS - KUPOKO

STYLES - KILEKI

SU - KU

SUAN - KUANA

SUAT KING - KUAKA KINE

SUBHA - KUPOHA

SUBHALAXMI- KUPOHALAKAMI

SUCO - KUKO

SUCHITA - KUKIKA

SUDA - KUKA

SUDIE - KUKIE

SUE - KU

SUEANN - KUEANA

SUEDETTE - KUEKEKE

SUE-LING - KU-LINE

SUELLEN - KUELENI

SUFI - KUPI

SUGANYA - KUKANIA

SUGAR - KUKALA

SUH - KUHO

SUHEY - KUHEI

SUJATA - KUIAKA

SUJI - KUII

SUKHJIT - KUKOHIIKE

SUKHMANI - KUKOHOMANI

SUKI - KUKI

SUKIE - KUKIE

SULAIMAN - KULAIMANA

SULEMA - KULEMA

SULLIVAN - KULIWANA

SULTAN - KULOKANA

SUMAIYA - KUMAIIA

SUMANGEL - KUMANELI

SUMARA - KUMALA

SUMAYAH - KUMAIAHA

SUMER - KUMELI

SUM HING - KUMO HINE

SUMIKO - KUMIKO

SUMIT - KUMIKE

SUMITRA - KUMILA

SUMMER - KAUWELA

SUMMERLIN - KUMELINE

SUNARTI - KUNAKI

SUNDANZ - KUNOKANAKA

SUNDAY - KUNOKAI

SUNDEEP - KUNOKEPI

SUNDER - KUNOKELI

SUNEETI - KUNEKI

SUNEL - KUNELI

SUNETTE - KUNEKE

SUNGHEE - KUNOHE

SUNIL - KUNILE

SUNITA - KUNIKA

SUNITHA - KUNIKA

SUNJAY - KUNIAI

SUNJAYA - KUNIAIA

SUNJOT - KUNIOKU

SUNLY - KUNOLI

SUNNI - KUNI

SUNNY - KUNI

SUNNYA - KUNIA

SUN OK - KONU OAKA

SUNORAH - KUNOLAHA

SUNSHINE - KUNOKINE

SUONG - KUONU

SUPHAROEK - KUPALOEKI

SUPNA - KUPONA

SURABHI - KULAPAHI

SURAJ - KULAI

SURAYIA - KULAIIA

SUREKHA - KULEKIHA

SUREN - KULENI

SURENDER - KULENIKELI

SURENDRA - KULENIKILA

SURESH - KULEKI

SUREYA - KULEIA

SURINA - KULINA

SURIYANI - KULIIANI

SURJIT - KULIIKE

SURY - KULI

SURYA - KULIA

SUSAN - KUKANA

SUSANA - KUKANA

SUSANNAH - KUKANAHA

SUSCIEL - KUKOKIELI

SUSETTE - KUKEKE

SUSIE - KUKE

SUTHIKSHNAN - KUKIKEKENANA

SUTINA - KUKINA

SUTTAN - KUKANA

SUTTON - KUKONU

SUWAN - KUWANA

SUWANNA - KUWANA

SUYEN - KUIENI

SUYIN - KUIINE

SUZAN - KUKANA

SUZANNA - KUKANA

SUZANNE - KUKANA

SUZELLE - KUKELE

SUZETTE - KUKEKE

SUZI - KUKI

SUZIE - KUKE

SUZITA - KUKIKA

SUZUKO - KUKUKO

SUZY - KUKI

SVEA - KAWEA

SVEIN - KAWEINE

SVEN - KAWENI

SVENJA - KAWENIA

SVETLANA - KAWEKILANA

SWAHILI - KAWAHILI

SWAPNA - KAWAPANA

SWAPNIL - KAWAPANILE

SWARDELLA - KAWALAKELA

SWARUPA - KAWALUPA

SWATHI - KAWAKI

SWATI - KAWAKI

SYMPHONY - KIMEPONI

SWEETA - KAWEKA

SYNDE - KINEKE

SWEETHEART - KAWEKEAKA

SYNDEL - KINEKELI

SWEETNESS -KAWEKINEKI

SYNDI - KINEKI

SYAMALA - KIAMALA

SYDNIE - KIKENIE

SYBIL - KEPILA

SYNISHA - KINIKA

SYBLE - KIPELE

SYNOVIA - KINOWIA

SYDAHNA - KIKAHANA

SYNPHONY - KINEPONI

SYDELLA - KIKELA

SYNSEAR - KINEKEALA

SYDIA - KIKIA

SYNTHIA - KINEKIA

SYDNEA - KIKENEA

SYONA - KIONA

SYDNEE - KIKENE

SYPRISS - KIPELIKE

SYDNEI - KIKENEI

SYREETA - KILEKA

SYDNEY - KIKENEI

SYTH - KIKE

SYDNI - KIKINI

SYVELLEAH - KIWELEAHA

SYLEINA - KILEINA

SYVERIA - KIWELIA

SYLMA - KILEMA

SYVIA - KIWIA

SYLVA - KILEWA

SZAKARY - KAKAKALI

SYLVAIN - KILEAINE

SZION - KAKIONU

SYLVANIA - KILEWANIA

SYLVANNAH - KILEWANAHA

SYLVANUS - KILEWANUKO

SYLVESTER - KILEWEKELI

SYLVIA - KILIWIA

SYLVIANE - KILEWIANE

SYLVIE - KILEWIE

SYMANTHA - KIMANAKA

SYMBERLY - KIMEPELI

SYMBRIA - KIMEPELIA

SYMONI - KIMONI

T

FIRST NAMES

TAB - KAPA
TABATHA - KAPAKA
TABBIE - KAPIE
TABBY - KAPI
TABEER - KAPELI
TABITHA - KAPIKA
TABIUS - KAPIUKO
TACARRA - KAKALA
TACE - KAKE
TACEY - KAKEI
TACO - KAKO
TAD - KAKA
TADASHI - KAKAKI
TADDER - KAKELI
TAE - KAE
TAEDRA - KAEKILA
TAEJAI - KAEIAI
TAELA - KAELA
TAELOR - KAELOLU
TAEWON - KAEWONU
TAFARA - KAPALA
TAFFY - KAPI
TAFT - KAPAKA
TAGEN - KAKENI
TAGG - KAKA
TAGGART - KAKAKA
TAHAMINA - KAHAMINA
TAHEERAH - KAHELAHA
TAHIR - KAHILE
TAHISHA - KAHIKA

TAHITUEY - KAHIKUEI
TAHLEE - KAHALE
TAHLIA - KAHALIA
TAHLYA - KAHALIA
TAHNAE - KAHANAE
TAHNI - KAHANI
TAHSEEN - KAHAKENI
TAHYA - KAHIA
TAI - KAI
TAIGAN - KAIKANA
TAILOR - KAILOLU
TAINA - KAINA
TAIR - KAILE
TAISA - KAIKA
TAITE - KAIKE
TAIYA - KAIIA
TAJ - KAI
TAJA - KAIA
TAJAL - KAIALA
TAJIA - KAIIA
TAJINDER - KAIINEKELI
TAJIRI - KAIILI
TAJJI - KAII
TAJSH - KAIKE
TAJUAN - KAIUANA
TAKAHIRO - KAKAHILO
TAKAO - KAKAO
TAKARA - KAKALA
TAKASHI - KAKAKI
TAKEISHA - KAKEIKA

TAKIYAH - KAKIIAHA

TALA - KALA

TALAKAI - KALAKAI

TALANI - KALANI

TALAYA - KALAIA

TALBERT - KALAPEKI

TALBOT - KALAPOKU

TALEEN - KALENI

TALEESHA - KALEKA

TALEISHA - KALEIKA

TALENT - KALENIKI

TALER - KALELI

TALI - KALI

TALIA - KALIA

TALIAH - KALIAHA

TALIB - KALIPE

TALICIA - KALIKIA

TALIENA - KALIENA

TALINE - KALINE

TALISA - KALIKA

TALISHA - KALIKA

TALISKA - KALIKEKA

TALITA - KALIKA

TALITHA - KALIKA

TALLI - KALI

TALLIE - KALIE

TALLIS - KALIKE

TALLON - KALONU

TALLULAH - KALULA

TALLUS - KALUKO

TALMA - KALAMA

TALMAGE - KALAMAKE

TALON - KALONU

TALOR - KALOLU

TALU - KALU

TALVIN - KALAWINE

TAM - KAMA

TAMAKI - KAMAKI

TAMALA - KAMALA

TAMANDA - KAMANAKA

TAMANTHA - KAMANAKA

TAMAR - KAMALA

TAMARA - KAMALA

TAMAREA - KAMALEA

TAMARSHALITA - KAMALAKALIKA

TAMAS - KAMAKA

TAMATHA - KAMAKA

TAMAYA - KAMAIA

TAMBARINE - KAMAPALINE

TAMBI - KAMAPI

TAMBRA - KAMAPALA

TAMECA - KAMEKA

TAMEEKA - KAMEKA

TAMEESHA - KAMEKA

TAMEIA - KAMEIA

TAMELA - KAMELA

TAMERA - KAMELA

TAMESHIA - KAMEKIA

TAMETRIA - KAMELIA

TAMI - KAMI

TAMIA - KAMIA
TAMICA - KAMIKA
TAMIKA - KAMIKA
TAMIKKA - KAMIKA
TAMIKO - KAMIKO
TAMINA - KAMINA
TAMIR - KAMILE
TAMIRA - KAMILA
TAMISHA - KAMIKA
TAMITRA - KAMILA
TAMLYN - KAMALINE
TAMMI - KAMI
TAMMIE - KAMIE
TAMMY - KAMI
TAMRA - KAMALA
TAMRI - KAMALI
TAMSIN - KAMAKINE
TAMYRA - KAMILA
TAN - KANA
TANA - KANA
TANASIA - KANAKIA
TANDERA - KANAKELA
TANDIE - KANAKIE
TANDY - KANAKI
TANESHA - KANEKA
TANESSA - KANEKA
TANETTE - KANEKE
TANEYA - KANEIA
TANG - KANA
TANGELA - KANELA

TANGERINE - KANELINE
TANGIE - KANIE
TANI - KANI
TANIA - KANIA
TANIAH - KANIAHA
TANICE - KANIKE
TANIKA - KANIKA
TANIKIA - KANIKIA
TANIS - KANIKE
TANISHA - KANIKA
TANITH - KANIKE
TANJA - KANIA
T'ANNA - KA'ANA
TANNA - KANA
TANNAZ - KANAKA
TANNEN - KANENI
TANNER - KANELI
TANNISH - KANIKE
TANNO - KANO
TANNOR - KANOLU
TANO - KANO
TANSON - KANAKONU
TANU - KANU
TANVEER - KANAWELI
TANVI - KANAWI
TANWA - KANAWA
TANYIKA - KANIIKA
TANYA - KANIA
TANYS - KANIKE
TA'QUAN - KA'AKANA

TAQUINA - KAKINA

TARA - KALI

TARANEH - KALANEHI

TARAS - KALAKA

TARASA - KALAKA

TAREQ - KALEKI

TARI - KALI

TARIK - KALIKE

TARINA - KALINA

TARIQ - KALIKE

TARLYN - KALINE

TARMI - KALAMI

TARNI - KALANI

TAROLYN - KALOLINE

TARON - KALONU

TARQUIN - KALAKINE

TARREL - KALELI

TARRISHA - KALIKA

TARSH - KALAKA

TARUN - KALUNO

TARVINDER - KALAWINEKELI

TARYN - KILANA

TARZAN - KALAKANA

TAS - KAKA

TASHA - KAKA

TASHANA - KAKANA

TA'SHAY - KA'AKAI

TASHEBA - KAKEPA

TASHELLE - KAKELE

TASHEUAL - KAKEUALA

TASHINA - KAKINA

TASVIRA - KAKAWILA

TASHIA - KAKIA

TAMISHA - KAMIKA

TASHJIA - KAKIIA

TASIA - KAKIA

TASNIM - KAKANIME

TASVIRA - KAKAWILA

TATE - KAKE

TATENDA - KAKENIKA

TATIA - KAKIA

TATIANA - KAKIANA

TATILIA - KAKILIA

TATJANA - KAKIANA

TATRI - KALI

TATS - KAKA

TATSUO - KAKUO

TATUM - KAKUMO

TATY - KAKI

TATYANA - KAKIANA

TAUNYA - KAUNIA

TAUREAN - KAULEANA

TAURINE - KAULINE

TAUSHI - KAUKI

TAVAN - KAWANA

TAVARA - KAWALA

TAVEE - KAWE

TAVEH - KAWEHI

TAVEN - KAWENI

TAVIA - KAWIA

TAVIE - KAWIE
TAVO - KAWO
TAWANDA - KAWANAKA
TAWEH - KAWEHI
TAWNIE - KAWANIE
TAWNIESHA - KAWANIEKA
TAWANNA - KAWANA
TAWAU - KAWAU
TAWNEE - KAWANE
TAWNY - KAWAN
TAWNYA - KAWANIA
TAY - KAI
TAYA - KAIA
TAYAH - KAIAHA
TAYAH-LEA - KAIAHA-ALEA
TAYARAMMA - KAIALAMA
TAYARI - KAIALI
TAYDEN - KAIKENI
TAYE - KAIE
TAYEN - KAIENI
TAYLA - KAILA
TAYLAN - KAILANA
TAYLAR - KAILALA
TAYLEN - KAILENI
TAYLER -KAILELI
TAYLIN - KAILINE
TAYLOE - KAILOE
TAYLON - KAILONU
TAYLOR - KAILOLU
TAYON - KAIONU

TAYSHA - KAIKA
TAYSHEA - KAIKEA
TAYTE - KAIKE
TAYTEN - KAIKENI
TAYTOM - KAIKOMA
TAYTUM - KAIKUMA
TAYVEN - KAIWENI
TAZE - KAKE
TEA - KEA
TEAGAN - KEAKANA
TEAH - KEAHA
TEAKIA - KEAKIA
TEAL - KEALA
TEALA - KEALA
TEANDRA - KEANAKALA
TEANNA - KEANA
TEARA - KEALA
TEARIAN - KEALIANA
TEARL - KEALA
TECHANDRA - KEKANAKALA
TECKBENG - KEKIKIPENI
TECORA - KEKOLA
TED - KEKA
TEDDRA - KEKILA
TEDDY - KEKI
TEE - KE
TEEA - KEA
TEENA - KENA
TEERAWAT - KELAWAKA
TEESHA - KEKA

TEFFANY - KEPANI

TELMA - KELIMA

TEGAN - KEKANA

TESLA - KEKILA

TEHANA - KEHANA

TEMILY - KEMILI

TEHILLAH - KEHILAHA

TEMIKA - KEMIKA

TEHYA - KEHIA

TEMISHA - KEMIKA

TEIGAN - KEIKANA

TEMORA - KEMOLA

TEILA - KEILA

TEMPER - KEMIPELI

TEI'QUAN - KEI'EKANA

TEMPEST - KEMIPEKI

TEIRSON - KEILEKONU

TEMPLE - KEMIPILE

TEIYA - KEIIA

TENA - KENA

TEJA - KEIA

TENAYA - KENAIA

TEJAI - KEIAI

TENCHIA - KENIKIA

TEJAL - KEIALA

TENE - KENE

TEJNOOR - KEINOLU

TENEE' - KENE'I

TEJU - KEIU

TENIA - KENIA

TEJVIR - KEIWILE

TENICIA - KENIKIA

TEKE - KEKE

TENILE - KENILE

TEKEISHA - KEKEIKA

TENLEY - KENILEI

TEKEYAH - KEKEIAHA

TENNEYCE - KENEIKE

TEKI - KEKI

TENNILLE - KENILE

TEKINA - KEKINA

TENNIS - KENIKE

TEKRISHA - KEKILIKA

TENNY - KENI

TELEENA - KELENA

TENYSHIA - KENIKIA

TELESE - KELEKE

TENZIN - KENIKINE

TELIA - KELIA

TEO - KEO

TELICIA - KELIKIA

TEODORO - KEOKOLO

TELINA - KELINA

TEOFILO - KEOPILO

TELISA - KELIKA

TEORNY - KEOLUNI

TELLA - KELA

TEPY - KEPI

TELLY - KELI

TEQUIA - KEKIA

TEQUILA - KEKEILA

TERA - KELA

TERAH - KELAHA

TEREA - KELEA

TEREISHA - KELEIKA

TEREK - KELEKI

TERELA - KELELA

TEREN - KELENI

TERESA - KELEKA

TERESAK - KELEKAKA

TERESE - KELEKIA

TERESITA - KELEKIKA

TERESSA - KELEKA

TEREZA - KELEKA

TERI - KELI

TERICE - KELIKE

TERIN - KELINA

TERINA - KELINA

TERNITA - KELINIKA

TERRA - KELA

TERRAN - KELANA

TERRELL- KELELI

TERRENCE - KELENIKE

TERRENESHA - KELENEKA

TERRI – KELI

TERRIANNE - KELIANE

TERRILYNN - KELILINE

TERRI-LYNNE - KELI-ELINE

TERRINA - KELINA

TERRIS - KELIKE

TERRON - KELONU

TERRY – KELI

TERRYSTAN - KELIKANA

TERYL - KELILE

TESHAE - KEKAE

TESHIA - KEKIA

TESLIN - KEKILINE

TESS - KEKI

TESSA - KEKA

TESSIE - KEKIE

TESSIN - KEKINE

TEVIN - KEWINE

TEVON - KEWONU

TEWANNA - KEWANA

TEX - KEKI

TEYA - KEIA

TEYLOR - KEILOLU

TEYME - KEIME

TEZ - KEKI

THABEN - KAPENI

THACH - KAKA

THAD - KAKA

THADDEUS - KAKEUKO

THADIOUS - KAKIOUKO

THAI - KAI

THAINE - KAINE

THAIS - KAIKE

THALIA - KALIA

THALISSA - KALIKA

THALYNN - KALINE

THANDI - KANAKI
THANG - KANA
THANH - KANAHA
THANNO - KANO
THAO - KAO
THAREN - KALENI
THAVONE - KAWONE
THEA - KEA
THEARY - KEALI
THEIN - KEINE
THEISSON - KEIKONU
THELMA - KAMA
THEO - KEO
THEODORA - KEOKOLA
THEODORE - KEOKOLE
THEOPHANO - KEOPANO
THERESA - KELEKA
THERESE - KELEKIA
THERIAN - KELIANA
THERON - KELONU
THEYNONIA - KEINONIA
THI - KI
THIAGO - KIAKO
THIAMI - KIAMI
THIANHUAT - KIANAHUAKA
THIERRY - KIELI
THIES - KIEKI
THIDA - KIKA
THIMAPPA - KIMAPA
THOA - KOA

THOM - KOMU
THOMAS - KOMA
THOMASA - KOMAKA
THOMASINA -KOMAKINA
THOMI - KOMI
THONGSOTH - KONUKOKU
THOR - KOLU
THORA - KOLA
THORBJORN - KOLUPIOLUNU
THORNEL - KOLUNELI
THORSTEN - KOLUKENI
THORUNN - KOLUNO
THORVAL - KOLUWALA
THOUKI - KOUKI
THRISHALA - LIKALA
THRUSH - LUKO
THU - KU
THUC - KUKO
THULA - KULA
THUNDER - KUNOKELI
THUMPER - KUMOPELI
THURMAN - KULOMANA
THURMON - KULOMONU
THUY - KUI
THUYEN - KUIENI
THYME - KIME
THYRA - KILA
TIA - KIA
TIAHNA - KIAHANA
TIAJA - KIAIA

TIAMARIE - KIAMALIE
TIAN - KIANA
TIANA - KIANA
TIANIE - KIANIE
TIANNA - KIANA
TIANNAH - KIANAHA
TIANYUN - KIANIUNO
TIARA - KIALA
TIARE - KIALE
TIARNE - KIALANE
TIARRA - KIALA
TIAUDA - KIAUKA
TIBBS - KIPEKE
TIBEE - KIPE
TICE - KIKE
TIEN - KIENI
TIERNAN - KIELINANA
TIERNEY - KIELINEI
TIERRA - KIELA
TIERRE - KIELE
TIERS - KIELIKI
TIETTA - KIEKA
TIEYESSIA - KIEIEKIA
TIFANE - KIPANE
TIFANNY - KIPANI
TIFFANI - KIPANI
TIFFANIE - KIPANIE
TIFFANY - KIPANI
TIFFENY - KIPENI
TIFFIANI - KIPIANI

TIFFINI - KIPINI
TIFFINY - KIPINI
TIFFONI - KIPONI
TIGER - KIKELI
TIGGER - KIKELI
TIGHE - KIKEHE
TIGRESS - KIKELEKI
TIILONI - KILONI
TIIU - KIU
TIJUANA - KIIUANA
TIJON - KIIONU
TIKI - KIKI
TILDEN - KILENI
TILL - KILE
TILLIE - KILIE
TILLIESA - KILIEKA
TILMAN - KILEMANA
TIM - KIMO
TIMANE - KIMANE
TIMARI - KIMALI
TIMBER - KIMEPELI
TIMBERLIE - KIMEPELIE
TIMBRA - KIMEPELA
TIMBREY - KIMEPELEI
TIMARIE - KIMALIE
TIMERRA - KIMELA
TIMEX - KIMEKI
TIMIKA - KIMIKA
TIMILLIE - KIMILIE
TIMIONA - KIMIONA

TIMM - KIME

TIMMI - KIMI

TIMMY - KIMI

TIMOLEE - KIMOLE

TIMOTHEE - KIMOKE

TIMOTHIA - KIMOKIA

TIMOTHY - KIMOKEO

TIN - KINE

TINA – KINA

TINDY - KINEKI

TINE - KINE

TINEKA - KINEKA

TING TING - KINE KINE

TINNELLE - KINELE

TINK - KINEKE

TINKERBELL - KINEKELIPELI

TINO - KINO

TINUS - KINUKO

TINY - KINI

TIONA - KIONA

TIONDRA - KIONUKULA

TIONETTE - KIONEKE

TIONNA - KIONA

TIONNI - KIONI

TIP - KIPE

TIPHANI - KIPANI

TIPPER - KIPELI

TIPPIN - KIPINE

TIRA - KILA

TIRZAH - KILEKAHA

TISA - KIKA

TISART - KIKAKA

TISH - KIKE

TISHA - KIKA

TISHALL - KIKALA

TISHARA - KIKALA

TIRSHATHA - KILEKAKA

TISHAWN - KIKAWANA

TISHNA - KIKENA

TISHUNNA - KIKUNA

TITA - KIKA

TITIANA - KIKIANA

TITO - KIKO

TITUS - KIKUKO

TIYAH - KIIAHA

TIYANNA - KIIANA

TIYOSHA - KIIOKA

TIZIANA - KIKIANA

TJITS - KIIKE

T'KEYAH - KA'AKEIAHA

T'NIYZSA - KA'ANIIKEKA

TOBE - KOPE

TOBIAS - KOPIAKA

TOBIE - KOPIE

TOBIN - KOPINE

TOBY - KOPI

TOCASHE - KOKAKE

TODD - KOKA

TOI - KOI

TOKI - KOKI

TOKIYO - KOKIIO

TOKS - KOKUKU

TOLEDO - KOLEKO

TOLLEENA - KOLENA

TOLOYA - KOLOIA

TOM - KOMA

TOMARA - KOMALA

TOMARO - KOMALO

TOMAS - KOMAKA

TOMBRA - KOMUPULA

TOMEI - KOMEI

TOMEISHA - KONEIKA

TOMELLAR - KOMELALA

TOMEK - KOMEKI

TOMEKA - KOMEKA

TOMI - KOMI

TOMIKA - KOMIKA

TOMILYNN - KOMILINE

TOMMACITA - KOMAKIKA

TOMMIE - KOMIE

TOMMISINA - KOMIKINA

TOMMY - KOME

TOMOKO - KOMOKO

TOMOMI - KOMOMI

TOMORAH - KOMOLAHA

TOMRIS - KOMULIKE

TONDA - KONUKA

TONERIA - KONELIA

TONESSA - KONEKA

TONETTE - KONEKE

TONI - KONI

TONIA - KONIA

TONIANN - KONIANA

TONIKA - KONIKA

TONITA - KONIKA

TONJA - KONIA

TONJUS - KONIUKO

TONNA - KONA

TONY - KONI

TONYA - KONIA

TOODY - KOKI

TOOMAS - KOMAKA

TOONNY - KONI

TOOTER - KOKELI

TOOTSIE - KOKIE

TOPANGA - KOPANA

TOPHER - KOPELI

TORASHA - KOLAKA

TORBEN - KOLUPENI

TORCUATO - KOLUKUAKO

TOREATHA - KOLEAKA

TOREE - KOLE

TORGEIR - KOKEILE

TORI - KOLI

TORIA - KOLIA

TORIE - KOLIE

TORLAN - KOLANA

TORONTO - KOLONUKO

TORRA - KOLA

TORREN - KOLENI

TORRENCE - KOLENIKE
TORREVIO - KOLEWIO
TORREY - KOLEI
TORRIE - KOLIE
TORRODD - KOLOKU
TORYN - KOLINE
TOSCA - KOKUKA
TOSH - KOKU
TOSHA - KOKA
TOSIN - KOKINE
TOT - KOKU
TOUA - KOUA
TOULA - KOULA
TOVA - KOWA
TOVIA - KOWIA
TOWNES - KOWUNEKI
TOYA - KOIA
TOYETTA - KOIEKA
TOYIE - KOIIE
TOYIKA - KOIIKA
TOYOKO - KOIOKO
TOYYA - KOIA
TRABILLE - LAPILE
TRACE - LAKE
TRACEE - LAKE
TRACEY - LAKEI
TRACI - LAKI
TRACIE - LAKIE
TRACY - KALAKI
TRACYE - LAKIE

TRAE - LAE
TRAER - LAELI
TRAJAN - LAEIANA
TRALANA - LALANA
TRALISA - LALIKA
TRALONDA - LALONUKA
TRAMIA - LAMIA
TRAML - LAMALA
TRAMMELL - LAMELI
TRAN - LANA
TRANG - LANA
TRAPPER - LAPELI
TRASE - LAKE
TRAVER - LAWELI
TRAVERSE - LAWELIKE
TRAVES - LAWEKI
TRAVIA - LAWIA
TRAVIE - LAWIE
TRAVIS - KALAWIKA
TRAVON - LAWONU
TRAY - LAI
TRAYCE - LAIKE
TRAYLOR - LAILOU
TRAYONA - LAIONA
TRAYTON - LAIKONU
TRAYVIS - LAIWIKE
TRE' - LE
TREA - LEA
TREASURE - LEAKULE
TRECIA - LEKIA

TRECIANA - LEKIANA

TRECY - LEKI

TREECE - LEKE

TREENA - LENA

TREGAR - LEKALA

TREINA - LEINA

TREJOR - LEIOLU

TRELLA - LELA

TRELLI - LELI

TRELLIS - LELIKE

TREMAINE - LEMAINE

TREMAYNE - LEMAINE

TREMELL - LEMELI

TRENA - LENA

TRENACE - LENAKE

TRENDY - LENIKI

TRENISHA - LENIKA

TRENT - LENIKI

TRENTON - LENIKONU

TRES - LEKI

TRESE' - LEKE'I

TRESHINE - LEKINE

TRESLYNNE - LEKILINE

TRESSA - LEKA

TRESSIE - LEKIE

TRESSIA - LEKIA

TRESTIAN - LEKIANA

TRESTYN - LEKINE

TRESON - LEKONU

TREVA - LEWA

TREVAN - LEWANA

TREVEN - LEWENI

TREVIN - LEWINE

TREVINA - LEWINA

TREVIS - LEWIKE

TRE'VON - LE'IWONU

TREVOR- LEWOLU

TREVYN - LEWINE

TREY - LEI

TREYCE - LEIKE

TREYSON - LEIKONU

TREYVON - LEIWONU

TREZUR - LEKULO

TRIANA - LIANA

TRICIA - LIKIA

TRIESTA - LIEKA

TRIFFICA - LIPIKA

TRIFON - LIPONU

TRIIN - LINE

TRIINU - LINU

TRIJA - LIIA

TRILBY - LILEPI

TRILLIUM - LILIUMO

TRINA - LINA

TRINDA - LINEKA

TRINE - LINE

TRINEKA - LINEKA

TRINELL - LINELI

TRINETTE - LINEKE

TRINH - LINE

TRINITA - LINIKA

TRINITY - LINIKI

TRINKA - LINEKA

TRINT - LINEKE

TRIP - LIPE

TRIPP - LIPE

TRISH - LIKE

TRISHA - LIKA

TRISSY - LIKI

TRISTA - LIKA

TRISTAN - LIKANA

TRISTEN - LIKENI

TRISTIAN - LIKIANA

TRISTIN - LIKINE

TRISTON - LIKONU

TRIVA - LIWA

TRIXIBELLE - LIKIPELE

TRIXIE - LIKIE

TROE - LOE

TROIA - LOIA

TRON - LONU

TROND - LONUKU

TROOPER - LOPELI

TROTTY - LOKI

TROY - LOI

TRUDA - LUKA

TRUDI - KALUKI

TRUDY - KALUKI

TRUETT - LUEKI

TRULIE - LULIE

TRUMAN - LUMANA

TRYG - LIKE

TRYNITY - LINIKI

TRYSTAN - LIKANA

TRYSTINA - LINIKA

TRYSTON - LIKONU

TSERENDORJ - KELENIKOLI

TSERINA - KELINA

TSIONA - KIONA

TSUME - KUME

TSUNEYUKI - KUNEIUKI

TU - KU

TUAN - KUANA

TUCKER - KUKOKELI

TUCKY - KUKOKI

TUESDAY - KUEKIKAI

TULAY - KULAI

TULIN - KULINE

TULLE - KULE

TULLIO - KULIO

TULLY - KULI

TULSA - KULOK

TULU - KULUA

TUNDE - KUNOKE

TUNG - KUNO

TUNISHA - KUNIKA

TUOMAS - KUOMAKA

TURIYA - KULIIA

TURK - KUKO

TURNEISHA - KULONEIKA

TURNER - KULONELI

TURTLE - KUKOLE

TUSHAR - KUKALA

TUY - KUI

TUYEN - KUIENI

TUYET - KUIEKI

TUZZINA - KUKINA

TWANETTA - KAWANEKA

TWANNESHA - KAWANEKA

TWEED - KAWEKI

TWIGGY - KAWIKI

TWILLA - KAWILA

TWINK - KAWINEKE

TWYLA - KAWILA

TY - KI

TYANA - KIANA

T'YANNA - KA'IANA

TYBRIE - KIPELIE

TYCAL - KIKALA

TYCHANDER - KIKANAKELI

TYCHO - KIKO

TYDE - KIKE

TYE - KIE

TYEE - KIE

TYENESHA - KIENEKA

TYESHA - KIEKA

TYGER - KIKELI

TYGIMA - KIKIMA

TYJAI - KIIAI

TYJSHA - KIIKA

TYKAVON - KIKAWONU

TYKEVIAN - KIKEWIANA

TYLA - KILA

TYLAN - KILANA

TYLE - KILE

TYLEE - KILE

TYLENE - KILENE

TYLER - KILEKI

TYMBER - KIMEPELI

TYNIECH - KINIEKI

TYLISHA - KILIKA

TYLOR - KILOLU

TYLYN - KILINE

TYMORI - KIMOLI

TYNANA - KINANA

TYNEZHIA - KINEKIHIA

TYNISHA - KINIKA

TYRA - KILA

TYREE - KILE

TYREK - KILEKI

TYREIK - KILEIKE

TYRELL - KILELI

TYREN - KILENI

TYRENA - KILENA

TYRENE - KILENE

TYRESE - KILEKE

TYRISHA - KILIKA

TYRITHA - KILIKA

TYRON - KILONU

TYRONE - KAILONE

TYRUS - KULO

TYSHAH - KIKAHA

TYSIE - KIKIE

TYSON - KIKONU

TY'TANNA - KI'EKANA

TYUS - KIUKO

TY'WAN - KI'EWANA

TYZAJAYLA - KIKAIAILA

TZIPPORAH - KAKIPOLAHA

TZIPPY - KAKIPI

U

FIRST NAMES

UACERKIU - UAKEKIU

UARDA - UALAKA

UBAID - UPAIKE

UCHE - UKE

UDAWNA - UKAWANA

UDHANTH - UKOHANAKA

UGASHREE - UKAKALE

UGO - UKO

UJVAL - UIWALA

ULAH - ULAHA

ULANDA - ULANAKA

ULF - ULOPO

ULISES - ULIKEKI

ULLA - ULA

ULRIC - ULOLIKE

ULRIKA - ULOLIKA

ULRIKE - ULOLIKE

ULTI - ULOKI

ULTIMINIO - ULOKIMINIO

ULYSSES - ULEKI

UMA - UMA

UMANG - UMANA

UMAR - UMALA

UMASHANKAR - UMAKANAKALA

UMBERTO - UMOPEKO

UMIKA - UMIKA

UNA - UNA

UNDERWOOD - UNOKELIWOKU

UNEEDA - UNEKA

UNIA - UNIA

UNIQUE - UNIKE

UNIQUEWEYA - UNIKEWEIA

UNIS - UNIKE

UNISSA - UNIKA

UNITY - UNIKI

UNJANETTA - UNIANEKA

UNREE - UNOLE

URANUS - ULANUKO

URBANO - ULOPANO

URIAH - ULIAHA

URIEL - ULIELI

URIJAH - ULIIAHA

URSULA - ULUKULA

URVASHI - ULOWAKI

URWANA - ULOWANA

USAMA - UKAMA

USHA - UKA

USHER - UKELI

USMAN - UKOMANA

UTA - UKA

UTE - UKE

UVELA - UWELA

UWE - UWE

UYENNGA - UIENA

UZIEL - UKIELI

UZMA - UKOMA

V

FIRST NAMES

VADA - WAKA
VADELIA - WAKELIA
VALDEN - WALENI
VADIM - WAKIME
VAHAN - WAHANA
VAHE - WAHE
VAHTA - WAHAKA
VAIDEHI - WAIKEHI
VAIDEN - WAIKENI
VAIL - WAILE
VAISHALI - WAIKALI
VAISHNAVI - WAIKENAWI
VAITI - WAIKI
VAL - WALE
VALAIRE - WALAILE
VALAREE - WALALE
VALARIE - WALALIE
VALARY - WALALI
VALDA - WALA
VALDEAN - WALEANA
VALDIS - WALIKE
VALEDA - WALEKA
VALEENA - WALENA
VALEENE - WALENE
VALEN - WALENI
VALENE - WALENE
VALENCIA - WALENIKIA
VALENTE - WALENIKE
VALENTINA - WALENEKINA
VALENTINE - WALENEKINE

VALENTINO - WALENIKINO
VALERA - WALELA
VALERIA - WALEIA
VALERICK - WALELIKEKE
VALERIE - WALELIA
VALESHA - WALEKA
VALETA - WALEKA
VALICIA - WALIKIA
VALICITY - WALIKIKI
VALIK - WALIKE
VALINDA - WALINEKA
VALKYRIE - WALAKILIE
VALLEN - WALENI
VALLIE - WALIE
VALLIER - WALIELI
VALMA - WALAMA
VALORIE - WALOLIE
VALOUNY - WALOUNI
VALYNN - WALINE
VALYSSA - WALIKA
VAN - WANA
VAN ESSEN - WANA EKENI
VANA - WANA
VANASTACIA - WANAKAKIA
VANCE - WANAKE
VANDA - WANAKA
VANDELL - WANAKELI
VANDRA - WANAKALA
VANDY - WANAKI
VANEET - WANEKI

311.

VANEKA - WANEKA

VANESA - WANEKA

VANESHA - WANEKA

VANESHREE - WANEKILE

VANETTA - WANEKA

VANGIE - WANIE

YANGSTE - IANAKE

VANIA - WANIA

VANIDI - WANIKI

VANISHA - WANIKA

VANITA - WANIKA

VANESSA - WANEKA

VANIA - WANIA

VANIECE - WANIEKE

VANIK - WANIKE

VANILA - WANILA

VANNIE - WANIE

VANNI - WANI

VANNEY - WANEI

VANNY - WANI

VANSA - WANAKA

VANTANEE - WANAKANE

VANYA - WANIA

VAQAS - WAKAKA

VAREE - WALE

VARINIA - WALINIA

VARLEY - WALEI

VARO - WALO

VARRICK - WALIKEKE

VARSHA - WALAKA

VART - WAKA

VARUN - WALUNO

VASANTH - WAKANAKA

VASANTHI - WAKANAKI

VASANTI - WAKANAKI

VASCO - WAKAKO

VARSHINI - WALAKINI

VASHTI - WAKAKI

VASILE - WAKILE

VASILI - WAKILI

VASSY - WAKI

VASU - WAKU

VASYANA - WAKIANA

VAUGHN - WANA

VEANNA - WEANA

VEATRICE - WEALIKE

VECILE - WEKILE

VEDA - WEKA

VEDIA - WEKIA

VEE - WE

VEEDERS - WEKELIKI

VEENA - WENA

VEENISHA - WENIKA

VEERAL - WELALA

VEEVO - WEWO

VEGA - WEKA

VEGARD - WEKALAKA

VEGO - WEKO

VEHLILAH - WEHILILAHA

VEL - WELI

VELANI - WELANI
VELDA - WELA
VELEKA - WELEKA
VELERIA - WELELIA
VELIA - WELIA
VELIDA - WELIKA
VELISA - WELIKA
VELLIA - WELIA
VELLINDA - WELINEKA
VELMA - WELAMA
VELORA - WELOLA
VELTA - WELIKA
VELVET - WELIWEKI
VENECIA - WENEKIA
VENEDA - WENEKA
VENEE - WENE
VENEIGH - WENEIKEHE
VENESSA - WENEKA
VENGELIN - WENELINE
VENITA - WENIKA
VENKATA - WENIKAKA
VENKATESH - WNEIKAKEKI
VENNA - WENA
VENNIE - WENIE
VENONIA - WENONIA
VENSO - WENIKO
VENTURA - WENIKULA
VENUS - WENUKO
VEONNA - WEONA
VERA - WILA

VERCELLY - WELIKELI
VERDA - WELIKA
VERDAN - WELIKANA
VERDELL - WELIKELI
VERENA - WELENA
VERENYA - WELENIA
VERISHA - WELIKA
VERL - WELI
VERLA - WELA
VERLENE - WELENE
VERIL - WELILE
VERITY - WELIKI
VERLIN - WELINE
VERLINE - WELINE
VERLIS - WELIKE
VERMAN - WELIMANA
VERNA – WELENA
VERN - WELINI
VERNARD - WELINALAKA
VERNEDA - WELINEKA
VERNEL - WELINELI
VERNER - WELINELI
VERNESSA - WELINEKA
VERNIE - WELINIE
VERNIQUE - WELINIKE
VERNITA - WELINIKA
VERNON - WENONA
VERNUS - WELINUKO
VERON - WELONU
VERONA - WELONA

VERONICA - WALONIKA

VERONIKE - WELONIKE

VERONIZ - WELONIKE

VERSARY - WELIKALI

VERSIE - WELIKIE

VERSIL - WELIKILE

VERTA - WEKA

VERTLENE - WEKILENE

VERY - WELI

VESNA - WEKINA

VESTA - WEKA

VESTIE - WEKIE

VETA - WEKA

VEYDA - WEIKA

VI - WI

VIANCA - WIANAKA

VIANNE - WIANE

VIC - WIKE

VICCI - WIKI

VICENTE - WIKENIKE

VICHITRA - WIKILA

VICKI - WIKI

VICKIE - WIKEKIE

VICKY - WIKI

VICTOR - WIKOLI

VICTORIA - WIKOLIA

VICTORY - WIKOLI

VIDA - WIKA

VIDAL - WIKALA

VIDHI - WIKEHI

VIDHYA - WIKEHIA

VIDISHA - WIKIKA

VIDYA - WIKIA

VIENNA - WIENA

VIETTE - WIEKE

VIGGO - WIKO

VIHAN - WINHANA

VIIVI - WIWI

VIJAY - WIIAI

VIJAYA - WIIAIA

VIJU - WIIU

VIKA - WIKA

VIKKI - WIKI

VIKRAANT - WIKELANAKA

VIKRAM - WIKELAMA

VILANI - WILANI

VILATE - WILAKE

VILE - WILE

VILEO - WILEO

VILIUS - WILIUKO

VILLA - WILA

VILLARAZA - WILALAKA

VILLIERA - WILIELA

VILLIERS - WILIELIKI

VILMA - WILEMA

VILULA - WILULA

VIMA - WIMA

VIMAL - WIMALA

VINA - WINA

VINAYA - WINAIA

VINCE - WINIKE
VINCENT - WINIKENEKE
VINCENZA - WINEKENIKA
VINCETTA - WINEKEKA
VINETA - WINEKA
VINO - WINO
VINSON - WINEKONU
VIRIAN - WILIANA
VINICIUS - WINIKIUKO
VIRINDA - WILINEKA
VINITA - WINIKA
VINNIE – WINI
VIOLA - WINI
VIOLET - WAIOLEKA
VIOLETA - WIOLEKA
VIPIN - WIPINE
VIRDYA - WILEKIA
VIRDEN - WILEKENI
VIRGA - WIKA
VIRGIE - WIKIE
VIRGIL - WILIKILIA
VIRGILIE - WIKILIE
VIRGILIO - WIKILIO
VIRGINE - WIKINE
VIRGINIA - WILIKINIA
VIRGINIE - WIKINIE
VIRGIS - WIKIKE
VISHAL - WIKALA
VISHNU - WIKENU
VISION - WIKIONE

VISRUTI - WIKELUKI
VITA - WIKA
VITALY - WIKALI
VITO - WIKO
VITTARIO - WIKALIO
VIV - WIWE
VIVA - WIWA
VIVAN - WIWIANA
VIVEK - WIWEKI
VIVI - WIWI
VIVIA - WIWIA
VIVIAN - WIWIANA
VIVIANA - WIWIANA
VIVIANE - WIWIANE
VIVIANNA - WIWIANA
VIVIARA - WIWIALA
VIVID - WIWIKE
VIVIENE - WIWIENE
VIVIENNE - WIWIENE
VIVOLYN - WIWOLINE
VLADA - WALAKA
VLADIC - WALAKIKE
VLADIMIR - WALAKIMILE
VO - WO
VOGLE - WOKULE
VON - WONU
VONCEIL - WONUKEILE
VONDA - WIKONUKA
VONDRENNA - WONUKULENA
VONE - WONE

VONEKA - WONEKA
VONI - WONI
VONJA - WONIA
VONJENAY - WONIENAI
VONK - WONUKU
VONNE - WONE
VONNETTA - WONEKA
VONNIE - WONIE
VONSHA - WONUKA
VONTAZE - WONUKAKE
VONYA - WONIA
VOULA - WOULA
VOYD - WOIKE
VRENI - WALENI
VRORA - WALOLA
VU - WU
VULLOY - WULOI
VUONG - WUONU
VY - WI
VYANNIS - WIANIKE
VYJU - WIIU
VYNGA - WINA
VYTAS - WIKAKA
VYTAUTAS - WIKAUKAKA

W

FIRST NAMES

WACILA - WAKILA   WARNER - WALANELI

WADDELL - WAKELI   WARNO - WALANO

WADE - WAKE   WARREN - WALENI

WAEL - WAELI   WARTHA - WAKA

WAGNER - WAKANELI   WARWICK - WALAWIKEKE

WAH - WAHA   WASHINGTON - WAKINEKONU

WAHID - WAHIKE   WASI - WAKI

WAJDI - WAIKI   WASKA - WAKAKA

WALDEAN - WALEANA   WATERMAN - WAKELIMANA

WALDEK - WALEKI   WATFA - WAKAPA

WALDO - WALO   WAUNITA - WAUNIKA

WALEED - WALEKI   WAVERLEY - WAWELEI

WALESKA - WALEKIKA   WAVERLY - WAWELI

WALKER - WALAKELI   WAVERY - WAWELI

WALLACE - WAIALE   WAWRZYNCA - WAWALAKINEKA

WALLY - WALI   WAYNE - WEINE

WALMOR - WALAMOLU   WAYLAND - WAILANAKA

WALT - WALAKA   WAYLON - WAIONU

WALTA - WALAKA   WAYMON - WAIMONU

WALTER - WALAKA   WEATHERLY - WEAKELI

WALTERENE - WALAKELENE   WEBB - WEPI

WALTON - WALAKONU   WEBELOS - WEPELOKU

WANA - WANA   WEDNESDAY - WEKINEKIKAI

WANDA - WANAKA   WEENA - WENA

WANDREA - WANAKALEA   WEIHU - WEIHU

WANNAH - WANAHA   WEIJUN - WEIIUNO

WANNELL - WANELI   WEILAND - WEILANAKA

WANNETTA - WANEKA   WEIQI - WEIKI

WARD – WALAKA   WEIZHONG - WEIKEHONU

WARLEY - WALEI   WELCOME - WELIKOME

WARNER - WALANI

WELDEN - WELENI

WELDON - WELONU

WELLES - WELEKI

WELTON - WELIKONU

WENCY - WENIKI

WENDA - WENIKA

WENDAL - WENIKALA

WENDALL - WENIKALA

WENDI - WENIKI

WENDEL - WENIKELI

WENDELL - WENIKELI

WENDELYN - WENIKELINE

WENDOL - WENIKOLU

WENDOLL - WENIKOLU

WENDY - WENIKI

WENG CHEONG - WENI KEONU

WENIKA - WENIKA

WENKY - WENIKI

WENONA - WENONA

WENTIAN - WENIKIANA

WERNER - WELINELI

WES - WEKI

WESLEY - WEKELI

WESTLEY - WEKELI

WESTON - WEKONU

WEZZIE - WEKIE

WHATLEY - WAHAKALEI

WHEATLEY - WAHEAKALEI

WHELLA - WAHELA

WHISPER - WAHIKEPELI

WHITFIELD - WAHIKEPIELI

WHITLEY - WAHIKELEI

WHITNEY- WIKELANI

WHITTEN - WAHIKENI

WHITWORTH - WAHIKEWOKU

WIAM - WIAMA

WIBKE - WIPEKE

WICKER - WIKEKELI

WIDLINE - WIKELINE

WIKUS - WIKUKO

WIL - WILE

WILBERT - WILEPEKI

WILBUR - WILEPULO

WILBURN - WILIPANA

WILDA - WILA

WILEEN - WILENI

WILETA - WILEKA

WILEY -WILEI

WILFORD - WILEPOLUKU

WILFRED – WILIPELEKE

WILFREDO - WILEPELEKO

WILFREN - WILEPELENI

WILHELMINA - WILEMINA

WILKERSON - WILEKELIKONU

WILL - WILE

WILLA - WILA

WILLARD - WILIKA

WILLEM - WILEMI

WILLEMIN - WILEMINE

WILLEMMA - WILEMA
WILLETTE - WILEKE
WILLIAM - WILIAMA
WILLIE - WILE
WILLIS - WILEKA
WILLOUGHBY - WILOUKOHOPI
WILLOW - WILOWU
WILLOWBEE - WILOWUPE
WILLY - WILI
WILMA - WILEMA
WILMER - WILEMELI
WILMONT - WILEMONUKU
WILMOT - WILEMOKU
WILSON – WILIKONA
WILTON - WILEKONU
WINAH - WINAHA
WINDEE - WINEKE
WINDELL - WINEKELI
WINET - WINEKI
WINIFRED - WINIPELEKE
WINK - WINEKE
WINNIBERRTO - WINIPEKO
WINNIE - WINIE
WINOLA - WINOLA
WINONA - WINONA
WINSLOW - WINEKELOWU
WINSON - WINEKONU
WINSTON - WINIKONA
WINTA - WINEKA
WINTER - WINEKELI

WINTON - WINEKONU
WIRTJO - WIKIO
WISBEL - WIKEPELI
WISSAM - WIKAMA
WITT - WIKE
WOLF - WOLUPU
WOLFGANG - WOLUPUKANA
WOLLETT - WOLEKI
WOODY - WOKI
WOON - WONU
|WORRELL - WOLELI
WREDE - WALEKE
WREYNN - WALEINE
WRIGHT - WALIKEHEKE
WUSHIZHE - WUKIKEHE
WYATT - WIAKA
WYLAND - WILANAKA
WYLDER - WILELI
WYLENE - WILENE
WYLIE - WILIE
WYLONDA - WILONUKA
WYMAN - WIMANA
WYNELL - WINELI
WYNELLE - WINELE
WYNETTA - WINEKA
WYNETTE - WINEKE
WYNN - WINE
WYNTER - WINEKELI
WYNTON - WINEKONU
WYOLENE - WIOLENE

322.

X

FIRST NAMES

XAKERY - KAKELI

XAMANTHA - KAMANAKA

XAN - KANA

XANDER - KANAKELI

XANDY - KANAKI

XANTOS - KANAKOKU

XAO - KAO

XAQ - KAKA

XARIE - KALIE

XAVIER - KAWIELI

XAVIERA - KAWIELA

XAVION - KAWIONU

XELA - KELA

XENA - KENA

XENIA - KENIA

XENIE - KENIE

XENIELLE - KENIELE

XENIFER - KENIPELI

XENO - KENO

XENOS - KENOKU

XIA - KIA

XIANA - KIANA

XIANG-KE - KIANA-AKE

XIAOKE - KIAOKE

XIAOQING - KIAOKINE

XIN - KINE

XINING - KININE

XINRONG - KINELONU

XIOMARA - KIOMALA

XIONG - KIONU

XOCHITL - KOKIKELE

XOL - KOLU

XU - KU

XUAN - KUANA

XUEMEI - KUEMEI

XUXA - KUKA

XVANTE - KAWANAKE

XYLINE - KILINE

XYLON - KILONU

Y

FIRST NAMES

YAAKOV - IAKOWU

YACINTHE - IAKINEKE

YACIRA - IAKILA

YADIANE - IAKIANE

YADIANN - IAKIANA

YADIRA - IAKILA

YADRE - IAKALE

YAEL - IAELI

YAFFA - IAPA

YAGEL - IAKELI

YAGESHNIE - IAKEKINIE

YAHAIRA - IAHAILA

YAHEL - IAHELI

YAHJAIRA - IAHIAILA

YAHNIQUE - IAHANIKE

YAICHA - IAIKA

YAINET - IAINEKI

YAIRA - IAILA

YAISMIN - IAIKEMINE

YAITZEL - IAIKEKELI

YAJAIRA - IAIAILA

YAKEA - IAKEA

YAKELIN - IAKELINE

YAKIR - IAKILE

YALEXIS - IALEKIKE

YALITZA - IALIKEKA

YAMIL - IAMILE

YAMILEX - IAMILEKI

YAMINA - IAMINA

YAMMA - IAMA

YAN - IANA

YANA - IANA

YANAL - IANALA

YANAMI - IANAMI

YANCO - IANAKO

YANCY - IANEKI

YANELI - IANELI

YANELIS - IANELIKE

YANESA - IANEKA

YANG - IANA

YANIA - IANIA

YANIE - IANIE

YANIKA - IANIKA

YANIRA - IANILA

YANIV - IANIWE

YANIXY - IANIKI

YANNA - IANA

YANNIC - IANIKE

YANNIS - IANIKE

YANNISYA - IANIKIA

YAP - IAPA

YAPHET - IAPEKI

YARDAN - IALAKANA

YARDLEY - IALAKALEI

YARELY - IALELI

YARITZA - IALIKEKA

YARON - IALONU

YAS - IAKA

YASAMIN - IAKAMINE

YASH - IOKO

YASHAN - IAKANA

YASHICA - IAKIKA

YASHIRA - IAKILA

YASHMIN - IAKAMINE

YASIAH - IAKIAHA

YASMEEN - IAKAMENI

YASMIN - IAKAMINE

YASMINE - IAKAMINE

YASSIER - IAKIELI

YASSYR - IAKILE

YATES - IAKEKI

YATHREB - IALEPI

YAUNETTE - IAUNEKE

YAVNA - IAWANA

YAXCHE - IAKAKE

YAYAH - IAIAHA

YAZAN - IAKANA

YAZMIN - IAKAMINE

YDANIA - IKANIA

YEAN - IEANA

YECHESKIEL - IEKEKIKIELI

YEDI - IEKI

YEE - IE

YEGOR - IEKOLU

YEHUDA - IEHUKA

YEHUDI - IEHUKI

YEISSEN - IEIKENI

YELENA - IELENA

YELSEN - IELIKENI

YEMALA - IEMALA

YEMILI - IEMILI

YEMOND - IEMONUKU

YEN - IENI

YENCE - IENIKE

YEONHEE - IEONUHE

YER - IELI

YERBIE - IELIPIE

YESENIA - IEKENIA

YESICA - IEKIKA

YESSENIA - IEKENIA

YESSINIA - IEKINIA

YETI - IEKI

YETZEL - IEKIKELI

YUEPHENG - IUEPENI

YEVETTE - IEWEKE

YEVONNE - IEWONE

YEWWAH - IEWAHA

YEZAN - IEKANA

YI - II

YIFANG - IIPANA

YILDIZ - IILIKE

YING – I'INE

YINN YII - IINE II

YISHAE - IIKAE

YITING - IIKINE

YITZIE - IIKEKIE

YLANG - ILANA

YLANI - ILANI

YLEANA - ILEANA

YLIANA - ILIANA

Y'LLON - I'ELONU

YMA - IMA

Y'NITA - I'ENIKA

YO - IO

YOCHEVED - IOKEWEKI

YODA - IOKA

YODAIME - IOKAIME

YODET - IOKEKI

YODIT - IOKIKE

YOGESH - IOKEKI

YOGI - IOKI

YOKO - IOKO

YOLA - IOLA

YOLAINE - IOLAINE

YOLANDA - IOLANA

YOLANDE - IOLANAKE

YOLANDIE - IOLANAKIE

YOLIE - IOLIE

YOLINDA - IOLINEKA

YOLLI - IOLI

YOMARIE - IOMALIE

YONASE - IONAKE

YONATHAN - IONAKANA

YONG - IONU

YONGJUN - IONIUNO

YONGKONG - IONUHONU

YONI - IONI

YONIE - IONIE

YONJA - IONIA

YONOUS - IONOUKO

YOOK-LUN - IOKU-ULUNO

YOON JOO - IONU IO

YORI - IOLI

YSABEL - IKAPELI

YOSAN - IOKANA

YOSEF - IOKEPI

YOSELINE - IOKELINE

YOSEPH - IOKEPI

YOSH - IAKA

YOSHEKA - IOKEKA

YOSHI - IOKI

YOSHIKO - IOKIKO

YOUA - IOUA

YOUNG - IOUNO

YOUSSEF - IOUKEPI

YOUWEN - IOUWENI

YOVANIA - IOWANIA

YOYA - IOIA

YRA - ILA

YREN - ILENI

YSA - IKA

YSABELLA - IKAPELA

YSÉ - IKEÉE

YSIDRO - IKIKELO

YTOSSIE - IKOKIE

YUANPENG - IUANAPENI

YUDA - IUKA

YUDIDIAN - IUKIKIANA

YUDIT - IUKIKE

YUGAN - IUKANA

YUI - IUI

YUIKO - IUIKO

YUJI - IUII

YUKARI - IUKALI

YUKO - IUKU

YULISA - IULIKA

YULISSA - IULIKA

YUMI - IUMI

YUMIKO - IUMIKO

YUNG - IUNKI

YUNHAN - IUNOHANA

YUNI - IUNI

YURI - IULI

YURIKA - IULIKA

YURONG - IULONU

YUSEF - IUKEPI

YUSEPTH - IUKEPIKI

YVANNA - IWANA

YVENS - IWENIKI

YVES - IWEKI

YVETTE - IWEKE

YVON - IWONU

YVONNA - IWONA

YVONNE - IWONE

Z

FIRST NAMES

ZABADOO - KAPAKO

ZABEL - KAPELI

ZABREE - KAPALE

ZABRINA - KAPALINA

ZAC - KAKA

ZACARY - KAKALI

ZACARYRAY - KAKALILAI

ZACH - KAKALI

ZACHARIAH - KAKALIAHA

ZACHARY - KAKALI

ZACHERY - KAKELI

ZACK - KAKAKA

ZACKARY - KAKAKALI

ZACKORY - KAKAKOLI

ZACKRE - KAKAKALE

ZAD - KAKA

ZADA - KAKA

ZADE - KAKE

ZADEN - KAKENI

ZADIA - KAKIA

ZADOK - KAKOKU

ZAE - KAE

ZAF - KAPA

ZAFIRO - KAPILO

ZAHAIRA - KAHAILA

ZAHAR - KAHALA

ZAHAVA - KAHAWA

ZAHEER - KAHELI

ZAHI - KAHI

ZAHIR - KAHILE

ZAHNE - KAHANE

ZAHRA - KAHALA

ZAHRAH - KAHALAHA

ZAHRAIN - KAHALAINE

ZAHUR - KAHULO

ZAID - KAIKE

ZAIDA - KAIKA

ZAINA - KAINA

ZAINAB - KAINAPA

ZAINE - KAINE

ZAINEB - KAINEPI

ZAIRA - KAILA

ZAIRE - KAILE

ZAIRRIN - KAILINE

ZAK - KAKA

ZAKAI - KAKAI

ZAKARIAH - KAKALIAHA

ZAKIA - KAKIA

ZAKKE - KAKE

ZAKKEKIA - KAKEKIA

ZALEMA - KALEMA

ZALENA - KALENA

ZALI - KALI

ZAMARA - KAMALA

ZAMIR - KAMILE

ZAN - KANA

ZANDER - KANAKELI

ZANDRA – KANAKALA

ZANDRIA - KANAKALIA

ZANDY - KANAKI

ZANE - KANE

ZANETTA - KANEKA

ZANIAH - KANIAHA

ZANNA - KANA

ZARA - KALA

ZARAH - KALAHA

ZARIA - KALIA

ZARIN - KALINE

ZARIUS - KALIUKO

ZARMINE - KALAMINE

ZARQUIS - KALAKIKE

ZATANA - KAKANA

ZAVIK - KAWIKE

ZAWADI - KAWAKI

ZAYA - KAIA

ZAYAUNA - KAIAUNA

ZAYD - KAIKE

ZAYDA - KAIKA

ZAYETH - KAIEKI

ZAYNAB - KAINAPA

ZAYNE - KAINE

ZBIGNIEW - KAPIKENIEWI

ZDENA - KAKENA

ZDENEK - KAKENEKI

ZEAIRRA - KEAILA

ZEALAN - KEALANA

ZEB - KEPI

ZEBULON - KEPULONU

ZECHARIAH - KEKALIAHA

ZEDRA - KEKILA

ZE'EV - KE'EWI

ZEFERINO - KEPELINO

ZEHRA - KEHILA

ZEINA - KEINA

ZEINAB - KEINAPA

ZEKE - KEKE

ZELDA - KELA

ZELIA - KELIA

ZELICA - KELIKA

ZELIMIR - KELIMILE

ZELJKA - KELIKA

ZELL - KELI

ZELLEIGH - KELEIKEHE

ZELMA - KELIMA

ZELMIRA - KELIMILA

ZEMAH - KEMAHA

ZEN - KENI

ZENA - KENA

ZENAIDA - KENAIKA

ZENDA - KENIKA

ZENDRA - KENIKILA

ZENIA - KENIA

ZENIQUE - KENIKE

ZENO - KENO

ZENOBIA - KENOPIA

ZENON - KENONU

ZENOUA - KENOUA

ZENTHIA - KENIKIA

ZENY - KENI

ZEOLA - KEOLA

ZEONZALEE - KEONUKALE

ZEPH - KEPI

ZEPHANIAH - KEPANIAHA

ZEPRINA - KEPILINA

ZERA - KELA

ZEREULLA - KELEULA

ZERITA - KELIKA

ZERRA - KELA

ZERYN - KELINE

ZETH - KEKI

ZE-TOTO - KE-IKOKO

ZETTA - KEKA

ZETTIE - KEKIE

ZEUS - KEUKO

ZEV - KEWI

ZEYAD - KEIAKA

ZEZEANA - KEKEANA

ZEZENYA - KEKENIA

ZEZETTE - KEKEKE

ZHAFIR - KAHAPILE

ZHANIECE - KAHANIEKE

ZHANNA - KAHANA

ZHARA - KAHALA

ZHARFA - KAHALAPA

ZHAYDA - KAHAIKA

ZHIVAGO - KAHIWAKO

ZHIVKA - KAHIWEKA

ZIA - KIA

ZIANA - KIANA

ZILDA - KILA

ZIG - KIKE

ZIGGY - KIKI

ZII - KI

ZII KUANG - KI KUANA

ZILENIA - KILENIA

ZILMA - KILEMA

ZILVINAS - KILEWINAKA

ZIMA - KINA

ZINA - KINA

ZION - KIONU

ZIPPORAH -KIPOLAHA

ZIQI - KIKI

ZIREYA - KILEIA

ZIRON - KILONU

ZITA - KIKA

ZIXIAO - KIKIAO

ZOANNE - KOANE

ZOBIDA - KOPIKA

ZOE - KOE

ZOEBEL - KOEPELI

ZOEY - KOEI

ZOHAIR - KOHAILE

ZOIE - KOIE

ZOILA - KOILA

ZOLA - KOLA

ZONA - KONA

ZONDRIA - KONUKULIA

ZONIA - KONIA

ZOPHIA - KOPIA

ZORA - KOLA

ZORAYA - KOLAIA

ZORAYMA - KOLAIMA

ZOREL - KOLELI

ZOREN - KOLENI

ZORIN - KOLINE

ZORINA - KOLINA

ZORKA - KOKA

ZORRO - KOLO

ZORTH - KOKO

ZOSHA - KOKA

ZOWIE - KOWIE

ZOYA - KOIA

ZSA-ZSA - KAKA-AKAKA

ZSOLT - KAKOLUKU

ZUBEEDA - KUPEKA

ZUELLA - KUELA

ZUHA - KUHA

ZUL - KULO

ZULAIDA - KULAIKA

ZULAYMIS - KULAIMIKE

ZULAYNAH - KULAINAHA

ZULEMA - KULEMA

ZULFIAN - KULOPIANA

ZULMA - KULOMA

ZUMA - KUMA

ZURAMA - KULAMA

ZURI - KULI

ZURIEL - KULIELI

ZUZANA - KUKANA

ZUZU - KUKU

ZVI -KAWI

ZYAIRE - KIAILE

ZYE - KIE

ZYON - KIONU

ZYRA - KILA

ZYTAJSHA - KIKAIKA

About the Author Kim Crinella

Kim Crinella first visited Oahu, Hawaii on her honeymoon in June 1989 where she and her husband Mike fell in love with island life. They made the move to Oahu from Massachusetts in 1993 and enjoyed learning about Hawaii's unique culture, history, environment, and island activities. Kim enjoys exploring Hawaii's unique marine and rain forest environments and researches to learn more about what she encounters while hiking and snorkeling.

In 1998 Kim completed the State of Hawaii Tour Guide Certification course at Kapiolani Community College. The course covered Hawaii's unique cultural and natural history from the time the islands were formed to modern time. This certification training gave Kim a deeper appreciation and understanding of the Hawaiian culture and Hawaii's history.

Kim wanted to share her love and knowledge of Hawaii with others and began volunteering weekly at the Waikiki Aquarium, where she was a volunteer for over 7 years. Kim learned a lot about Hawaii's unique marine life through training and literature provided by the Aquarium. Kim worked at an interactive exhibit called "Edge of the Reef" where she would show and tell visitors about creatures they may encounter in different parts of the reef and answered questions.

In 1999 Kim created a website AlohaFriends.com where she shared information about Hawaii, photos taken by her and her husband, tips and recipes to have luau or

Hawaii themed wedding anywhere, tips on how to move to Hawaii, Hawaii vacation tips and activity reviews, and phonetic first name translations into Hawaiian.

Kim and Mike have offered several personalized Hawaii related services over the past 25 years including Airport and Hotel Lei Greeters, Photography for Couples and Families in Outdoor Settings Around Oahu, Personal Tour Guide of Oahu, Fresh Lei and Island Treasures Shipped Anywhere in USA, Oahu Vacation Itinerary Planner, Luau and Hawaii Theme Wedding Advisor For People Outside of Hawaii, Licensed Hawaii Wedding Officiant.

Kim became an ordained minister in 2016 and began officiating personalized love centric nonreligious wedding ceremonies, elopements and vow renewals. She currently assists traditional and same sex couples in getting married in a simple courthouse style wedding at her office or a personalize love centric nonreligious ceremony at a beach, park, garden, waterfall, scenic lookout, or venue anywhere on Oahu.

Kim now shares the Hawaii resources and tips she created from **AlohaFriends.com** on **WeddingsOnOahu.com** to help couples simplify getting married on Oahu as well as to provide resources to have a Luau celebration anywhere and for couples anywhere to have a Hawaii theme wedding and/or wedding reception! Kim also shares resources to make moving to Hawaii a reality.

Author Kim Crinella

Aloha!

"Aloha is the unconditional desire to promote
the true good of other people in a friendly spirit
out of a sense of kinship."
Rev. Abraham K. Akaka

"Aloha is not just a word, it's a way of life, an
attitude, and a perspective on the World."
Author Unknown

"Spread Aloha wherever you go, and you'll leave a
trail of kindness and warmth."
Author Unknown

341.

If you are getting married on Oahu or are planning a Luau or Hawaii theme wedding ANYWHERE in the World WeddingsOnOahu.com has FREE resources including:

- Instructions on How to Apply for a Hawaii Marriage License
- Resource of Oahu Beaches, Parks, Gardens, and Venues for Weddings Including Links to Videos to Get a Virtual View
- Explanation of Popular Hawaii Wedding Traditions
- Unique Oahu Honeymoon Ideas for Couples
- List of What Needs to be Updated After Marriage
- Hawaii Travel Tips for Visitors to Have a More Enjoyable Experience
- How to Grow a Pineapple from a Fresh Pineapple Top Tutorial
- Ideas for Using Pineapples to Decorate with and Eat at Luaus or Hawaii Theme Weddings and Vow Renewals
- Fun Hawaii Theme Games for Luaus
- Popular Luau Recipes
- Decorating Ideas to Easily Create a Luau or Hawaii Theme Wedding Anywhere
- Fun Easy to Make Hawaii Theme Table Centerpiece Ideas
- Full Menu With Recipes to Add a Hawaii Twist to Your Thanksgiving including Pineapple Turkey Table Centerpiece Tutorial
- Hawaii Theme Christmas Party Resource Games and Recipes
- Learn to Hula Dance Resource
- Learn to Play The Ukulele Resource
- Orchid Lei Making Tutorial

- Popular Hawaiian Words and Phase with English Translations
- Largest Collection of First Name Phonetic Translations into Hawaiian on the Internet
- Resource on How to Create and Cook in a Traditional Hawaiian Imu Pit (underground oven)
- Hawaii Theme Wedding Ceremony and Vow Suggestions
- Hawaii Theme Sand Unity Ceremony and Candle Unity Suggestions
- Incorporating Couple or Family Lei Unity Ceremony into a Wedding or Vow Renewal Ceremony
- The Lords Prayer Translated into Hawaii
- Popular Phrases of Love in Hawaiian with English Translations
- Tips and Resources for Moving to Hawaii
- Answers to Frequently Asked Questions About Hawaii
- Directory to Listen to Hawaii Radio Stations Online
- Sharks Found Around the Hawaiian Islands and Why They Attack
- Educational Resources Related to Hawaii for Students, Teachers, and Parents Home Schooling

WeddingsOnOahu.com

9 798888 368637